Spiritual Economies

EXPERTISE

CULTURES AND
TECHNOLOGIES
OF KNOWLEDGE

EDITED BY DOMINIC BOYER

SPIRITUAL ECONOMIES

Islam, Globalization, and the Afterlife of Development

DAROMIR RUDNYCKYJ

CORNELL UNIVERSITY PRESS
ITHACA AND LONDON

All photographs are by the author unless otherwise noted.

First published 2010 by Cornell University Press
First printing, Cornell Paperbacks, 2010
Printed in the United States of America

Library of Congress Cataloging-in-Publication Data

Rudnyckyj, Daromir
    Spiritual economies : Islam, globalization, and the afterlife of development / Daromir Rudnyckyj.
        p. cm. — (Expertise: cultures and technologies of knowledge)
    Includes bibliographical references and index.
    ISBN 978-0-8014-4850-8 (cloth : alk. paper)
    ISBN 978-0-8014-7678-5 (pbk. : alk. paper)
    1. Islam—Indonesia—21st century.   2. Islamic renewal—Indonesia.
3. Islam—Economic aspects—Indonesia.   4. Krakatau Steel, PT—
Employees—Training of.   5. Krakatau Steel, PT—Employees—Religious
life.   6. Economic development—Religious aspects—Islam.   I. Title.
II. Series: Expertise: cultures and technologies of knowledge.
    BP63.I5R834   2010
    297.09598'090511—dc22   2010022632

Cornell University Press strives to use environmentally responsible suppliers and materials to the fullest extent possible in the publishing of its books. Such materials include vegetable-based, low-VOC inks and acid-free papers that are recycled, totally chlorine-free, or partly composed of nonwood fibers. For further information, visit our website at www. cornellpress.cornell.edu.

Cloth printing   10 9 8 7 6 5 4 3 2 1
Paperback printing   10 9 8 7 6 5 4 3 2 1

For Anissa, Maksym, and Amira

CONTENTS

ACKNOWLEDGMENTS

First and foremost I acknowledge all those in Indonesia who have given their time, expertise, and friendship over the past ten years. Although the human subjects protocols under which I conducted research preclude me from thanking many individuals by name, this does not indicate a lack of appreciation. Many employees of Krakatau Steel, inhabitants of Banten and Jakarta, and participants in Emotional and Spiritual Quotient (ESQ) training shared a great deal, and to them I extend my most sincere gratitude. Among those I can acknowledge by name, I especially thank two successive CEOs of Krakatau Steel, Sutrisno and Danaeulhay, who facilitated my research at the company and allowed me access to its operations beyond my expectations. I also acknowledge the support of Tubagus Yayat Sukiyat, Alfauzi Salam, and Ali Kusumo for aiding my research at the company. I am also grateful for the kindness of all the employees of the ESQ Leadership Center who patiently tolerated my entreaties in person and by email. Ary Ginanjar graciously enabled me to participate in ESQ and treated me exceptionally well, as did his brother Rinaldi Agusyana. To them I extend my deepest gratitude. Pak Ary also generously gave permission to use several images in this book. I hope that all those affiliated with ESQ will recognize this as a fair and accurate appraisal of their hopes

x   *Acknowledgments*

and desires for Indonesia, even if my interpretations do not exactly match theirs.

Without the support of a number of other institutions and individuals in Indonesia I would not have been able to write this book. Foremost, I thank Azyumardi Azra, the former rector of the State Islamic University (UIN) in Jakarta, who was my research counterpart in Indonesia and generously provided me with institutional sponsorship. He was supportive of my research both logistically and intellectually, for which I am extremely grateful. UIN provided me with a scholarly home in Indonesia, and Faisal Badroen, Komaruddin Hidayat, and Jamhari Makruf gave me advice and guidance during fieldwork. Two students at the university, Hudri and Afri, provided assistance with transcriptions. In Banten I benefited from the advice, insight, and support of Imat Tihami and Ilzamuddin of STAIN Serang. Without Ali Nurdin's assistance I probably never would have made it to Banten, and without Tubagus Ace Syadely I would not have enjoyed it half as much. Others who provided advice or assistance over the years I spent in Indonesia include Harry Bhaskara, Heddy Sri Ahimsa Putra, Scott Guggenheim, Tauvik Muhammad, Yudhi Junaedi, the Rochmadi family, the Wewengkang family, and the family of Ibu Darmawan. The staff of the Fulbright office in Jakarta, and Nelly Paliama in particular, provided me with essential support in Indonesia. I also thank Ruben Silitonga and the rest of the staff at the Indonesian Institute of Sciences (LIPI), which facilitated my research clearance and residence permission. Above all I acknowledge the support of Norbertus Nuranto and Sarah Maxim. Their friendship greatly enriched my experience of Indonesia.

I made research trips to Indonesia in 2003–2005, 2006, and 2008, and without the material support of a number of institutions, such extensive fieldwork would have been impossible. These organizations include the International Dissertation Research Fellowship program of the Social Science Research Council, the Wenner-Gren Foundation for Anthropological Research, the Fulbright-Hays Doctoral Dissertation Research Abroad Program, the Pacific Rim Research Program of the University of California, the Sumitro Fellowship Program of the United States–Indonesia Society, and an Internal Research Grant from the University of Victoria.

This book owes a great deal to the sage guidance of Aihwa Ong. The clarity of Aihwa's thought set a high standard and pushed me to be as clear as possible with my own. She provided a model of how to conduct rigorous, cutting-edge research to create anthropology that is both relevant and conceptually inventive. I hope this book does justice to all I have learned from her. I also benefited a great deal from my other mentors: Charles Hirschkind, Nancy Peluso, and Paul Rabinow. Jeffrey Hadler and Donald Moore played critical roles in laying the groundwork this project. As an undergraduate I first experienced the sheer pleasure of anthropological thought in courses with Raymond Fogelson, Marshall Sahlins, George Stocking Jr., and James Wilde.

The ideas and methods in this book were developed over a number of years and have benefited immensely from the incisive and insightful comments of a number of scholars who shared their knowledge with me in locations ranging from conference panels to coffee shops. These include Suraya Afif, Carlo Bonura, Philippe Bourgois, John Bowen, Joseph Bryan, Leslie Butt, Simon Coleman, Émile Fromet de Rosnay, Maneesha Deckha, R. Michael Feener, Zeynep Gürsel, Robert Hefner, Laura Hubbard, Benjamin Gardner, Daniel Goldstein, Kevin Karpiak, Celia Lowe, William Mazzarella, Christopher Morgan, Lucinda Ramberg, Analiese Richard, Roger Rouse, Lincoln Shlensky, James Siegel, Rachel Silvey, Mary Steedly, Christopher Vasantkumar, Scott Watson, Jerome Whitington, and Sylvia Yanagisako. The final version of the book has greatly benefited from careful readings by Sonja Luehrmann and Anissa Paulsen, who both graciously read the entire manuscript. Tuong Vu and Kevin Fogg provided me with some timely citations. Jos Sances of Alliance Graphics did inspired work on the maps for the book. All outstanding errors are mine alone. The material presented in this book was improved through comments and questions I received from audiences at Colorado University, National University of Singapore, Stockholm University, Royal Netherlands Institute of Southeast Asian and Caribbean Studies (KITLV) at the University of Leiden, University of California Berkeley, University of Bergen, University of Puget Sound, University of Washington, and Yale University. I thank the American Anthropological Association for permission to include material in chapter 3 of this book from my article "Spiritual Economies: Islam and Neoliberalism in Contemporary Indonesia," *Cultural Anthropology* 24(1): 104–141.

Completing this book was enabled by the warmth and support I received from my family: Caitlin, Ishai, Jill, Jos, Robbin, Sorrel, Xenia, and Zhdan. Mark and Eric kindled my interest in anthropological thinking from an early age. Above all my immediate family have inspired me to see this long project through to completion. Amira gave me a real deadline. Maksym provided welcome diversions, particularly when he told me to stop writing and play baseball or build trains with him. Without Anissa's care it would have never happened.

Spiritual Economies

Introduction

Spiritual Reform and the Afterlife
of Development

At 7:45 in the morning on May 4, 2004, I sat in an audience consisting of about two hundred and fifty Krakatau Steel employees in Banten, Indonesia. We were assembled in a large auditorium at the company's education and training center, and we listened as Ary Ginanjar introduced spiritual training, a program that combined business leadership, human resources, and life-coaching techniques with Islamic practice. A thickset, broad-shouldered man wearing a well-tailored black business suit and a neatly trimmed mustache, Ginanjar lectured against a background of the saccharine sounds of "Silk Road," an instrumental composition by the prolific New Age musician Kitaro. In dramatic tones he told us that enhanced Islamic practice was indispensible to productivity and prosperity in the global economy.

Equating Muslim virtues with corporate values, Ginanjar represented globalization as a divine challenge that could be met through the intensification of Islamic faith. The government's recent decision to eliminate tariffs on imported steel was the source of acute anxiety among Krakatau Steel employees because it would end the company's privileged position

competing against producers located outside Indonesia. However, Ginanjar construed this not as a political decision but rather as a challenge posed
by God directly to company employees. "Ladies and gentlemen," he bel-
lowed, "our faith [*iman*] in Allah is the key to all the problems that we face
in this global era! This era has brought the elimination of import tariffs on
steel. For humans it is darkness, but for Allah it is light! The reduction of
import tariffs to zero percent is a sign of Allah's mercy [*rahmat*]!" Amid
the quickening pace and rising timbre of the inspirational music, Ginanjar continued with weighty conviction. He proclaimed that the increased
competition faced by the steel company was an effect of a visible hand inspired by an invisible force:

> Allah wants to raise us up [*meningkatkan*] to become a company, to become
> an *ummah,*[1] that can look past our own self-interest. Achieving our potential
> is not dependent on the government! We can compete with outside compa-
> nies! The way things are going in Indonesia and international competition—
> these are the challenges with which Allah has confronted us.... Allah wants
> us to raise Krakatau Steel up to another level now that two thousand of you
> have finished this program. Allah wants to show the company that we have
> entered the global era [*kita masuk di era* global] and that we are able to com-
> pete. Allah wants us to renounce our egoism with these zero percent tariffs.
> This is not the government's doing, but Allah via the hand of the govern-
> ment [*Allah melalui tangan pemerintah*]!

The audience listened in rapt attention as the huge projection screens behind Ginanjar displayed three serial images of a corporate logo that simultaneously evoked electrons circling a nucleus, planets in orbit around a
sun, and what Ginanjar would later refer to as the "universal *tawaf.*"
    The hall, darkened and cool, was filled with music conveying buoyant
optimism as Ginanjar deployed metaphorically rich language to assert that
globalization required employees to become different kinds of workers.
He likened the personal changes that employees must make in this "global
era" to the metamorphosis of a caterpillar, explaining, "Krakatau Steel is
not just a place that produces iron pellets and steel, but a place that produces human beings with the mentality of steel [*mengeluarkan manusia ber-
mental baja*]! ... The reduction of import tariffs to zero percent is the hand

---

1. This is an Arabic term that refers to the Islamic religious collectivity.

of Allah putting you into a cocoon. When you begin to move and break out, you will soar high like a butterfly that brings a new culture [*peradaban*] to Krakatau Steel."

According to Ginanjar globalization required nothing less than a cultural change. This was precisely what he sought to bring about through three days of employee training in which he and his staff would seek to demonstrate that success in this global era could be achieved through enhancing Islamic faith. It was a message that managers and other employees of Krakatau Steel found compelling as their faith in Indonesia's decades-long project of state-led nationalist developmentalism appeared to be almost out of steam. Proponents of enhancing Islamic faith sought to reconfigure the company to meet unprecedented challenges in the wake of thirty-two years of authoritarian political rule, an economy that was no longer configured in mainly national terms, and the looming specter of privatization that cast an ominous shadow over the company.

In analyzing this convergence I argue that, whereas much of the postcolonial history of what were formerly called developing nations was characterized by "faith in development" (Ferguson 1999, 247), efforts to merge Islamic practice with corporate norms represent efforts instead to develop faith. On the one hand, faith in development refers to the "expectations of modernity" (Ferguson 1999, 11–17) and the nationalist projects of state-led modernization to facilitate economic growth that occurred in much of Asia, Africa, and Latin America (Apter 2005; Escobar 1995; Gupta 1998; Li 2007). On the other hand, developing faith refers to concrete initiatives designed to intensify religious practice under the presumption that doing so will bring the work practices of corporate employees in line with global business norms and effect greater productivity and transparency. Developing faith is related to but somewhat different from faith-based development. Erica Bornstein has examined development as a moral project and shown how religious NGOs have supplanted the state in Africa (Bornstein 2005). Analyzing a parallel development albeit one that differs in fundamental ways, this book focuses on how the ethical dispositions rooted in religion are cultivated to enable the transition away from state-led modernization. Developing faith is not a complete break with faith in development, however, because both share the similar conviction that worldly problems can be solved through the proper application of technical knowledge (Scott 1998). Furthermore, developing faith sustains the utopian visions that provided the impetus for faith in development.

I argue that efforts to develop faith represent not the end of development (Rahnema and Bawtree 1997; Sachs 1992) but rather its afterlife. The
afterlife of development is neoliberal because it entails the introduction of
economic rationality and calculative reason into domains from which they
were previously limited or excluded. Thus, the afterlife of development
captures the shift from modernization supported through state investment
in the space of the nation, to a market-based system that caters to private,
transnational capital. Faith in development was premised on the nation-
state as the principle agent of modernization, insofar as it was anointed
with the power to bring about the utopian visions upon which development was founded. However, in Indonesia and much of the rest of the
developing world, state-led development has largely failed to bring about
these dramatic transformations (Aragon 2000; Collins 2007).

The afterlife of development illuminates the consequences of failed
schemes for national modernization in which the state is no longer the
principal agent responsible for improving the lives of its citizens (Elyachar
2005; Leve and Karim 2001; Richard 2009). Instead, this duty is transferred
to citizens themselves, who are empowered to become individually responsible for bringing about the kind of economic growth that the nation-state
has become unable to guarantee. In Indonesia, proponents of developing
faith sought to bring about this change by creating a spiritual economy
and governing through affect. Thus, the afterlife of development entailed
reframing the project of development from one premised on large-scale industrial and technological investment by the nation-state to one premised
on the individual religious practices of corporate workers. Indonesia's economic crisis and the failure of modernization schemes were reconfigured
as a moral crisis and made into the object of intervention. In this reconfiguration, Islam was substituted for the nation as the common denominator
for subjects of the new spiritual economy, a project that precipitated tensions with Indonesia's history of nationalist pluralism.

This analysis of the afterlife of development provides new insight into
the anthropology of globalization. Most anthropologists have approached
globalization as a culture, era, system, or space (Appadurai 1996; Harvey
2006; Hannerz 1989). These discussions are sometimes vague and overly
general, as globalization is often represented as an abstract, almost transcendental, force that is outside the world yet remakes it in profound ways.
The actual practices and actions that constitute globalization are often left

unaddressed or assumed. In contrast, I focus on globalization as a set of concrete practices.[2] This book provides a detailed, fine-grained analysis of the specific interventions that proponents of developing faith designed to enhance corporate productivity and survival in the aftermath of faith in development. I show how the transformations associated with transnational economic integration are not abstract processes in contemporary Indonesia.

There are two ways in which I analyze globalization as practice. First, I examine practices specifically designed to meet the challenges posed by what participants in this research project identified as globalization. These practices are intended to enable corporate competitiveness and productivity in an economy that is increasingly defined in transnational, rather than national, terms. They are designed to enable corporate survival amid the increasing integration of production systems, financial activities, and labor markets across national borders. Second, these practices are "global assemblages" (Ong and Collier 2005) because they are fabricated from an array of forms that are taken to be universally valid, such as human resources management, science, and Islam. The spiritual economy I describe consists of a diverse assemblage of Islamic prayer, management knowledge, Qur'anic recitation, and popular psychology. Approaching globalization as the reconfiguration and standardization of practices enables a more modest, empirical, and ultimately more anthropological approach to the phenomenon.

Objects and Sites: Islam and the Legacy of Nationalist Development

This book analyzes a particular convergence of forces that shapes contemporary human life in Indonesia and beyond: a legacy of nationalist

---

2. In developing this approach I have found useful Ferguson and Gupta's call to connect the everyday practices of state power with the new modes of government characteristic of transnational economic integration (Ferguson and Gupta 2002). They call for examination of the "spatiality of contemporary practices of government as an ethnographic problem" (994). In contrast, my approach does not focus so much on the spatiality of global practices but rather the conditions, processes, and effects of their assemblage. In so doing, I demonstrate how it became possible in contemporary Indonesia to combine business management knowledge and Islamic practice as a panacea to the challenge presented by globalization.

development, a resurgence of religious practice, and economic transformations associated with neoliberalism. The evidence for my arguments is drawn from the widespread phenomenon that I refer to as developing faith and that participants in my research referred to as "spiritual reform" (*reformasi spiritual*). Spiritual reform was manifest in a number of initiatives in the years following the end of authoritarian rule in Indonesia, but I focus mainly on Ary Ginanjar's popular human resources program called Emotional and Spiritual Quotient (ESQ) training. A successful businessman, Ginanjar had experienced his own religious renaissance in middle age, after launching businesses in health insurance and telecommunications. He was familiar with human resources management primers and employee training programs from efforts to improve the performance of his companies. Ginanjar concluded that many of the same principles for business success were evident in Islamic practice, history, and doctrine. Thus, he designed ESQ to enhance the Islamic piety of Indonesian workers, including employees of state-owned enterprises, government offices, and private companies.

Managers of state-owned Krakatau Steel introduced ESQ to increase company productivity, eliminate corruption, become more internationally competitive, and prepare the workforce for privatization. For decades the factory was a key site in the project of nationalist development but in the late 1990s was faced with a new political and economic landscape characterized by the cessation of formerly reliable state investment and the reconfiguration of the domestic economy such that it was no longer defined in primarily national terms. Proponents of spiritual reform expected that by enhancing the Islamic practice of employees they could ensure the company's survival in a rapidly changing economic landscape. The unprecedented initiative of spiritual reform involved subjecting workers to training sessions totaling forty hours over three days.

Spiritual reform is anthropologically significant because it represents a larger formation in which religious values are mobilized to address the challenges of globalization in contemporary Indonesia and beyond (Csordas 2009a; Silverstein 2008). In Indonesia, ESQ was one of a growing number of similar Islamic reform initiatives that also included Management of the Heart, Syariah Management, and Celestial Management. Proponents of these initiatives considered Indonesia's current economic crisis an effect of the separation of religious ethics from economic practice. They declared this disjunction resulted in rampant corruption, inefficiency, and a lack of discipline in the workplace. The participants in these initiatives sought to achieve what was termed "management of the heart" by combining Islamic doctrines with human resources methods and life-coaching principles to enhance individual discipline and collective economic performance.

In the years following the New Order (the period of President Suharto's authoritarian rule) programs combining Islamic practice and management knowledge spread widely across Indonesia.[3] ESQ and other manifestations of spiritual reform were implemented at some of Indonesia's largest and most prominent state-owned enterprises and government institutions including the Department of Taxation, Pertamina (the state oil company), Telkom (the national telecommunications company), and Garuda (the nation's flag air carrier). Current and former military generals were avid participants in ESQ, and training sessions were repeatedly delivered at the army's officer candidate training school in Bandung. In 2004 Indonesia's minister of state-owned enterprises, Sugiharto, announced that ESQ training would be required for employees of every state-owned firm in the country—more than 180 companies. However, Ary Ginanjar's plans for ESQ did not end at the limits of the nation-state. He saw the program as a universally valid method of human resources training, and his ultimate goal for ESQ was to, in his words, "go global." The first overseas ESQ training was held in April 2006 in Kuala Lumpur, and by 2007 regularly scheduled ESQ trainings were being delivered in Malaysia on a bimonthly basis. In addition, versions of the training have been offered in Singapore, the Netherlands, Qatar, Australia, and Brunei, and in late 2008 Ginanjar brought the program to Houston and Washington, DC. Ary Ginanjar also took his unique brand of Islam-inspired management training to the very heart of Islamic learning by introducing ESQ to an audience at Al-Azhar University in Cairo in 2006.

Ary Ginanjar created the ESQ program after experiencing his own spiritual renaissance. With an upbeat demeanor and charismatic disposition, Ginanjar is one of the many new religious leaders who have emerged across the Muslim world in recent years (Deeb 2006; Eickelman and Anderson 2003; Hirschkind 2006; Schulz 2006). He saw strengthening Islamic

---

3. The New Order lasted from 1965 until 1998. Suharto coined the term to contrast his rule with Indonesia's Old Order under Sukarno.

piety as a means to address his country's "multidimensional crisis" and explained to me that "at the root of Indonesia's political and economic crises is a moral crisis." He viewed this moral crisis as a result of the fact that "although most Indonesians are Muslims," they do not adhere to the tenets of Islam "so at the moment here religion is only like a ritual...just a ritual without spirituality." Developing faith was a way to redress the moral crisis that he saw was at the root of Indonesia's crisis of faith in development.

ESQ drew on different forms of management knowledge and practice that have greatly expanded in North America, Asia, and Europe. By management knowledge I refer to the "soft management skills" and applied practices of business success and personal development used by corporations and detailed in the vast human resources, life-coaching, and self-help literatures (Olds and Thrift 2005; Thrift 1998, 2005).[4] Ary Ginanjar argued that principles conducive to business success and effective corporate management can be found in Islamic practice and Qur'anic doctrine. For example, participants in ESQ were informed that the third pillar of Islam, the duty to give alms (*zakat*), is divine sanction for "strategic collaboration" and exercising a win-win approach in both business transactions and relations with coworkers. Ginanjar further asserted that the fourth pillar of Islam, the duty to fast during Ramadan, is a model for self-control. Based on this principle, ESQ seeks to inculcate the duty to constrain worldly desires to ensure otherworldly salvation. Corruption, a major problem at state-owned firms, was understood as the result of an uncontrolled desire for material wealth and was depicted as contrary to divine injunctions for self-management.

In 2002 I selected Krakatau Steel as a site to conduct ethnographic research because it appeared to offer an ideal setting to analyze the articulation of development, religion, and globalization. Fieldwork in Indonesia consisted of three trips, including an eighteen-month period between 2003 and 2005, with shorter return visits in 2006 and 2008. When I first selected the site I had no idea that I would find anything as fascinating as the spiritual training sessions held on a regular basis at the company. Rather, I chose the field site because it contained a convergence of compelling dynamics,

---

4. Thrift notes that "'soft' management skills like team leadership, creativity, [and] emotional thinking" represent "an alternative tradition of management...that stresses human interaction and self-fulfillment as general elements of organizational success" (Thrift 1999, 62).

including a legacy of nationalist development, a region with a long tradition of Islamic devotion, and a major state-run enterprise planned for
privatization. Indonesia contains the world's largest Muslim population
and Muslims dwarf the country's other religious groups, constituting
about 90 percent of the total population (Hefner 2000, 6). At state-owned
enterprises such as Krakatau Steel the percentage of Muslim employees is
even higher than the national rate because these companies were used by
the Suharto regime as vehicles for enhancing the material circumstances of
so-called indigenous Indonesians who were economically disadvantaged
in comparison to those labeled Chinese under the Dutch colonial regime
(Hadler 2004; Rush 1990).

The company is located in Banten, which was formerly part of the province of West Java but became an independent province in 2000. Banten is
based on the boundaries of an Islamic sultanate that was a prosperous node
in early modern Southeast Asian trade networks and has long been connected to other parts of Asia and the Pacific (Meilink-Roelofsz 1962; Reid
1988; van Leur 1955). Islam is an oft-cited feature of the identity of inhabitants of Banten, whom other Indonesians consider as second only to the
Acehnese in the strength of their Islamic piety (Williams 1990). During the
colonial period, the sultanate was rendered ineffectual by the Dutch and
fell into poverty and underdevelopment (Djajadiningrat 1913; Multatuli
1868). After the Indonesian revolution of 1945–1949 the region was the
site of several prominent development initiatives. Banten's accessibility to
sea-based trade networks was central to the 1956 decision by Sukarno's nationalist government to build, with Soviet support, Indonesia's first steelworks. Although construction ceased following the military coup of 1965
that brought Suharto to power, it was resuscitated with Western backing
in the early 1970s as a centerpiece of national development. Krakatau Steel
produces a material that was considered absolutely critical to the state's ambitious development agenda and occupied an iconic position in the nation,
receiving frequent visits from Indonesian political leaders and visiting dignitaries. Today the company is the largest steel factory in Southeast Asia
and manufactures half of the steel produced in Indonesia (Akbar 2003).

Over the past four decades Krakatau Steel received billions of dollars in state development aid. However, the Asian financial crisis of 1998
and the downfall of the Suharto regime heralded the twilight of state-led
schemes for nationalist modernization. The period following the end of

the New Order is widely referred to as *reformasi* (reform). *Reformasi* simultaneously refers to political changes in the form of increasing democratic governance, and economic changes in the form of greater transparency, government accountability, free markets, and merit-based (rather than patronage-based) systems of competition, compensation, and promotion. *Reformasi* had wide-ranging effects on Krakatau Steel and coincided with a set of neoliberal economic reforms that included the cessation of state investment and protective tariffs and plans to privatize state-owned firms. For years the central government had invested generously in technological modernization and these funds had guaranteed the company's viability, but such outlays had become impossible after the near bankruptcy of the Indonesian government and subsequent International Monetary Fund (IMF) bailout in 1998. Tariffs on imported steel that had long protected the company from international competition were eliminated in April 2004. Furthermore, China emerged as a global steel superpower, and employees feared that when the demand for steel within China ebbed, companies based there would flood the Indonesian market with cheaper imported steel. Finally, after the end of the authoritarian regime workers obtained new rights to organize, which offered unprecedented possibilities for political mobilization. At Krakatau Steel this precipitated the formation of a new labor union that was for the first time not directly tied to the state.

By the early 2000s many company employees, journalists, NGO activists, and academic observers felt the economic challenges associated with *reformasi* would ultimately lead to the privatization of Krakatau Steel. Privatization of state-owned enterprises was a critical condition of the IMF's $40 billion loan package to the Indonesian government in the wake of the financial crisis. Under the terms of this agreement, private ownership was expected to create "efficient and viable enterprises" and foreign capital would fund plant modernization (Government of Indonesia 2000). Privatization was a contentious political issue in Indonesia (Prasetyawan 2006) and Krakatau Steel employees heatedly debated its merits. Those opposed to privatization feared widespread job losses after the shift from state to private ownership. Arguments in favor of privatization were motivated by the anxiety that the company could no longer rely on state investment for the modernization of aging production facilities and thus would be unable to compete in an increasingly global steel market without foreign investment and expertise.

Methods: Subjects by Design

In my ethnographic work on the convergence of religious reform, economic globalization, and the twilight of nationalist development, I have
found particularly useful the work of Max Weber and Michel Foucault.
This book draws on convergences in their writings by attending to historical contingency, rationalization, the reflexive relationship between subject and object, and ethics, understood as "practices of embodied existential
and conceptual self-transformation through inquiry and reflection on self
and others" (Rabinow 2008). Although both writers have been influential
in anthropology, few scholars have addressed the affinities in their work.[5]
The convergences in their respective intellectual endeavors offer genera-
tive insights for the anthropology of modernity.

Both Weber and Foucault deployed genealogical methods that emphasized historical contingency and empirical specificity as opposed to approaches guided by a search for ultimate causes (Foucault 1997; Weber
1990, 92, 183). Through detailed empirical studies both sought to understand how facets of modern life came to be such as they are and not otherwise. Weber demonstrated how Protestant practices created the conditions
of possibility for the emergence of what he called the "spirit of capitalism"
(Weber 1951, 1958b, 1990, 47–78). Foucault analyzed how scientific knowledge (medicine, criminology, psychology, and political economy) and the
institutions in which it was deployed (hospitals, prisons, schools, and factories) constituted modern human beings (Foucault 1973, 1977, 1978). Their
discomfort with causal analysis was rooted in a common recognition of the
inherent reflexivity of modernity, as modern human beings are ensnared
in what Foucault called an "empirico-transcendental doublet" (Foucault
1970, 319). By this he meant that modern humans stand in a paradoxi-
cal, doubled relationship with themselves because they are simultaneously
the subjects *and* objects of knowledge. Thus, the human appears as "a fact
among other facts to be studied empirically, and yet as the transcendental
condition of the possibility of all knowledge" (Dreyfus and Rabinow 1983,
31). Foucault and Weber both recognized that this existential doubling

---

5. There are several notable exceptions in anthropology (Ong 1987; Ong and Collier 2005;
Rabinow 1996, 2003; Zaloom 2006). Scholars outside anthropology have also identified resonances
in the work of Weber and Foucault (Martensson 2007; Szakolczai 1998).

posed a methodological problem for the human sciences because it illuminated the pitfalls inherent in any claims to universal or transcendental knowledge about humans. Their recognition of this problem led both Weber and Foucault to eschew attempts at generalization and universal explanation: what Weber called "universal significance" (Weber 1990, 13). Thus, both authors concentrated on the empirical investigation of historical singularities, recognizing the West as but one contingent historical formation among many others.[6]

Further, both Weber and Foucault investigated rationalization, the reflexive application of knowledge to human practice to achieve optimal standards of efficiency and productivity, because they recognized it as a constitutive feature of modern life. According to Weber, the sober, austere way of life practiced by the Protestants and their ontological heirs is an effect of the methodical application of Calvin's doctrine of predestination to their everyday existence. In contrast to Catholics, "the God of Calvinism demanded of his believers not single good works, but a life of good works combined into a unified system.... The moral conduct of the average man was thus deprived of its planless and unsystematic character and subjected to a consistent method for conduct as a whole" (Weber 1990, 117). Similarly, Foucault's pivotal concepts of governmentality and biopower both emerge out of inquiry into the effects of rationalization on human life. Governmentality (which he also called governmental rationality) refers to the statistical practices of calculation and enumeration deployed by early modern states to effectively manage populations (Foucault 2007). The related notion of biopower "brought life and its mechanisms into the realm of explicit calculations and made knowledge/power an agent of the transformation of human life" (Foucault 1978, 143). For both authors rationalization was not an inevitable effect of history, but a practice implemented

---

6. For example, in the first sentence of *The Protestant Ethic,* Weber cautions that the aspiration to universally valid knowledge was a problem that emerged initially in the West. He writes, "A product of modern European civilization, studying any problem of universal history, is bound to ask himself to what combination of circumstances the fact should be attributed that in Western civilization, and in Western civilization only, cultural phenomena have appeared which (as we like to think) lie in a line of development having *universal* significance and value" (Weber 1990, 13). Similarly, in *The Order of Things,* Foucault argues that the crisis of modern representation emerged when the human was recognized as simultaneously the subject and object of knowledge (Foucault 1970). He distinguishes three domains (life, labor, and language) through which the sovereign *subject,* the human, was constituted as the *object* of scientific knowledge (Rabinow 2003, 13).

in multiple domains of modern life by a range of experts who sought to optimize human life by subjecting it to an array of specialized modes of knowledge.

Finally, both Weber and Foucault focused on ethics and practices rather than ideas or mental states. The dominant anthropological interpretation of Weber has led to overly mentalist readings of his work in the discipline (Geertz 1973b). Geertz's definition of culture as composed of webs of meaning disregarded Weber's emphasis on ethics, as embodied practices, that is central to his analysis. Indeed, the central question of Weber's comparative sociology of world religions (Weber 1920) was how work, perhaps the signature practice of modernity, became a moral duty for Protestants and their ethical successors. Thus, Weber's sociology is best read not so much as an idealist counterpoint to Marx but rather as an inquiry into the peculiar attachment of moral worth to hard work.[7]

Although Foucault is often read as focusing primarily on discourse, he was perhaps less interested in mental states than in the bodily techniques through which subjects were inculcated in particular ways of being in the world. This emphasis on embodied practices is apparent in his work on both docile bodies and technologies of the self. Docile bodies, such as those of soldiers, school children, hospital patients and factory workers, were those that could be "subjected, used, transformed and improved" (1977, 136). After the eighteenth century Foucault describes how, in modernity, the body became treated like a machine: the object of targeted, repeated, precise interventions to maximize its economic capacity. The modern body was subjected to techniques of rationalization to become efficient, organized, and productive. Technologies of the self, on the other hand, involve less external manipulation. Rather they focus on how individuals are enlisted in the project of working on themselves to achieve desired states complicit with certain moral values. These technologies involve enlisting individuals in "operations on their own bodies and souls, thoughts, conduct, and way of being, so as to transform themselves in order to attain

---

7. Although Weber positions his approach against what he called "the doctrine of the more naïve historical materialism" (1990, 55), he does not discount material conditions. Rather he looks at the recursive relationship between ideas, most notably the Protestant doctrines of the calling and predestination, and the embodied practice of material production, work. Thus, Weber's approach is instructive because it does not treat ideas and matter as separate, but rather shows how they are mutually constitutive.

a certain state of happiness, purity, wisdom, or immortality" (Foucault 1988, 18).

In addition to the insights I draw from Weber and Foucault, several additional methodological principles guided my research and provide confidence in my analysis. First, I did not assume that I grasped the predicament faced by those who participated in this research project better than they did themselves (Ricœur 1970).[8] This required me to understand the ways in which Indonesians understood and acted on the broader economic and political predicament that they faced from their own perspective. I was specifically interested in documenting the arguments and practices that Indonesians developed to meet the demands of the day as they saw them. This approach contrasts with other scholarly approaches that privilege the position of the analyst by presuming that he or she has a superior vantage point from which to understand the challenges faced by those under study (Comaroff and Comaroff 2000). Thus, many of the conceptual concerns in the book emerge directly from the way in which those with whom I interacted represented the predicament with which they were confronted. For example, globalization was not an abstract problem for those who participated in my research, as the event I describe at the beginning of this chapter demonstrates. Quite to the contrary, it was a topic that was frequently discussed and was the subject of an ongoing set of applied practices and technical interventions designed specifically to address the challenge that it posed.

My research stance required that I suspend my own skepticism (and at times aversion) to some of the events I observed and practices I describe to achieve a position of scholarly objectivity (Weber 1949). Two recent anthropological studies of contemporary religious phenomena provided models of how to achieve such a stance, *The Book of Jerry Falwell* (Harding 2000) and *Investing in Miracles* (Wiegele 2005). These works examine movements that might appear bizarre to secular liberals, and some anthropologists might even dismiss out of hand. However, in their incisive yet empathetic portrayals these books provided models of how to treat the movements they studied as serious social phenomena and demonstrated why they were worthy of anthropological scrutiny. From these works I

---

8. Ricœur terms this position, which he associates with approaches to social analysis inspired by Marx and Freud, the "hermeneutics of suspicion."

draw the lesson that anthropology is not only composed of what anthropologists think is important or relevant but rather what those who participate in our fieldwork identify as significant. The anthropologist's objective therefore is to understand phenomena encountered during fieldwork and reflect on them to show how they increase anthropological understanding. Ultimately these approaches pave the way to an anthropology that does not romanticize the exotic but rather enables a discipline capable of comprehending the diverse forms of *logoi* (knowledge) that are entailed in creating contemporary *anthropoi* (humans) (Rabinow 2003).

The methodological orientation I develop contributes to what Douglas Holmes and George Marcus have recently termed "para-ethnography," which frames anthropological investigation as inquiry into practices that are analogous to, but go beyond, ethnography (Holmes and Marcus 2005, 2006; Holmes 2009; Marcus 2007). They write that the subjects of anthropological study "have developed something like an ethnography of both their own predicaments and those who have encroached on them. . . . Their knowledge practices in this regard are in some sense parallel to the anthropologist's and deserving of more consideration than mere representation in the archive of the world's peoples that anthropologists have created" (2006, 35). Such an approach suggests that anthropologists analyze the knowledge and theoretical models deployed by those with whom we engage ethnographically. Taking reflexivity as both a methodological tactic and a characteristic feature of modern knowledge (Beck 1992; Beck, Giddens and Lash 1994; Luhmann 1998), Holmes and Marcus suggest that anthropologists should narrow the chasm between anthropological practice and the practices that anthropology documents and analyzes. Such ethnography is not oriented toward transparently reproducing the native's point of view to successfully interpret a preexisting cultural whole (Geertz 1973b). Instead it develops what might be thought of as ethnographic double vision, in which research projects are configured to illuminate the reciprocity between disciplinary questions and the concerns of those with whom anthropologists engage to answer those questions. Thus, para-ethnography elucidates the specific problems confronted by participants in anthropological research projects and the interventions that are developed to address them.

I find the formulation of para-ethnography useful because those who participated in my project (including spiritual reformers, company managers, and line operators) were engaged in practices that were analogous to ethnography but went beyond it as they actively sought to transform the situation under diagnosis. Those who sought to develop Islamic faith to resolve Indonesia's development crisis were posing a question that has long been asked by anthropologists: How do cultural norms inflect economic action (Geertz 1963b; Mauss 1990; Peacock 1978; Scott 1976)? However, they also surpassed anthropological description because this was not posed as an abstract question. Those who sought to enhance the Islamic practice of corporate employees did so to better equip Indonesian companies to compete in an increasingly global economy. They promoted a set of ethics they identified as intrinsic to Islamic practice and conducive to success in a new economic configuration. This entailed nothing less than the creation of a theoretical model of human nature and the deployment of sophisticated practices and technological apparatuses to instill this model in Indonesian workers.

Para-ethnography also directs anthropological inquiry toward projects to design specific types of subjects and social orders. Thus, my approach describes how reformers in contemporary Indonesia sought to design a subject (a worshipping worker) and social formation (a spiritual economy).[9] Management knowledge is particularly amenable to para-ethnographic investigation, as it involves both an empirical diagnosis of and reflexive action on what is often conceived of as culture. I draw on Nigel Thrift's conceptualization of management knowledge as the practical theory of capitalism because it consists of the actual empirical practices and concrete models deployed by corporations to optimize the efficiency and productivity of their workers (Thrift 2005).

Furthermore, para-ethnography avoids making an artificial split between theory and method in anthropology.[10] Rather than imposing a theoretical model on a preexisting empirical reality, I focus on the way in which contemporary Indonesians posed questions about their contemporary lives that might enable anthropologists to view the theoretical approaches that

---

9. Although spiritual reformers explicitly sought to reconfigure corporate labor as a form of religious worship, the term spiritual economy is one I developed to capture the social formation that those involved referred to as "spiritual reform."

10. Other anthropologists have also recently sought to develop approaches that suture the gap between anthropological theory and method (Maurer 2002; Miyazaki 2004; Riles 2000).

we deploy in a different light (Boyer 2001). This book works reflexively between the disciplinary concerns of anthropology and the Indonesians whose knowledge practices are reproduced. Thus, it is not so much dedicated to uncovering what kind of definitive statements anthropology can make about its subjects but rather what the implications of the knowledge practices of the subjects of anthropological inquiry are for the discipline's engagement with the empirical world.

Another point of methodological departure was that close attention to public events, especially training sessions dedicated to spiritual reform, complemented interview and questionnaire data. Regular attendance at these events enabled the collection of discourse and the observation of practices that I did not directly elicit. Spiritual training sessions demonstrated how Indonesians represented to themselves the conjunction of a legacy of nationalist development, a resurgence of Islamic practice, and the economic changes they took as associated with globalization. These sessions provided a rich site for documenting how Indonesians were posing profound existential questions about who they were and who they wanted to become in a way that did not require the direct intervention of the analyst.

This method differed in fundamental ways from earlier anthropological approaches that approached culture as "an ensemble of texts... which the anthropologist strains to read over the shoulder of those to whom they properly belong" (Geertz 1973a, 452). I do not analyze a culture as a static script. Rather the object of this study is the reflection on past practices and the interventions devised to develop new practices (de Certeau 1984; Ortner 1984). Although the subjects in Geertz's interpretive accounts reflect on their culture, they do so to reinforce it. In contrast, the protagonists in my account reflect on their practices with the explicit goal of changing them. Further, unlike a culture, for which (at least according to Geertz) proper ownership is known, possession of the assemblages of practice that I analyze is by no means settled. These practices are global because they entail diverse influences and they are represented as universally valid. Claims to ownership of these practices, discussed in chapter 2, are grounded in their combination rather than in their origins.

The final methodological principle that undergirds this book concerns the scale that it addresses. By the 1990s anthropologists had become acutely aware of the problems that the discipline confronted in representing formations beyond the localized, small-scale cultural units that had constituted the traditional objects of anthropological inquiry (Asad 1994; Gupta and Ferguson 1997a; Hannerz 1989; Marcus 1998; Ong 1999). Although my research is grounded in the up-close, experience-based empirical fieldwork methods that have historically characterized anthropological fieldwork (Evans-Pritchard 1969; Malinowski 1922), the book addresses a formation that extended well beyond the perspective of a lone ethnographer. This is due not least to the fact that the assemblage of a legacy of nationalist development, religious resurgence, and economic restructuring was occurring not only at Krakatau Steel but also at a number of similar sites in contemporary Indonesia and beyond.

The spiritual reform initiative that I describe was a replicable form, repeated hundreds of times at numerous state-owned firms, government offices, and private companies across Indonesia. Although the particular circumstances were not identical in every case, the broader formation consisted of similar characteristics. The problems that spiritual reform was designed to address were not specific to Krakatau Steel, but were evident in a broad range of institutions in contemporary Indonesia. By December 2008 over 616,000 people had completed the ESQ program and the alumni network was growing at over 200,000 per year. In addition, ESQ is part of a family of similar initiatives in contemporary Indonesia that merge Islamic ethics with business management practices and life-coaching theories. Thus, the analysis of the specific material I observed represents a larger formation, a spiritual economy, in which religious values are mobilized to address the challenges posed by the failure of state-supported development and the move toward transnational economic integration.

Conceptual Interventions: Religion as Globalization and Neoliberal Reason

The conceptual approach that is developed in this book examines the convergence of religion and globalization. Few human scientists have examined the global religious resurgence and economic globalization in the same analytical frame. On the one hand, a number of authors have looked at dimensions of the global religious resurgence (Asad 2007; Bowen 2007; Hale 1998; Hansen 1999; Mahmood 2005). On the other hand, there have been a number of studies addressing globalization (Appadurai 1996; Hannerz 2004; Ong 1999; Sassen 1998). Few scholars have examined the simultaneity of the global religious resurgence and economic globalization. For example, three edited collections on globalization contain a total of only four essays that address religion (Inda and Rosaldo 2002; O'Meara, Mehlinger and Krain 2000; Ong and Collier 2005).

This book argues that religious practice can be conducive to globalization and is not necessarily opposed to it. In the few cases in which religion and globalization have been treated in the same analytical frame, they have often been seen as contradictory. Thus, I offer a counterpoint to research that concludes that religious resurgence is either a realm of refuge from, or means of resistance to, economic globalization (Castells 1997; Comaroff and Comaroff 2000). Spiritual reformers in contemporary Indonesia advocated religious virtues based on the understanding that doing so would create greater productivity, enhanced competitiveness, and the reduction of chronic corruption.

In analyzing religion as globalization, my approach differs from that of a 2009 edited volume that examines the "globalization of religion" and "globalization as religion" (Csordas 2009a).[11] Building on my treatment of globalization as practice, I document how religious practices are reconfigured to optimize the efficiency and productivity of workers in an increasingly global economy. Spiritual reformers in Indonesia have designed a form of Islamic practice that inculcates an ethics of accountability, personal responsibility, and self-discipline that they see as conducive to corporate success.

This book also clarifies and provides greater analytical purchase on discussions in anthropology that analyze neoliberalism (Ferguson 2006; Harvey 2005; Postero 2007; Rofel 2007; Sawyer 2004). I do not treat neoliberalism as an epoch, a culture, an age, or a space. To mark a neoliberal age as a historical period exists in the mind of the analyst denoting such an age and does not necessarily relate to any empirical phenomena taking place in

---

11. The studies in that volume examine the "globalization of religion" in which certain religious practices travel across vast distances, for example the increasing allure of Pentecostalism in the New Guinea highlands and the growing popularity of Buddhism in France. It also explores the "globalization as religion" which refers to the reverence with which devotees of the free market regard neoliberal principles.

the world. Further, I do not take neoliberalism to be a culture diffused on a global scale (Comaroff and Comaroff 2000). This volume demonstrates the inherent flexibility and adaptability of neoliberalism as it has the ability to combine with other forms to create novel assemblages. During the period of my research neoliberalism was not a native category. Virtually no one aside from a handful of activists used the term while I was conducting research in Indonesia between 2003 and 2005.[12]

In contrast, I use neoliberalism as an analytical category that refers to a specific type of rationality. Thus, I use the term to refer to a practical method for organizing human conduct. I build on Foucault's analysis, which treats neoliberalism as comprising pragmatic techniques to introduce economic rationality into domains that were previously considered external to market logic (Foucault 2008). Foucault writes that "the problem of neoliberalism is...how the overall exercise of political power can be modeled on the principles of a market economy" (2008, 131). Thus, neoliberalism is not so much a matter of "freeing empty space" but rather of taking "the formal principles of a market economy and...projecting them on to a general art of government" (2008, 131). Foucault further argues that neoliberalism entails "extending the economic model of supply and demand and of investment-costs-profit so as to make it a model of social relations and of existence itself, a form of relationship of the individual to himself, time, those around him, the group, and the family" (2008, 242). Several scholars have drawn on Foucault's farsighted account. Nikolas Rose refers to "advanced liberalism" as a technique of government in which all "aspects of social behavior are now reconceptualized along economic lines—as calculative actions undertaken through the universal human faculty of choice" (Rose 1999, 141). Cris Shore and Susan Wright have sought to understand how "neoliberal governmentality" creates an "audit culture." Thus, they analyze "a wholesale shift in the role of government premised on using the

---

12. This changed during the Indonesian presidential election of 2009 when the incumbent president, Susilo Bambang Yudhoyono, was accused of being a neoliberal. The charge became particularly acute after he selected Boediono, a post–New Order technocrat with a PhD in economics from the University of Pennsylvania's Wharton School of Business, as his vice presidential running mate. (Yudhoyono's first-term vice president, Jusuf Kalla, ran a losing campaign against him as a rival candidate in the 2009 election). When the term was invoked during the campaign, it was primarily used in an attempt to rekindle Indonesia's legacy of nationalist self-sufficiency by pejoratively referring to the country's increasing integration with the global economy.

norms of the free market as the organizing principles not only of economic life, but of the activities of the state itself and, even more profoundly, of the conduct of individuals" (Shore and Wright 2000, 61).

Building on Foucault's work and the accounts of those who have been inspired by him, I define neoliberalism as a relatively mundane but increasingly ubiquitous practice of making economic calculation a universal standard for the organization, management, and government of human life and conduct. This approach does not entail treating neoliberalism as a homogenizing force. Rather I document ethnographically the novel and unique formations that emerge as the imperative to rationalization merges and combines with previously existing norms (Collier and Ong 2005; Ong 2006). Thus, I describe how spiritual reformers in contemporary Indonesia found justification for neoliberal norms in Islamic doctrine and practice. These reformers found precedent and expression for the neoliberal injunctions to self-discipline, accountability, and transparency in Islamic virtues. Furthermore, I analyze the introduction of economic rationality and calculation into a set of domains that were previously organized in ways that did not strictly conform to the logic of the market. At Krakatau Steel there was a conscious attempt underway to transform the company from one organized according to a social mission to one organized according to a business mission. Employees described the company as "not a pure business" (*bisnis murni*) but rather as one that was intended to "support the livelihoods of the masses" (*hajat hidup orang banyak*). State-owned enterprises, which had previously been organized (at least in part) according to a social logic of nationalist development, were being reconfigured to comply with the imperatives of economic rationality. Efforts to develop Islamic faith were taken as directly conducive to the goal of reorganizing the company according to a strictly market rationality.

This spiritual economy, however, did not only represent the neoliberalization of an enterprise whose earlier mandate as a catalyst of national development had extended beyond merely returning the greatest profit. Instead, it entailed the neoliberalization of religion, as Islamic practice was interpreted as setting a precedent for market reason. Islam was reconfigured according to calculative rationality insofar as Islamic values (such as hard work, honesty, transparency, and self-discipline) were promoted because of their economic benefit. Enhanced religious practice was seen as conducive to greater profitability.

At the same time as spiritual reformers sought to endow religious practice with economic justification, they also sought to bestow religious sanction on economic practice. According to them, one was a good Muslim if one worked hard, but economic rationality was also represented as a religious value. Thus, the spiritual economy represented not only the neoliberalization of Islam but also the Islamicization of neoliberalism. Spiritual reform was as much designed to produce better Muslims as it was to produce better workers. To read spiritual reform as only a function of market imperatives would be to consign the piety of those involved to "false consciousness" (Engels 1968; Lukács 1920, 64–72) and risk discounting the agency of those described in the succeeding chapters who professed profound spiritual experiences during ESQ training (Mahmood 2001). Furthermore, spiritual reformers saw their paramount goal as moral reform, after which political and economic reform would necessarily follow.

Treating globalization as practice reveals that it does not lead to homogenization. In combining Islamic practices with principles drawn from North American and European business primers, Indonesians enmeshed in the resulting spiritual economy did not become just like Westerners, but neither did they remain who they were beforehand. They worked on themselves to change themselves. The resulting spiritual economy involves the assemblage of two modes of practice, Islam and neoliberalism, that are represented and enacted as universally valid. What emerges is a new way of life that, while not unconnected from what preceded it, is irreducible to it.

Overview

This book is divided into three parts. In general, these sections document the context, implementation, and effects of efforts to merge Islamic practice with market ethics. Part 1 documents the milieu from which this spiritual economy emerged by examining the transition from faith in development to developing faith. Chapter 1 argues that the Suharto period in Indonesia was characterized by faith in development because poverty and underdevelopment were assumed to be capable of resolution through technological intervention and the appropriate application of scientific and engineering knowledge. Chapter 2 argues that, in the post-Suharto period, the faith in development characteristic of the New Order was replaced by efforts instead to develop faith. I describe how ESQ training and other popular movements for spiritual reform were designed to enhance religious practice under the presumption that doing so would instill ethics conducive to greater transparency, productivity, and competitiveness.

Part 2 analyzes the contours of a spiritual economy by describing the specific interventions that spiritual reformers devised to address Indonesia's economic crisis and the failure of developmentalism. Chapter 3 describes how spiritual economies are formed by reconfiguring work as a form of religious worship, producing spirituality as an object of intervention, and inculcating ethics of individual accountability and responsibility among workers. The creation of a spiritual economy involved elucidating and implementing a number of compatibilities in the ethical practice constitutive of both Islam and neoliberalism. While most scholarly research on neoliberalism suggests the creation of individualized and detached subjects, in chapter 4 I argue that the mobilization of affects was critical to creating a spiritual economy. I show how Islamic spiritual reform in contemporary Indonesia entailed governing through affect. By this I refer to the way in which affect served as a medium for a new mode of governing employees and citizens.

Part 3 analyzes the effects of the emergence of a spiritual economy and how spiritual reform articulated with the configuration of religious, national, and class identities in contemporary Indonesia. Chapter 5 argues that the dissolution of an economy defined in national terms is linked to the reconfiguration of national identity. I examine Indonesia's legacy of nationalist pluralism on two scales: that of a single individual of mixed heritage and the workforce of Krakatau Steel as a whole. The chapter shows how Islamic spiritual reform at what was a key site in the project of national development challenged how non-Muslims and those who identified as of mixed heritage understood their membership in the nation. Chapter 6 describes how a group of employees creatively reworked the terms of spiritual reform to suit their own interests. I argue that spiritual reform did not induce blind obedience nor did it provoke spontaneous resistance. Rather it created a new frame in which employees devised new ways to advance their interests within an emerging spiritual economy.

Ultimately, the emergence of the spiritual economy described in this book demonstrates how a large and visible Muslim constituency designed a mode of Islamic practice compatible with the afterlife of development.

Thus, in contrast to accounts that represent Islam in conflict with modernity (Barber 1996; Huntington 1993); spiritual reformers suggest a certain reconciliation between Islam and modernity. However, this should not be understood as a celebratory account of transnational harmony brought about through the panacea of globalization. There is no small measure of caution in this tale. My intention is to inspire reflection on what is perhaps the most fateful force of our time: the increasing extension of economic rationality and calculative reason into diverse domains of human life. Indeed, in wake of the financial crisis of 2008 and the debates about government reform taking place in various guises around the world in its aftermath, this cold, calculative reason may in fact be tightening its icy grip on our souls...and spirits.

Part I

MILIEU

1

FAITH IN DEVELOPMENT

From Jakarta, Indonesia's capital city, the most common trip to Krakatau Steel takes place on one of the country's few four-lane toll roads. During the roughly one-hundred-kilometer journey to the western extremity of the island of Java the landscape goes through several alterations. After one passes through the first set of toll gates the city itself changes from densely packed storefronts sporting signs and banners that appear more grandiose than their interiors, to a more open spatial distribution where once rural villages butt up against recent housing developments catering to the capital region's middle and upper classes. Several massive shopping malls sprout up on the landscape like giant fungi after a warm monsoon rain and eventually the landscape gives way to flat rice paddies (*sawah*) bordered by banana trees and simple wooden shelters. When one enters the province of Banten, which lies alongside the eastern border of Jakarta, these tranquil fields are dissonantly interspersed with more recently built factories that seek to take advantage of proximity to the city's infrastructure, capital, and consumers.

Driving the road can be a knuckle-whitening experience as huge buses ply this route at breakneck speeds, their doors ripped off and their engines belching great volumes of noxious black exhaust. Roaring imperiously down the tollway and swerving recklessly from lane to lane, they obey the only real rule that seems to govern Indonesian roads: the largest vehicle always possesses the right of way. These buses are headed to towns in Banten; many routes end in Merak, at the western tip of Java, where passengers can catch ferries that will take them to the southernmost extremity of the neighboring island of Sumatra. Brightly painted cargo trucks with elaborately airbrushed images of fierce forest fauna and scantily clad women also compete for space on the highway, albeit at somewhat lower speeds and with considerably less maneuver. In this direction, they mostly carry industrial goods back to Sumatra having deposited shipments of that island's agricultural commodities, such as coconuts, durians, and cows, in the Jakarta region.

The stretch of road between Jakarta and Merak seems to be perpetually under construction as workers, who sleep in makeshift camps just off the shoulder, pound at concrete and asphalt with pitifully small metal hammers and carry away barefoot the debris in handwoven baskets. Indonesia's nouveau riche also travel the highway in spruced up Toyota Kijang SUVs and sometimes more opulent German sedans, commuting from Jakarta to managerial jobs in Banten's scattered factories or on weekends making a trip to the beach at Anyer, which seems to be of interest based more on its past reputation rather than its contemporary appearance. Depending on the season and air quality, Gunung Karang, a dramatic, forest-flanked tropical volcano will come into view about midway through the journey. The size and position of the mountain on the horizon indicates roughly how close one is to Serang (Banten's recently designated provincial capital), Banten Lama (the seat of the prominent sultanate of Banten during its period of peak influence in the sixteenth and seventeenth centuries), and Cilegon (the city that services Krakatau Steel and the cluster of industries that it has attracted).

After a trip of roughly two hours from Jakarta, traffic delays notwithstanding, one arrives in Cilegon, or Steel City (*Kota Baja*), as it is sometimes called by Indonesians. Leaving the toll road at the east Cilegon exit and driving toward the factory zone takes one through the municipality itself, which bears the hallmarks of a frenzied town that perhaps grew

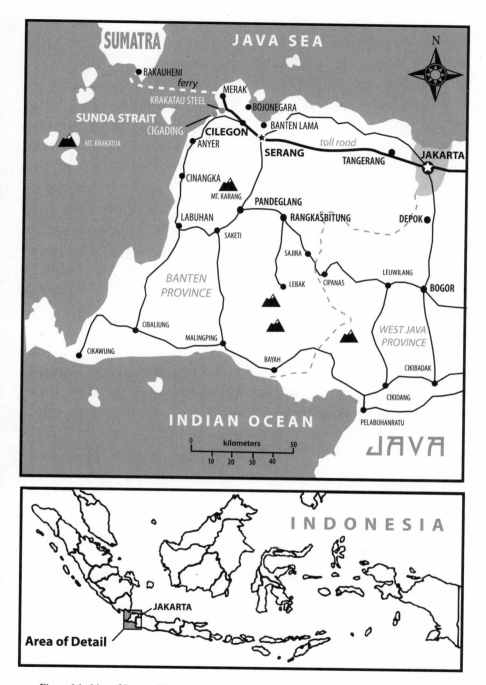

Figure 1.1. Map of Banten. This new province was created in 2000. Credit: Jos Sances, Alliance Graphics.

too rapidly and definitely without much foresight or organization. The main road through town was originally part of the infamous Daendels Road that the Dutch colonial administration, using corvée labor, had constructed from one end of Java to the other in the early nineteenth century. A four-lane strip of asphalt, the road is crowded with horse-drawn carts, massive trucks, and all manner of transportation in between. It is the main artery for this city of roughly three hundred thousand inhabitants and serves a dense sequence of storefronts and businesses. A wide range of consumer goods—electric rice cookers, television sets, and Chinese motorbikes—is visible from the roadway, baking in the blazing sun that seems ubiquitous in Cilegon even in the rainy season. Three boxy shopping malls, decidedly less opulent than their enormous cousins in Jakarta, are evenly spaced through the city along the main artery: Ramayana at the east end, Matahari close to the city's central square, and the chaotic, stifling SuperMal Cilegon, which lies at the city's west end about seventy-five meters down the road from the Al-Hadid mosque. The mosque was built by Krakatau Steel in the 1970s as compensation for a mosque that was previously located on land that the company "absorbed" during a period of rapid expansion. It once must have been one of the most impressive buildings in Cilegon, but after three decades it bears the tired visage of a dilapidated modernism that characterized a number of company-constructed structures.

While I was conducting research in Cilegon and its environs, the main road was incessantly clogged with minivans (*angkot*) that plied several routes through town. Usually there were more of these buses than there were passengers, which caused their drivers to drive extremely slowly while looking for passengers and then become exceptionally aggressive when a prospective rider appeared, lurching spasmodically to the curb. This unpredictable traffic led to bottlenecks and backups; a source of constant consternation among some employees of Krakatau Steel and other automobile-owning inhabitants of the region, who usually explained the erratic nature of the drivers by asserting, as if it was a self-evident fact, that they "lacked education" (*kurang ajar*). Most employees of the company were from other parts of Indonesia, while those who drove the buses were the offspring of people with families who had lived in Banten for several generations, if not longer. These two groups, locals (*putra daerah*) and newcomers (*pendatang*), coexisted in an uneasy détente and seldom mixed

Figure 1.2. The main road through town with SuperMal Cilegon in the background.

outside the market, evoking what James Furnivall had some decades earlier referred to as a "plural society" (Furnivall 1948, 304–305).

Just beyond the Al-Hadid mosque the main road forks with one branch heading to the west, passing along the southern boundary of the Krakatau Steel factory zone to the factory's port at Cigading. It then curves to the south toward the beach at Anyer where one can take a speedboat to visit an active remnant of the Krakatau (which in English is often spelled Krakatoa) volcano, which was immortalized in both a Hollywood film and a *New York Times* bestseller (Winchester 2003). Alternatively, the northwest branch road passes several municipal buildings before continuing on to the factory zone and then to the ferry terminal at Merak. Taking this branch leads one past the new regional parliament that was constructed in the aftermath of Indonesia's 1999 regional autonomy (*otonomi daerah*) laws that were intended to decentralize decision making in Indonesia by reducing

Figure 1.3. Krakatau Steel's main gate with the buses used to transport workers on the right.

the influence of the central government (Kimura 2007; Mietzner 2007). Just beyond the parliament, on the right, sits the local police headquarters. Once past this building the traffic speeds up considerably and the road cuts along the edge of the sprawling industrial zone associated with Krakatau Steel. Offices and production facilities sit on the left side of the road, and on the right are located the employee housing complex and company-built recreation facilities. After about half a kilometer the company's education and training center, where ESQ training sessions were held, is on the left immediately adjacent to Tirtayasa University. The university, named after one of Banten's preeminent seventeenth-century sultans, was built by Krakatau Steel and offers degrees to local students, mainly in technical fields. Shortly thereafter the main road comes to a four-way stop where one can turn left onto an expansive four-lane road containing far less traffic than neighboring arteries, as it is used only by traffic to or from Krakatau Steel and its adjacent industrial zone. This broad thoroughfare leads,

Figure 1.4. The interior of the billet steel plant.

after roughly two kilometers, to the main gates of the factory compound where the primary steel production facilities are located.

Passing through the gates one encounters the first of the six major mills that compose the steel-making facilities at Krakatau Steel. Beginning at the main gate and lined up from north to south these include a cold rolling mill, a wire rod mill, a hot strip mill, a billet steel plant, a slab steel plant, and a direct reduction plant. The steel production process begins at the direct reduction plant, which is most distant from the main factory gate but closest to the Cigading port. Direct reduction is an alternative to coal smelting and involves heating iron ore (imported from Brazil, Chile, and on occasion Sweden) to a temperature of twelve hundred degrees Celsius which destroys impurities and transforms it into sponge iron. The main fuel source in this process is natural gas which arrives at the factory via an offshore pipeline from fields near Cirebon, three hundred kilometers to the east.

After the sponge iron is created it is conveyed to the billet steel and slab steel plants, which are the most dangerous and uncomfortable mills in the entire compound. Here the iron is heated past its melting point in electric arc furnaces and combined with scrap metal, carbon, and other minerals to produce molten steel alloy. The sound of the furnace is deafening, and a fine black carbon dust lingers perpetually in the air creating an oddly diffuse light while coating virtually everything in the factory with a fine, charcoal blanket. The molten alloy is poured from giant black cauldrons into casting machines where it is formed into either billets or slabs. The billets, which weigh between one and two thousand kilograms, are then shaped into bars and rods at the wire rod mill. Adjacent to the billet plant is the slab steel mill where a continuous casting machine is used to create massive slabs weighing between ten and thirty tons. After the slabs have cooled and cured, they are transported across a small roadway to the hot strip mill, an immense and cavernous edifice over half a kilometer long. There they are again heated to over a thousand degrees until they glow bright orange and then are thunderously flattened into smooth sheets of coiled steel.

Like the bars and rods, the hot rolled coils are commodities. They can be fashioned into plates and other objects used in construction and other industrial applications. However, not all are sold, and many of these coils are sent for further forming to the final plant in the production zone, the cold rolling mill. The cold rolling mill was the cleanest and most comfortable plant. In contrast to the other mills it felt almost antiseptic in its absence of dust and other airborne grime and was not nearly as noisy. It had been built most recently and thus had less time to fall into disrepair, as some of the other mills had. A job in the cold rolling mill was a plum position for Krakatau Steel employees, and morale among workers in the mill appeared to be the highest among employees in any of the other plants.

These plants, indispensible to what company officials proudly described as a "fully integrated" steel factory (one that could turn iron ore into commodities), were part of the resuscitation of the steel factory, after construction had gone dormant following the military coup of 1965 and Indonesia's turn away from the Soviet bloc and toward the West. The period between 1972 and 1995 marked the heyday of Krakatau Steel, as the company and its workers were flush with cash and halcyon fantasies of industrial

Figure 1.5. The interior of the hot strip mill.

utopianism. Under the patronage of the longtime minister of research and technology and later vice president, B. J. Habibie, the Suharto government had spared little expense to bring the most up-to-date high technology steelmaking equipment to Krakatau Steel. After construction of the first direct reduction plant in 1972, a series of new plants were brought on line. By 1979 the billet plant and the wire rod mill were completed. In 1983 President Suharto officially opened plants constructed under the company's "second stage development" plan, including the steel slab plant and the hot strip mill. In 1993, the hot strip mill was expanded and modernized, leading to a corresponding expansion in the organization of the company and more managerial jobs. Suharto again visited the company after a major expansion of the facilities in 1995, when the third direct reduction facility, called Hyl 3, and another slab steel plant were completed (*Metal Bulletin Monthly* 1996). As long as the company was building new plants, there was a corresponding expansion of managerial positions for employees who had worked at the factory and felt entitled to promotions.

Modernization on the Margins: Faith in Development

Under both Indonesian presidents, Sukarno (1945–1966) and Suharto (1966–1998), national development was seen as a technological problem (Barker 2005). During Suharto's New Order modernization became a national obsession to the extent that Suharto branded himself "Mister Development" (*Bapak Pembangunan*). He justified authoritarian political rule based on continually improving Indonesian living standards. Suharto's influential protégé B. J. Habibie envisioned that the country would import technological innovations to bring about modernization and national development. Habibie's faith in development was premised on assumptions most notably articulated by Walt Rostow, who argued that individual nation-states move uniformly through discrete "stages of economic growth" (Rostow 1960, 4–16). Operating within this paradigm of modernization, Habibie believed that by importing expertise and modern technology from Europe and North America, Indonesia could leapfrog some of these development stages and bring living standards characteristic of Rostow's ultimate epoch, "the age of high mass consumption," to Indonesia.[1] Habibie expected that a critical mass of scientists and engineers trained outside the country would return to Indonesia and accelerate the process of modernization (Amir 2007b). Habibie's optimistic conviction in technology and development was a general characteristic of the developing world during the paradigm of modernization, where massive state-directed investment was expected to raise living standards in the formerly colonized countries of Asia and Africa (Abu-Lughod 2005; Ferguson 1999; Gupta 1997; Mazzarella 2003).

Although construction of a steel factory had gone dormant following the military coup of 1965 that culminated in Suharto's ascension to

---

1. The nationalist obsession with technological development was perhaps most conspicuous in the massive outlays that Habibie funneled to the state-owned aircraft company PT Dirgantara (Amir 2004). These expenditures ultimately yielded little return. After years of labor strife following the end of the New Order the company declared bankruptcy in 2007 and now operates at a fraction of its former size.

president of the republic, it was resuscitated in the early 1970s as a centerpiece of national development under the import substitution industrialization prong of Indonesia's New Order development strategy (Arndt 1975; Hill 2000; Rock 2003). Under Habibie's patronage, the engineers who championed these policies encouraged technological development and cultivated bureaucratic power in what the government labeled "strategic industries." Many employees at Krakatau Steel were graduates of the Institut Teknologi Bandung (ITB or Bandung Institute of Technology),[2] which was an important base for the network that Habibie had created.[3]

Like the other ten companies that fell under the rubric of strategic industries and were held by a state-owned Strategic Industries Supervisory Agency (Bahana Prakarya Industri Strategis or BPIS), Krakatau Steel occupied a critical place in the Indonesian national imaginary.[4] Steel is not only a potent symbol of modernity but enables modern life in an undeniably material fashion. Quite simply much of the infrastructure that makes modernity possible could not exist without steel. As one employee told me, steel is in everything from "screws to office towers." The faith in development held by Suharto and his technologically minded acolytes was premised on the domestic capacity to produce this crucial commodity. Thus, Krakatau Steel occupied an iconic position in the nation, receiving frequent visits from President Suharto and other official dignitaries.

During the years of the late 1970s and 1980s when Indonesia's oil boom lubricated national development, Cilegon also became known as Dollar City (*kota dollar*) (Hikam 1995). State development funds largely garnered from the extraordinary oil profits that Indonesia accumulated during the oil shocks of the 1970s flowed thickly into the city and fostered the expansion

---

2. Habibie was granted an honorary professorship at ITB in 1977 although he never taught there (Amir 2008, 319).

3. This group of engineers and scientists advocated development through massive state investment in technology and industrialization. As such they were at odds with another influential group of technocrats, who were primarily economists. This latter group, referred to as the "Berkeley mafia" because many of them had obtained doctoral degrees at the University of California, Berkeley, advocated open borders, private ownership of the means of production, and foreign investment as the keys to national development. They supported private, market-based investment and were generally less sanguine about the massive state outlays for modernization advocated by the engineers (Amir 2008).

4. For accounts of the construction of Indonesian nationalism see Boellstorff 2005; Keane 2003; Laffan 2003; Mrázek 2002; Rutherford 2003.

of Krakatau Steel, which grew to become the largest steel mill in Southeast Asia. Citizens from across Indonesia flocked to Cilegon. Some sought the salaried jobs that the company offered while others came to the growing town to open businesses that serviced the company and its growing pool of employees, including restaurants, auto repair shops, pharmacies, and other operations offering goods and services.

One manifestation of faith in development was the construction of an unabashedly modernist planned community that Krakatau Steel built just to the northwest of Cilegon. This extensive complex contained approximately eighteen hundred sturdy, concrete houses featuring long, horizontal lines and open floor plans—a tropical version of the prairie school. Initially all permanent employees of the company were provided with a house, but by the 1980s the number of employees had expanded so much that only those at the level of supervisor or above were provided with this benefit. Consequently almost no foremen or operators lived in the complex.[5] The houses were rationally arranged in orderly rows along attractively planted median strips. In 2003 the orderly planned community, although somewhat dilapidated, stood in verdant contrast to the unplanned, cluttered streetscapes of Cilegon, with its warrens of alleyways and haphazardly constructed residences. Walking through the complex, however, was mildly disconcerting. In contrast to the rest of urban Indonesia where invariably there are people on the streets, this complex was eerily devoid of people lingering at food stalls or at makeshift rest stops.[6]

In addition to the housing development, Krakatau Steel optimistically built many of the accoutrements of a modernist planned community: a hospital, schools, a university, parks, and several community centers. Recreation facilities constructed by the company included an Olympic-size swimming pool, an eighteen-hole golf course, and several sets of tennis courts. A stadium was erected that could hold over ten thousand spectators and served as a venue for employee rallies and public events, such as the annual commemoration of Indonesia's independence on August 17. The

---

5. In descending order of status, the employee hierarchy at Krakatau Steel, with the total number of positions as of January 2003 in parentheses, consisted of: president director or CEO (1), director (5), general manager (29), manager (80), assistant manager (47), superintendent (274), assistant superintendent (251), supervisor (842), foreman (1827), and operator (2509).

6. Holston observes a similar phenomenon in a prototypical modernist city, Brasilia (Holston 1989).

Figure 1.6. Employee housing in the Krakatau Steel factory complex. These townhomes were occupied by employees at the level of supervisor and above.

company also sponsored a soccer team, Pelita Krakatau Steel, which competed in Indonesia's top division and held its home matches in the stadium. A number of employees were members of Volcano Mania, an organization of fervent supporters who choreographed raucous cheers during home matches. Many employees wistfully remembered nights at the cinema that was built at the center of the housing complex; however, the theater did not survive the proliferation of home movie players. By 2003 it had fallen into a state of profound disrepair with all the windows broken, graffiti scrawled on the exterior, and a loose network of stray cats inhabiting it.

Krakatau Steel had also spawned ten subsidiary companies, most of which were spun off during an initial wave of restructuring in the mid-1990s so that the company could focus on its core business of steel production. These companies provided everything from medical care to harbor

Figure 1.7. Krakatau Steel's defunct cinema. Employees fondly recalled past times watching films in the company cinema at the end of their work week.

management services. The land surrounding Krakatau Steel became the centerpiece of an ambitious attempt to attract both domestic and foreign capital to a vast development zone. This zone was spearheaded by Krakatau Industrial Estate Cilegon (KIEC). Like Batam (Lindquist 2008), Indonesia's largest and most successful attempt to attract foreign investment through what Aihwa Ong termed "graduated sovereignty" (Ong 2000), KIEC was established as a zone to attract investment to a region that was primarily agrarian and perceived by both those in the central government and locals as undeveloped.

When I began research for this project it was clear the optimism that massive industrial projects such as Krakatau Steel would enhance economic growth and national living standards through technological modernization had decreased. The grandiose developmental designs that had been deployed in the area around Cilegon had not achieved (and were

TABLE 1.1. Krakatau Steel's Subsidiary Companies

Name	Year established	Purpose
PT KHI Pipe Industries	1972	Makes steel pipes
PT Pelat Timah Nusantara	1983	Produces steel sheets backed with tin, used mainly as roofing material
PT Krakatau Wajatama	1992	Makes rebar
PT Krakatau Engineering	1988	Provides engineering consulting services
PT Krakatau Industrial Estate	1992	Manages industrial and commercial property
PT Krakatau Information Technology	1993	Provides high technology services
PT Krakatau Daya Listri	1996	Manages Krakatau Steel's 400-megawatt electrical power generation facility
PT Krakatau Tirta Industri	1996	Manages Krakatau Steel's industrial water reservoir and delivery system
PT Krakatau Bandar Samudra	1996	Manages Krakatau Steel's port at Cigading
PT Krakatau Medika	1996	Manages company hospital

not likely to ever achieve) the spectacular effects that were expected. The physical appearance of the production facilities and corporate offices reflected this malaise. It was not so much that things were falling apart but that they appeared to just barely be held together. With the exception of a brand new building that housed the offices of the most senior managers, many of the office buildings dated to the 1970s and had become dilapidated. Within the factory itself, production facilities experienced regular breakdowns, causing entire mills to cease production. Leaking pipes were commonplace. Many control rooms were in bad need of several coats of paint. Krakatau Steel employees lamented the outdated technology and equipment, dismissing my awe at the fire, heat, and light with nonchalance while bemoaning the technological inferiority of the company's machinery in comparison with steel mills in North America or Europe.

The signs of a development initiative in the shadow of its prime were also ubiquitous in the company's housing complex. Some employees attributed this to the fact that inhabitants had little incentive to invest in the upkeep of houses to which they did not hold title. Often employees who had retired from the company continued to live in the houses with which they had been provided as part of their initial appointment. However, the value of pensions had declined greatly due to rampant inflation following the financial crisis of 1998 when the purchasing power of the rupiah declined to only 20 percent of its precrisis value against the U.S. dollar. Incomes had declined so precipitously that pensioners had little money available for property maintenance. Thus, whenever a house in the complex turned over the new occupant often had to invest a tidy sum to return the property to habitability.

Krakatau Steel's offices, production facilities, and company-owned houses all bore the distinct look of an enterprise whose best days had passed but also one that had never fully achieved the grand vision of the bureaucrats, planners, and government officials who saw steel as the key to development and modernization. Several times employees compared the company to Pohang Iron and Steel (Posco), the gigantic South Korean conglomerate that was established at roughly the same time as Krakatau Steel. However, in the intervening years Posco had far outpaced its Indonesian cousin, producing about 50 million tons of steel in 2003 in comparison to the meager 2.5 million tons made by Krakatau Steel.

Similarly, the optimistic plans to make Krakatau Steel the centerpiece of an industrial development zone attractive to foreign investment were still unrealized. It was not that these plans failed completely. Several transnational corporations had invested in the zone and built substantial factories, including the Japanese chemical giant Asahimas, the Australian company BlueScope Steel, and the French industrial gas producer Air Liquide. However, the plans for expansion had not achieved expected levels and extensive land holdings sat parched and undeveloped, overgrown with weeds, and forlornly waiting for the fecundity of foreign capital. A dilapidated sign was prominently posted on one overgrown plot and proudly proclaimed that the German multinational company BASF would be constructing a chemical plant on the site. When I asked a senior manager about how plans for attracting the German company to the development zone had faired, he told me that in 2000 BASF had made initial plans to build a production facility in the zone and signed a preliminary agreement toward that end. However, shortly thereafter violence between Dayaks and Madurese transmigrants broke out in Kalimantan (van Klinken 2007) and the international media, famished for the lurid appeal of ethnic strife, covered the conflict incessantly. When print and broadcast coverage of the discord swelled, BASF executives pulled out of the deal citing political instability in Indonesia, in spite of the fact that the clashes occurred over one thousand kilometers away on a completely different island and were precipitated by a set of historical events that had little connection to anything that had ever taken place in Banten.

By 2003, the appellation Dollar City no longer seemed to fit Cilegon, although the cost of living rivaled other big cities in Indonesia and there were examples of a degree of prosperity in the city and its immediate vicinity that marked it as clearly more affluent than many other parts of the country. These included a large cluster of both state-owned and privately-owned factories, three medium-sized shopping malls, bustling traffic, busy markets, and well-stocked storefronts. Yet it was also apparent that the optimistic projections of the developmentalist planners who had conceived of Krakatau Steel as the lynchpin of a rapidly developing industrial zone around Cilegon had not come to full fruition. Signs of not reaching those confident forecasts were ubiquitous. The private housing development Bukit Palem (Palm Hills), where I rented a house during fieldwork, was located adjacent to the Krakatau Steel housing complex. It consisted of about two hundred houses and was built for a managerial middle class that development planners anticipated would be drawn to employment possibilities at a thriving industrial zone. At least half of the residences were vacant or abandoned and many sported peeling paint, overgrown yards, broken windows, and shutters limply suspended on less than a full complement of hinges. Downtown, just off the main artery that ran through the center of Cilegon, large tracts of land that had been purchased to build commercial districts in the expectation of multitudes of future customers sat empty, with shuttered storefronts and few operating businesses.

Political Power in Banten

The ascent and subsequent slow, steady decline of state-led industrialization in northern Banten during the postcolonial period was mirrored by notable changes in the groups that occupied positions of political prominence in the region. Three different groups had emerged as influential local power brokers. Initially religious scholars known as *kyai* occupied the upper tier of political power. During the New Order they were replaced by military men who owed their positions and allegiance to the central government in Jakarta rather than local clients. They were largely Sundanese and viewed as outsiders by most Bantenese. In the wake of the New

Order, strongmen known as *jawara* emerged as the most politically influential group. The seeds for their emergence had indeed been laid during the New Order as they had strong ties to local military garrisons and were regarded as an informal security force to keep order in the region.

The religious politics of the *reformasi* period at Krakatau Steel and in the surrounding region were the effect of a series of historical contingencies that dated to before the Dutch consolidated colonial rule in what they called the East Indies. Banten was a powerful Muslim sultanate during the sixteenth and seventeenth centuries, primarily due to the fact that it was cosmopolitan node in the trade networks that connected the Java Sea with the Indian and Pacific Oceans (Reid 1988). Furthermore, unlike other Muslim trading ports on the north coast of Java such as Demak, Cirebon, and Giri, Banten did not fall under the sway of the Mataram Empire, which expanded from central Java to cover most of the island by the mid-seventeenth century. Michael Williams argues that Islam historically played a central role in Banten because it was never subjected to the syncretic kingdoms that emerged in central Java (Williams 1990). One illustration of the high degree of Islamic piety in the region is that by the nineteenth-century Banten had the highest per capita proportion of inhabitants who had completed the *hajj* of any region of Java (Kartodirdjo 1966, 332). Today Bantenese are considered by many Indonesians to be second only to the Acehnese in the strength of their faith. According to Williams, the fact that Banten never came under the shadow of central Javanese control endowed "Islam with an undisputed historical and cultural 'hegemony' denied it in many other regions of Java. Islam in Banten was untarnished and not married with Hindu and animist elements as elsewhere in Java" (Williams 1990, xxvii). This assertion, although perhaps overstated in its claims to religious purity, echoes representations that were often made by Bantenese themselves. Thus, it indexes how Bantenese invoke their adherence to Islam as a marker of distinctive identity.

The sultanate's influence waned as the Dutch East India Company accelerated its monopolization of trade routes in the archipelago. The port of Banten was eclipsed by the growing Dutch port of Batavia, and the sultanate became a Dutch protectorate in 1684. However, independent Bantenese political rule was not formally eradicated until 1832 when the Dutch colonial government consolidated control of Java following the termination of the Napoleonic wars and the British interregnum (Ricklefs 1981).

The dismantling of the sultanate led to "a history of peasant struggles in Banten" that are "not between peasant and lord, but between peasants and agents of outside government" (Williams 1990, xxvii). In contemporary Indonesia, Bantenese are often stereotyped as prone to quick tempers and violent behavior. Following the decline of the sultanate during nineteenth-century colonial rule, *kyai* were the most politically influential social group in Banten. *Kyai* (also called *ulama*) are well-respected religious leaders who in many cases acquired Islamic knowledge by studying overseas in places such as Medina, Baghdad, or Cairo, after which they returned to the Indonesian archipelago to establish Islamic boarding schools (*pesantren*).[7] *Kyai* were leading figures in major revolts against colonial rule that occurred in Banten in 1888 and 1926 and are respectively chronicled by Sartono Kartodirdjo and Michael Williams. The 1888 revolt was largely led by a network of *kyai* based in *pesantren* located in and around Cilegon. The revolt of 1926 was led by a coalition of *kyai* and political activists from the Indonesian Communist Party (PKI), an alliance that became increasingly less possible over the course of the twentieth century prior to exploding into the violent confrontation of the mass killings of accused communists in 1965 and 1966 (Robinson 1995; Roosa 2006).

In the postrevolutionary period, and particularly during the New Order, the influence of *kyai* steadily waned. Although during the Indonesian revolution of 1945–1949 *kyai* played an important role in the struggle against Dutch reoccupation forces, military officials were increasingly appointed to the paramount political positions in Banten by the Suharto-led state. Suharto was extremely wary of Islam in the aftermath of rebellions in the 1950s and 1960s that sought to establish an Islamic state in Indonesia (Dengel 1995; Gunawan 2000; van Dijk 1981). These rebellions had variously simmered and boiled against Sukarno's nationalist government in West Java, South Sulawesi, Kalimantan, and Aceh. Given the history of political rebellion in the province under the banner of Islam, the fledgling central government was deeply anxious about the potential political sway of Islam. In Banten, local government officials were largely drawn from the ranks of the Indonesian army's Siliwangi division based in Bandung.

---

7. A description of the position of *kyai* in Banten can be found in Kartodirdjo 1966, 92–96 and Williams 1990, 51–60. See Geertz 1960, 134–136, 177–198 for another description of the role of *kyai* in Indonesian Islam. A more recent account is Dhofier 1999.

Thus, during the New Order the regency heads (*bupati*) and city mayors (*walikota*) in Banten were typically former generals and colonels in the Indonesian military. Most were considered outsiders, as they were mostly from the upland Sundanese heartland around Bandung. These officials were ethnically Sundanese and were unfamiliar with the local Bantenese language and traditions. According to locals these outside leaders were perceived to have stronger connections with national political and military figures based in Jakarta than any demonstrated interest in representing inhabitants of Banten. The disconnect between local political leaders and the aspirations of the people (*aspirasi rakyat*) was one impetus many cited in the move toward regional autonomy that culminated in the formation of an independent province of Banten, based largely on the political boundaries of the former sultanate, on October 4, 2000.

In addition to the appointment of military men to official leadership positions, the Suharto regime cultivated relations with another potent political force in the province: the jawara (also called *pendekar*). This group had a long history in Banten, but their influence was grounded in decidedly different political networks than those of the *kyai* who had amassed their influence through Islamic schools.[8] Although there are analogues in other parts of Indonesia, jawara are considered characteristic of Banten.[9] They enthusiastically cultivate the reputation for toughness and violence for which Bantenese are stereotyped more broadly across the archipelago. Jawara are regarded as men of physical prowess who are also reputed to have supernatural abilities. According to popular representations they are physically powerful and dress all in black with thick, drooping mustaches. The physical prowess of jawara is attributed to their skills in martial arts, particularly the Bantenese version of *pancak silat,* an Indonesian martial art, and *debus.*[10] *Debus* practitioners are said to be able to repel metal objects with their bare skin. Thus, they are impervious to iron and steel and can resist cuts and punctures from knives or swords. More recent stories abound regarding *debus* practitioners who can repel bullets fired from rifles

---

8. Imat Tihami has compared the role of *kyai* and *jawara* in village politics in Banten (Tihami 1992).

9. Joshua Barker discusses the role of *jawara* in Bandung (Barker 1999). Also see Robert Cribb's treatment of the role of "gangsters" in the Jakarta people's militia during the Indonesian revolution (Cribb 1991).

10. For more on *pancak silat,* see Samudra 2008.

and pistols. It is perhaps not entirely coincidental that Indonesia's state-owned steelworks was located in a region in which some inhabitants are considered to have the ability to resist iron and steel with their bare skin.

Historically jawara were viewed as defenders of the dispossessed and were celebrated for their role in anticolonial political movements. During the Suharto period the jawara made a transition from marginal defenders of the dispossessed to influential power brokers affiliated with Suharto's authoritarian regime. As the *kyai* were increasingly marginalized during the postcolonial period, jawara became the most influential political elites in the new province after it was founded. While many parts of Indonesia greeted Suharto's downfall with optimism about the possibilities presented by democratization, in Banten an older set of powerful figures emerged as the most formidable in the province (Masaaki 2008a).

During the New Order jawara became the most politically and economically influential figures in Banten (Masaaki 2008b). By 2003 the richest and most powerful person in Banten was Chasan Sochib, who was the leader of the largest jawara network in contemporary Banten, the Union of Martial Arts and Bantenese Arts and Culture Guardians (Persatuan Persilatan Pendekar dan Seni Budaya Banten). Informally, Chasan was referred to as the "Governor General" (*Gubernur Jenderal* or simply "Gub-Jen"), which was the official title used during the colonial period to refer to the foremost Dutch official in the East Indies. This title was usually articulated with a wry smile as a testament to Chasan's mythic status but also to indicate the widely shared sense that his power was illegitimate and based on the violence and compulsion that characterized colonial rule. Chasan was a larger than life figure in the immediate post-Suharto period, and according to widespread accounts he had several wives and dozens of children.[11] Chasan initially worked organizing labor crews at Jakarta's rough and tumble Tanjung Priok port. Later he returned to Banten where he amassed his fortune by obtaining government contracts for public works projects. He also grew prosperous acting as a broker in land transactions in Cilegon during the period of Krakatau Steel's massive expansion in the 1970s. Chasan would convince small-scale peasants and farmers to sell off their small holdings, sometimes under the threat of violence, and then

---

11. For a short description of Chasan Sochib see Masaaki 2004.

quickly turn around and resell the land to business owners who were attracted to the Cilegon region due to its developing industrial infrastructure. Chasan's daughter, Atut Chosiyah, a Golkar politician, was selected vice governor of Banten in December 2001, and after the governor, Djoko Munandar, was implicated in a corruption scandal she became the governor in 2007, the first female provincial leader in Indonesia.[12] During the New Order Chasan was reputed to be a *centeng Cendana,* and many of the government contracts obtained by his company, PT Sinar Ciomas Raya, were reputed to be evidence of his close relations with Suharto.[13]

Although Chasan Sochib operated on a provincial scale from his base of operations in the capital of Serang, in Cilegon itself the most influential political figure was another jawara, Aat Syafa'at, who became the mayor (*walikota*) of Cilegon after it became an autonomous political unit in 1999. Syafa'at occupied the pinnacle of another patron-client network that was likewise rooted in jawara connections. Accounts of Syafa'at's rise to political and economic prominence varied. Some said that he had started out as an itinerant photographer (*tukang foto keliling*) rolling a rickety cart through the dusty *kampungs* (neighborhoods) lining Cilegon's back streets, taking pictures of families, children, and newlyweds. Other stories asserted that he had been a fish seller with a stall amid the chaos of Cilegon's new market, which lies just off the main road through town. According to some he had left Cilegon at a young age to seek his fortune, initially working as a lowly security guard (*satpam*) in Jakarta. The mystery surrounding his origins and path to a position of prominence was part of his aura. The fact that he was a self-made man who had overcome the rigid hierarchies that stifled mobility in other parts of Indonesia no doubt contributed to his widespread appeal. The story of his rise to power implicitly contrasted the possibilities for social mobility in Banten to other more rigidly hierarchical parts of the island of Java (Siegel 1986).

Managers at Krakatau Steel, who with several exceptions were not native to Banten, were openly dismissive of the local jawara leaders, whom they regarded as crude and unschooled in practices appropriate to modern

---

12. Golkar was the political party formed by Suharto that dominated Indonesian political life during the New Order and remained an influential political force thereafter.

13. *Centeng* can refer to a guard, a hired thug, or even a hit man. Pawns in the game of chess are also referred to as *centeng. Cendana* refers to a street in Menteng, Jakarta, on which Suharto occupied a private residence during and after his tenure as president of the republic. The appellation expresses Chasan Sochib's close relationship to Suharto and his family.

businessmen. In the *reformasi* period jawara controlled most of the major business associations in Banten, including the Builder's and Construction Association (Gabungan Pengusaha Konstruksi or Gapensi) and the Chamber of Commerce (Kamar Dagang Industri or Kadin). Chasan Sochib was the head of the Chamber of Commerce for Banten, and it was rumored that he had first choice of any government construction project in the province. One local activist told me that Chasan would not even consider bidding on a tender for a project valued at less than 50 million rupiah.[14]

Since political decentralization was initiated in 2000 local elites felt entitled to the largesse to which better connected national elites had previously held privileged access. The heads of Kadin were upset that Krakatau Steel had awarded them few contracts. A proposal to steer more company contracts to jawara-controlled businesses was broached at a meeting between senior Krakatau Steel directors and heads of the chambers of commerce for several localities in the Cilegon region. They wanted a portion of the lucrative business of supplying the company with the materials needed for production. Adit, a senior manager at Krakatau Steel, suggested that the jawara, while powerful, did not understand the basic principles of economic rationality and cost accounting that are critical to the survival of major corporations.[15] He lamented that "after regional autonomy (*otonomi daerah*) was implemented, the jawara in the Kadin wanted a piece of Krakatau Steel's business. They wanted to become suppliers for everything from spare parts to raw materials." He explained that "the company normally buys 60 percent of its needs directly from suppliers, particularly big ticket items like motors, transformers, and raw materials." Every piece of iron ore processed at Krakatau Steel came from overseas, but Adit incredulously told me, "Now the Kadin wants us to buy iron ore from them, at a markup over the market price, instead of getting it directly from the producers! It just doesn't make business sense."

In contrast to jawara, Krakatau Steel managers saw the economic and political reforms in the wake of the demise of the Suharto regime as holding the possibility of rationalizing the informal arrangements

---

14. This is equivalent to about $5,000.

15. Adit is a pseudonym. In keeping with anthropological practice and the human subjects protocols under which this research was conducted, I have used pseudonyms to protect the confidentiality of participants in this project. However, I have left the names of recognizable public figures in their actual form.

that threatened the economic viability of the factory given the incipient evaporation of state investment guarantees. In response to the demands of newly emboldened elites, Daenulhay (the president director of Krakatau Steel) introduced a plan to foster local development by building what Adit called "clustered industries" in partnership with local chambers of commerce. These companies would then supply products that they made themselves, such as packing materials, to Krakatau Steel. However, Adit said that the jawara were not interested; rather they wanted to become brokers in existing Krakatau Steel supply chains. He said, "Bantenese are descendents of traders. They don't understand modern business concepts, like the notion of clustered industries." Adit's account of the maneuvers by Kadin evoked the approach to commerce characteristic of Southeast Asian sultans (and subsequently the Dutch East India Company) in the early modern period who sought to monopolize trade routes. The strategy of the chambers of commerce centered on dominating the nodes of trade networks and profiting from existing commercial activity. This business model reflected the earlier economic rationality of *hulu-hilir* (upstream-downstream) exchange characteristic of premodern and early modern Southeast Asia (Bronson 1977). This pattern enabled sultans to amass opulent fortunes by controlling the points at which river systems met the sea and levying duties on upstream and downstream commerce.

Many *kyai* I spoke with resented their eclipse by jawara during the New Order. They saw the implementation of Islamic law as a means to regain political authority in the years following Suharto's downfall. One religious leader told me that the implementation of *syariah* (Islamic law) offered a strategy to "free Banten from the jawara" (*melepaskan Banten dari jawara*). In 2000 and 2001 Banten had made headlines in Indonesia when the new provincial parliament debated proposals for the implementation of *syariah*. Several *syariah* requirements were mandated, including a measure requiring female students to wear a scarf covering their hair and necks (*jilbab*) in state educational institutions. However, by 2003 most concurred that these initiatives had largely failed. Some viewed them as a brazen attempt by local *kyai,* who stood to become the arbiters of *syariah* in the province, to reconstitute their lapsed political power.

At Krakatau Steel managers feared that the implementation of *syariah* would frighten potential foreign investors from Europe and North America who they imagined would be uncomfortable with legal codes that, among other prescriptions, positively sanctioned corporeal punishment. Many employees at the company expressed reticence because they thought that the punishments called for by a *syariah* system were too severe. Like elsewhere in Indonesia (Rinaldo 2008), proposals to implement *syariah* in Banten seemed to be more smoke than fire as there was little interest in implementing *syariah* except from those who stood to become arbiters of the new law codes.

The Religious Politics of Industrialization

Kyai in northern Banten faced not only political eclipse due to the ascension of the jawara but also felt threatened by state-directed industrialization. The initial decision by the Sukarno-led government to locate steel production near Cilegon was somewhat unexpected and entirely unprecedented. On September 15, 1956, the Soviet Union pledged $100 million in "economic and technical development" assistance to Sukarno's government, a portion of which was earmarked for construction of a steel factory (Purwadi, Soemantri, Salam et al. 2003, 14). For several years thereafter the Indonesian government worked in concert with a Soviet survey team to find the best site in Indonesia in which to locate the factory. The final decision came down to two finalists: Cilegon and Probolinggo, a city in East Java midway between Surabaya and Situbondo. The one major advantage Cilegon had was that factory construction would not disturb any agricultural land, as the region lacked productive rice fields (Geertz 1963a; Lansing 1991, 2006). Probolinggo offered other advantages including a skilled labor force, a more developed infrastructure, and proximity to more industrial operations in and around Surabaya, which at the time was comparable to Jakarta in terms of the size of its population (Purwadi, Soemantri, Salam et al. 2003, 15–16).

The ultimate decision to locate the factory in Cilegon appeared to contravene conventional wisdom, as Probolinggo offered distinct advantages. The decision was likely the result of a number of contingent considerations, rather than one overriding imperative. Suzanne Moon notes that Cilegon was a symbolically important city because of Banten's precolonial prominence but had fallen into poverty as an effect of colonial rule. Drawing on speeches by government ministers, including Chaerul Saleh and

Subandrio, she interprets the decision to place a steelworks in Cilegon as a technique through which the state sought to favorably represent the nation as endowed with the capacity to return the region to its former prosperity. This would favorably contrast the nation with the previous colonial regime that had brought poverty to Cilegon and Banten (Moon 2009, 264–266).

People I spoke with in the community of Cilegon, many of whom were affiliated with the region's historically significant *pesantren,* expressed a similar interpretation. For example, Kyai Fathullah, an influential religious leader and Golkar politician, said that the factory was finally awarded to Cilegon because of the heroic role that Bantenese *ulama,* and particularly his father Kyai Syam'un, had played in the 1945–1949 Indonesian revolution. Local *ulama* supported bringing the factory to the province because they realized that opportunities for economic growth were constrained by the paucity of natural resources in the region. Later, when the Suharto regime began to promote the development of Krakatau Steel, Kyai Syam'un's son Rachmatullah (the half-brother of Fathullah) had taken over leadership of the influential Al-Khairiyah *pesantren* that Syam'un had established. The school was located on land that Suharto's technocrats wanted to use for the expanded steel production facilities that were much grander in scale than those initially planned by Sukarno's government. Rachmatullah con-sented to move the *pesantren* to the adjacent village of Citangkil. This was not without controversy due to the fact that there was a cemetery adjacent to the original school.[16] Ultimately, the human remains were left behind. Rachmatullah agreed to move the school in exchange for new facilities constructed by the company and, according to some of his rivals, personal financial benefits. Krakatau Steel's wire rod mill was located on the site formerly occupied by the Al-Khairiyah *pesantren* and several employees alleged that they had seen ghosts from the cemetery prowling about that factory and other mills during night shifts.

From the Soviet point of view strategic considerations likely came into play in the selection of Cilegon as the preferred site for the factory. In the escalating Cold War geopolitical climate, the Soviet Union was likely more inclined to support construction of a major industrial operation and

---

16. It is not uncommon for cemeteries to be located on or adjacent to the grounds of *pesant-ren.* Dhofier notes that the well-known pesantren of Tebuireng in East Java has a burial ground for the family of the founder, Kyai Hashim Ash'ari (1999, 79).

affiliated harbor adjacent to the Sunda Straits. This channel separates Java and Sumatra and for centuries has been a major lane for ships passing from the Indian to Pacific oceans. The construction of a steelworks with the participation of multiple Soviet advisors and engineers would provide access to a globally strategic shipping lane. In 2004 I was told that the port facility through which the iron ore processed at Krakatau Steel passed was the only harbor on Java that could accommodate Panamax freighters, the ocean-going freighters that are the largest possible vessels that can pass through the Panama Canal. This port is owned and operated by PT Krakatau Bandar Samudra, a subsidiary of Krakatau Steel, and handles cargo for surrounding industries and some shipments destined for Jakarta. Thus, it is a critical source of revenue for the company and one that local political elites eyed ravenously after political decentralization, anticipating that the new regional autonomy laws might enable them to assert control over this valuable harbor and the revenues that it generated.

In the late 1950s and early 1960s the central government's decision to place the initial iteration of Krakatau Steel, which Sukarno branded Trikora, in Cilegon was met by local political and religious leaders with enthusiasm but also with a measure of uncertainty.[17] First and foremost among their concerns was that a major industrial operation with workers from other parts of Indonesia and Soviet technical advisors (whom they assumed would be atheists) might spread ideas that would challenge the religious authority of the *kyai*. A story I was told several times attributed the lack of a Christian house of worship in Cilegon to an informal deal struck between local leaders and the national government at the time that the steelworks were being planned. Rizal, a local NGO activist, told me that "the *kyai* agreed to release land for construction of Krakatau Steel, but only on one condition. They said, 'We'll hand over the land for a factory, but no church should ever be built in Cilegon' [*jangan sampai ada gereja di Cilegon*]." According to another version of this story related to me by a Muslim employee of Krakatau Steel, the *kyai* had said, "All nationalities are welcome in Cilegon and anyone can do business here, but no churches will be built." According to these accounts, the local *kyai* realized that the

---

17. Trikora is an abbreviation for Tri Komando Rakyat (People's Triple Command). It comes from a speech that Sukarno gave in 1961 in which he advocated a popular mobilization to wrest West Papua from Dutch control and defend Indonesia from external attack.

influx of outsiders that would likely accompany industrial development would create a more heterogeneous population in the region. Perhaps due to a suspicion of the historical role of the Dutch colonial regime in fostering Christian missionary activity in the archipelago and weakening the political influence of Islamic leaders (Roff 1985), Cilegon *kyai* steadfastly refused the physical presence of a church in the city.

As a result, Christian employees of Krakatau Steel expressed feelings of discrimination. They had to trek twenty kilometers to Serang, the provincial capital, to worship at one of four Christian churches on Sundays. Stefanus, one of the small number of Catholics employed at the hot strip mill, said that Catholics had applied to build a church in Cilegon as early as 1993, but they never received a permit from the local government. He explained, "The land has already been purchased, but permission hasn't been granted." The plan was to put the church on the site of the Catholic school, called Mardiwana, which was located on Cilegon's main thoroughfare on the southern edge of town. Parents were concerned that the students were being exposed to pollution and dust from the main road and had purchased land in a less contaminated part of the city to relocate the school. They then planned to build a church on the original site, but their application to the local branch of the Department of Religion was never processed. In spite of the discrimination that they felt from the local government and religious leaders, Christian employees of Krakatau Steel felt that the company had historically been as supportive of Christianity as it had of any of Indonesia's other official religions. Stefanus told me that every Sunday the company provided buses that were normally used to bring workers to Krakatau Steel to transport Christian employees from Cilegon to one of the four churches in Serang.

Obtaining official statistics on the religious and ethnic composition of the workforce at Krakatau Steel proved impossible. However, most employees I spoke with estimated that between 95 and 97 percent of the labor force was Muslim. Stefanus told me that there were twelve Catholics, seven Protestants, and one Hindu working at the hot strip mill for a total of twenty non-Muslim employees out of over five hundred workers at the mill. For that particular plant employees who were identified as Muslim constituted 96 percent of the work force.

Furthermore, Christians at Krakatau Steel were resigned to the fact that conditions for non-Muslims were unlikely to change significantly.

Suharto-era employment policies looked to state-owned enterprises such as Krakatau Steel as vehicles of social promotion for so-called *pribumi* Indonesians. The word *pribumi* refers to those citizens who are considered autochthonous. Although the religion was established in the archipelago only in the thirteenth and fourteenth centuries, today Islam is a critical criterion for being considered *pribumi* in Indonesia. Religious affiliation is recorded on one's state-issued identity card and Islam is often a critical criterion that denotes a citizen as *pribumi*. *Pribumi* Indonesians were perceived to have suffered economically under colonial policies of administering the colonial plural society.

From "Extreme Right" to Right-hand Men

While Islam played a pivotal in configuring the identity of inhabitants of Banten who lived adjacent to Krakatau Steel, the religion was far less important inside the company during its early days. Factory workers, most of whom had migrated to Cilegon from other parts of Indonesia for work, told me that there was little interest in Islamic practice in the initial years of the company's existence. As one worker explained, "In those days we were young, we didn't think about what comes next, about the afterlife. Only when we got older did those things become important." Several employees related stories about their days as young bachelors who had just begun working at the factory. In those days they would occasionally get drunk and carouse at the end of their shifts. Others confided that they formerly liked to gamble and "chase women" in their younger days.

    In keeping with the general tendency to keep Islam at arm's length during the initial years of the New Order, there were few efforts by company managers to promote religion among employees. The inattention to Islamic strictures in the early days of the company's existence was evident in the company magazine *Bulletin Krakatau Steel*. In one issue published in 1977 there are photographs from a "cocktail party" in celebration of New Year's Day and hosted in the modernist residence of the CEO of the company, Tunky Ariwibowo (*Bulletin Krakatau Steel* 1977). In the photograph Indonesian engineers mingle casually with European consultants who were in Cilegon to provide technical advice for construction of the production facilities. They hold wineglasses and wear expressions of jovial conviviality. Freewheeling parties where alcohol was openly served were hard to imagine by the time I arrived to conduct fieldwork in the mid-2000s. When I attended a gathering organized by the current CEO at the same home in November 2003 I noticed that the bar in the house, located to the right of the front entrance, was conspicuously barren.

Based on the content of stories in the company magazine and conversations with employees, the company increasingly embraced Islam toward the end of the New Order and in the years that followed it. The pace of mosque construction in the production complex accelerated and each individual mill within the factory compound offered its own adjacent place of worship. Plant employees never had to walk far to attend a mosque. In addition, the company contracted popular local preachers to come to the plant mosques and give lectures during Friday prayers and other significant religious events. In the 1990s the factory began paying for senior-level employees to undertake the *hajj* pilgrimage and many employees at all levels participated in Qur'anic study groups (*pengajian*) (Weix 1998).

While efforts to enhance the Islamic practice of company employees were unprecedented, they did not emerge spontaneously. There were two critical historical events that made employees receptive to subsequent efforts to embrace initiatives to intensify Islamic practice. First was the movement for Islamic renewal (*tajdid*) at the Salman mosque in Bandung, and second was the formation of the Indonesian Association of Muslim Intellectuals (Ikatan Cendekiawan Muslim Indonesia or ICMI). These two events, which were themselves related, are critical to understanding not just the increasing visibility of Islamic practice at Krakatau Steel but the broader resurgence of Islam among middle-class Indonesians as a whole.

Contemporary efforts to develop faith are a legacy of the Salman mosque movement (*gerakan Salman*) (Rosyad 2006). While in the 1950s and 1960s Indonesian state universities operated under the presumptions of secular, nationalist modernization, in the 1970s there was a rapid rise in Islamic activism among university students. Central in this change was the Salman mosque movement, which was led by Imaduddin Abdulrahim, a professor of electrical engineering at Institut Teknologi Bandung (ITB). The Salman mosque was located on the campus of ITB, which has historically been Indonesia's leading science and engineering university and counts the nation's first president, Sukarno, among its graduates. The mosque became a center for the study of Islam by Indonesian university students

Figure 1.8. The An-Nur mosque at the wire rod mill. Adjacent to the mosque steel coils were stockpiled for shipment.

in the mid-1970s. Muslim students came from across the archipelago for short, intensive courses dedicated to religious study. The movement spread in rhizomatic fashion across the archipelago after students who had come to the Salman mosque returned to their home campuses to disseminate the religious lessons that they had been exposed to in Bandung (Rosyad 2006, 33). In courses offered as part of the Defending and Proselytizing the Faith Training (Latihan Mujahid Dakwah) and the Salman Mosque Youth Association (Keluarga Remaja Islam Salman), students learned the basic teachings of the Islam (Tirtosudiro 2002). Courses were often dedicated to personal problems that participants faced, and the mentors sought to offer solutions to these problems commensurable with Islam (Rosyad 2006, 34).

Although Imaduddin had an engineering degree and had never attended an Islamic institute of higher education, his father had studied at Al-Azhar

University in Cairo and provided him with instruction in Qur'anic recitation and interpretation while he was a child growing up in Langkat, North Sumatra (Rosyad 2006, 24). Widely known by the nickname "Bang Imad," Imaduddin became a well-educated and highly skilled engineer.[18] He obtained his bachelor's degree from ITB and later earned a master's degree in electrical engineering from Iowa State University in 1965. Imaduddin returned to Indonesia and became a member of the engineering faculty at ITB. He became increasingly interested in reform movements elsewhere in the Muslim world that sought to reconcile Islam with modernity. As the foremost activist in the Salman mosque, Imaduddin thought of the mosque as not merely a place of worship but also as an institution to educate young Muslims to be future national leaders. The training programs developed at the Salman mosque and then disseminated across Indonesia after students returned to their home universities sought to show how Islam offered solutions to the challenges of modern life and are an important precursor to the ESQ training program that followed it nearly thirty years later.

Bang Imad's efforts were viewed with suspicion by the Suharto-led state, which remained wary of public Islamic activity. The specter of the Darul Islam rebellions remained a fresh memory. Imaduddin was arrested by the New Order government and spent fourteen months in detention prior to his release in 1979. Prevented from returning to his previous position as a faculty member at ITB, Imaduddin left for the United States a second time to pursue another advanced degree. He graduated with a PhD in industrial engineering in 1985. However, his interests by this time had shifted from technical pursuits to human resources management, and his thesis was titled "Organizational Effectiveness of Universities in Malaysia" (Imaduddin 1985). The dissertation is framed by the problem of Indonesian national development. It takes human resources training as a pressing problem and, in language that was later echoed in ESQ, argues that "an effective education management system is the first and most important solution to the multicomplex problems" facing the country (Imaduddin 1985, 6).

In his later published work Bang Imad sought to make explicit the connection between Islamic principles and economic practice. One of his

---

18. *Bang* is a shortened, honorific form of *abang,* which literally means elder brother and is commonly used in Sundanese West Java, where ITB is located.

books, published in Malaysia, is titled *The Spirit of Tauhid and Work Motivation* (Imaduddin 1992). In this work Imaduddin drew on the notion of *tauhid,* the principle of the unity of Allah, to make an argument later taken up by ESQ and other contemporary spiritual reformers in Indonesia. *Tauhid* involves an acknowledgement of the oneness of Allah. Imaduddin and later Ary Ginanjar both argued that recognition of the unity of God meant that all of one's activity is conducted in the name of God, not just activities that were recognizable as religious, such as going to mosque or performing requisite prayers. Thus, Imaduddin laid out the argument that there was an economic ethic inherent in Islam that could facilitate Indonesian development.

The Salman movement was the bellwether of a broader transformation in the role of Islam in Indonesian public life. Robert Hefner writes that by "the early 1980s Salman-inspired outreach had become a feature of campus life at almost every university in Indonesia" (Hefner 2000, 123). The movement was historically significant because it marked a change in the way in which Islam was viewed by middle-class Indonesians. Bang Imad argued that Islam was commensurable with the scientific and technical educations in which many members of the growing middle class in Indonesia had been inculcated. As Suzanne Brenner has shown, the dramatic growth of interest in Islam that took place on university campuses in Indonesia in the 1970s and 1980s was not a reversion to tradition (Brenner 1996). Many of the women interviewed by Brenner adopted Islamic dress to explicitly contrast themselves with the practices of their parents and preceding generations.

Furthermore, Imaduddin's efforts to find the commensurabilities between Islam and modernity resonated with similar projects elsewhere in Southeast Asia. He had a long-lasting friendship with Anwar Ibrahim, the long-time protégé of Mahathir Mohamad, who became the deputy prime minister of Malaysia in 1993.[19] In 1967 Anwar, in his capacity as president of the Islamic youth organization Angkatan Belia Islam Malaysia, invited Imaduddin to Malaysia to lecture on Islam and modernization (Tirtosudiro 2002, 49).

---

19. Anwar later fell out of favor with Mahathir, was deposed from the cabinet, convicted of corruption and sodomy, and sentenced to prison.

Bang Imad's influence was significant at Krakatau Steel because historically the company drew heavily on graduates of ITB to fill its ranks of managers, engineers, and technical experts. Not only is the university Indonesia's foremost technical university, but it is also located in the province of West Java, in which Krakatau Steel was likewise located prior to the formation of the breakaway province of Banten in 2000. Many employees of the company were Sundanese and had strong connections to Bandung and ITB. Several employees stated that ITB alumni networks were often key factors in obtaining promotions to more prestigious and lucrative employment positions. Due to the fact that many Krakatau Steel employees graduated from ITB during the heyday of the Salman movement, they had been exposed to Imaduddin's arguments about how Islamic practice was conducive to national development. Several employees told me that they had heard Bang Imad lecture at the Salman mosque as undergraduates at the university.

The Salman movement was an important forerunner to ICMI, another institution in Indonesia that sought to dissolve the purported opposition between Islam and modernity. Following the emergence of a growing university-educated middle class inclined toward Islam, ICMI was established in 1990 under the leadership of Suharto's right-hand man, B.J. Habibie.[20] ICMI was intended to improve the economic standing of Muslim professionals. The establishment of this organization marked a significant transformation in Indonesia's New Order history because it represented a dramatic shift in Suharto's governing strategy. Whereas prior to the formation of ICMI Suharto had held Islam at arm's length, by encouraging some of his most trusted lieutenants to found such a high profile group Suharto signaled his growing embrace of Islam.

It is not coincidental that the founding of ICMI occurred as a generation of students who had been exposed to Salman-inspired Islamic outreach at the university assumed positions in government and industry in Indonesia. ICMI was established in December 1990 as Suharto sought to court the growing legions of middle-class Indonesians who embraced Islam. Suharto, who had previously been more interested in Javanese mysticism (*kejawen*), made the *hajj* pilgrimage in 1991 and symbolically adopted the

---

20. My discussion of ICMI draws on Hefner 2000, 128–166.

new name Haji Mohammed Suharto. Thus, the early 1990s marked the inception of a new political strategy in which Suharto began to openly court influential elites inclined toward Islam as he sought to balance shifting political tides in Indonesia. The change marked vindication for Imaduddin after his long period of persecution and imprisonment by the state during the New Order. He was asked to be a founding member of ICMI and became instrumental in coordinating the organization, recruiting members from the ranks of engineers and scientists inclined toward Islam who had been trained at ITB and other elite institutions of higher learning in Indonesia. He viewed the opportunity as a chance to redress long-time policies of the Suharto-led state that he saw as detrimental to Islam (Tirtosudiro 2002, 51–55).

This shift in the state's political strategy laid the foundations for managers at Krakatau Steel to adopt spiritual reform twelve years later. This transformation by the company was just as seismic as that which had taken place in national politics. One employee told me about how, until 1998, he had worked as a screener to weed out prospective company employees who were "of the extreme left and extreme right." By the former he meant anyone who had been affiliated with the Indonesian Communist Party. If their parents or more distant relatives had been in a labor union sympathetic to the Communist Party they would be denied employment at Krakatau Steel, even if they had never claimed membership in such an organization. In addition, he noted that the company was also intent on refusing employment to anyone linked to the "extreme right," which referred to Muslim militant groups that had fought to establish an Islamic state in Indonesia during the 1950s and 1960s.

To counter these political influences, the company had historically downplayed religious identification in favor of cultural participation.[21] One example of this was evident in photos from 1970s editions of *Bulletin Krakatau Steel* in which there were accounts and photos of practices identified with Javanese culture such as *slametan*.[22] These ritual feasts are associated with syncretic *abangan* forms of spiritual practice and created a

---

21. For an extended discussion of the role of culture as a domain of political intervention during the New Order see Pemberton 1994a. For an historical explanation see Roff 1985.

22. Barker has described how Javanese culture became a stand-in for Indonesian national culture during the New Order (Barker 2005).

"defined social group pledged to mutual support and cooperation" (Geertz 1960, 11). In the depictions of early versions of the company magazine, *slametan* took place to mark the opening of a new factory or the installation of a new piece of machinery. These rituals were a manifestation of "New Order policies…[to bring about] the relegation of Javanist spirituality to the sphere not of religion (*agama, din*) but of personalized religious belief (*kepercayaaan*)" (Hefner 2000, 84). In the wake of the violence and political conflict that had brought Suharto's regime to power, *slametan* at the factory in the 1970s were not so much religious activities but rather communal collective activities intended to build workplace solidarity and were perhaps intended to forestall the formation of class-based political affiliations (Wertheim 1977).

By the 1990s accounts of activities such as *slametan,* which Hefner has identified as "public Javanism" (Hefner 2000, 84), were increasingly rare in the company magazine. Instead there were many more articles and photographs with explicitly Islamic content, such as company commemorations of Idul Fitri (the holiday to mark the end of the fast) and Idul Adha (which marks the climax of the *hajj* pilgrimage). By 2004 there was a monthly column in the company magazine specifically dedicated to religion with exclusively Islamic content. These changes are the outcome of broader transformations in Indonesia reflected specifically in Suharto's embrace of Islam, the founding of ICMI, and the legacy of the Salman movement, and more generally in the departure from the regime's dual-pronged reliance on public Javanism, on the one hand, and pluralist nationalism, on the other, as means of forging a collective identity.

Even after the fall of the Suharto regime ICMI remained an influential organization. In 1993 it established *Republika* as a national Muslim newspaper (Hefner 1997). The publication offers an Islamic perspective in contrast to *Kompas* which, although acclaimed as Indonesia's newspaper of record for the high quality of its reporting and editing, is viewed with suspicion by some Muslims on account of the Catholic religious beliefs of the majority of its owners and editors. At Krakatau Steel, company offices received both *Kompas* and *Republika* daily. In 2005 a full page dedicated to ESQ began appearing in *Republika* every Tuesday. With articles such as "Raising Production through Spirituality" and a schedule of upcoming ESQ trainings, the full-page spread amounted to an advertisement for the training program. In addition to articles there were individual accounts of ESQ alumni who integrated spirituality into their work practices and a special section on "News for Alumni." The January 17, 2006, edition of "The ESQ Way" page included personal anecdotes supporting ESQ from the former minister of state-owned enterprises Rozy Munir and the Indonesian soap opera (*sinetron*) star Irfan Hakim (*Republika* 2006b).

The connection between ICMI as a representative organization of educated Muslims nationally and ESQ was solidified when Ary Ginanjar was appointed as a member of ICMI's Board of Experts (Dewan Pakar ICMI Pusat) in February 2006 (*Republika* 2006a). Other members of this board included national leaders identified with Islam such as Marwah Daud Ibrahim (a prominent Golkar politician who was named head of ICMI in December 2005), Hidayat Nur Wahid (leader of Partai Keadilan Sejahtera and head of the MPR, the People's Consultative Assembly), and Sugiharto (the minister of state-owned enterprises in the first Yudhoyono cabinet). In selecting Ary Ginanjar to the ICMI Board of Experts, Marwah Daud Ibrahim, who holds a PhD in communications from American University in Washington, DC, and was a candidate for vice president in the 2004 national elections, cited his vision for resuscitating Indonesian economic growth as the primary rationale for his appointment. In announcing the selection she invoked the concepts that Ginanjar had developed, stating, "We chose Ary Ginanjar because he is very concerned with developing human resources. This is in accord with the future mission of ICMI which is to develop human resources that are intelligent in their IQ, EQ, and SQ" (*Republika* 2006a). In an extremely complementary article that ran in *Republika* and was taken directly, without editing from a press release on ICMI's website, the newspaper asked rhetorically, "Isn't it true that ESQ has...a social plan [*tatanan masyarakat*] for intellectual, emotional, and spiritual intelligence? May this synergy be taken as the point of departure toward the glory of the unified nation of the Republic of Indonesia" (*Republika* 2006a). Ary Ginanjar's selection to the ICMI Board of Experts confirmed him as a pivotal Islamic leader at the national level in Indonesia and a prominent heir to the legacy of Bang Imad in seeking practical techniques to dissolve the opposition between Islam and modernity.

Privatization and the Predicament of Nationalist Development

Two related historical events precipitated the implementation of spiritual reform at Krakatau Steel: the Asian financial crisis of 1997–1998 and plans to privatize the company. While the Salman mosque movement and

the establishment of ICMI lay the critical social and intellectual groundwork for the introduction of ESQ training, the financial crisis and proposals to privatize Krakatau Steel made spiritual reform attractive in the
years following the end of the Suharto regime. The financial crisis called
into question the bargain that Indonesian citizens had made with President Suharto, who had enabled the economic well-being of the population
at the price of their political freedom. The crisis, which many Indonesians
referred to in its aftermath as *krismon* (a shortened form of *krisis moneter* or
monetary crisis), threatened to undo more than two decades of spectacular development success in Indonesia during which the country's economy
was among the fastest growing in the world, averaging nearly 7 percent
per year (Hill 2000).

Although the precise causes of the crisis are still a matter of some debate, the consensus among most economists and economic historians is that
Indonesia, like other Southeast Asian nations and South Korea, had bor-
rowed at unsustainable rates during the boom period of the early 1990s.
From a value of 2,450 per U.S. dollar in July 1997 the crisis saw the rupiah
bottom out at 17,000 per dollar by January 1998, meaning that some Indonesians saw the purchasing power of their money for some commodities
drop to less than one-sixth of its precrisis value (Soesastro and Basri 1998).
The crisis affected all levels of Indonesian society, from the upper-class Ja-
kartans who were compelled to sell household appliances out of the trunks
of their Mercedes-Benz sedans at impromptu street-side flea markets to
the hundreds of thousands of industrial employees who found themselves
jobless after the export-oriented factories in which they were employed
shut down when financing had evaporated. On May 21, 1998, Suharto
resigned in disgrace ending thirty-two years of authoritarian rule under
"Mister Development."

For Krakatau Steel the situation was not as dire as it was in other cor-
ners of the country. Although some employees expressed the sentiment
that they felt poorer because many commodities had become drastically
more expensive, there were no mass layoffs of employees at the state-
owned firm. Krakatau Steel actually became more profitable because the
depreciation of the rupiah against other foreign currencies meant that the
company's chief product could be sold more cheaply overseas. Nonetheless,
media reporting of hundreds of factory closures and almost weekly bank
collapses demonstrated that the country's development project had run

aground. The economic growth that had once been lauded by the World Bank as a development success story appeared to be more illusory than real. The financial crisis had decisively called the faith that many had held in Indonesia's development success into question.

The second reason that managers at Krakatau Steel were attracted to spiritual reform was that they thought that it would align the labor practices of company employees with global corporate norms and thus make Krakatau Steel more efficient, competitive, and ultimately attractive to private investors. They sought to reconfigure workers who had formerly been purveyors of national development into employees who could enable the company to be competitive in an economy no longer defined in national terms. The company was faced with a set of unprecedented challenges: privatization, the elimination of state subsidies to fund modernization of aging facilities, and the end of tariffs on steel imported into Indonesia. Proponents of spiritual reform concluded that Islam was a more effective technology of belonging than nationalism in garnering the support of workers as the company sought to adapt to these new economic conditions.

Privatization of the company, which had been first broached in the late 1990s, was perhaps the most ominous challenge facing the company. During the course of the New Order, Krakatau Steel had become accustomed to recurring government investment in technological upgrades that were regularly part of the state's Five-Year Development Plans (Rencana Pembangunan Lima Tahun or REPELITA). However, when I arrived at Krakatau Steel in 2003, it had been eight years since any new production facilities had been constructed, and there were no imminent plans to build new mills. In 1996 company directors had prepared a plan for future expansion to keep pace with rapid technological changes in steelmaking technology. Following a series of bailouts in which the government assumed the company's debt, the Ministry of Trade and Industry informed Krakatau Steel's directors that they would have to find outside investors to fund any future expansions or upgrades.[23]

Privatization of state-owned enterprises had become an increasing priority of the Indonesian government during the twilight of the New Order (Robison and Hadiz 2004, 77). After being spurned by the central

---

23. The most notable of these bailouts involved a transfer of the cold rolling mill from the tycoon Liem Sioe Liong to state ownership. This transaction is detailed in chapter 5.

government Krakatau Steel directors launched an ambitious plan to ensure the company's ability to keep pace with the rapidly changing steel market. The first attempt at privatization in early 1997 involved a joint venture with the South Korean steel company Posco. However, by July the Asian financial crisis hit, and by November Posco had pulled out of the deal. In spite of the worsening crisis, the Minister for State-Owned Enterprises, Tanri Abeng, proceeded full bore with plans to privatize the roughly 180 firms under his ministry. Krakatau Steel was projected to be one of the first to be dispensed. On May 5, 1998, the massive global steel conglomerate Ispat International put forward a $500 million bid for a 51 percent ownership stake in the company (Abeng 2001, 109–113). Ispat, under the leadership of the charismatic Indian billionaire Lakshmi Mittal, specialized in buying up distressed state-owned mills (many of which were located in the countries of the former Soviet Bloc) and making them profitable through austere management reforms, often including mass layoffs. When directors at Krakatau Steel caught wind of the new privatization plans they began to raise questions about the proposal. Senior managers at the company felt that the funds Ispat was planning to invest should be used to upgrade outdated production facilities, but government ministers, increasingly concerned about the state's financial solvency, wanted to direct the funds to national coffers as a way to recoup a portion of the government's massive investment in Krakatau Steel. When the directors were shown the memorandum of understanding that Abeng had reached with Ispat, they responded by obstructing the process, and a public quarrel broke out between the minister and the CEO of Krakatau Steel at the time, Soetoro Mangunsoewargo.

When political and religious leaders in Banten were informed of the plan to privatize the company they organized a series of raucous protests in front of the Ministry of State-Owned Enterprises in Jakarta. Particularly steadfast in their opposition to privatization were local religious leaders, especially those affiliated with the influential Al-Khairiyah Islamic school that had been relocated to facilitate Krakatau Steel's expansion during the early New Order. The head of the school, Kyai Satibi Ali Jaya, told me that when plans for privatization were announced he went to Jakarta to demonstrate against it "because if the land was sold to foreigners, the people here would be marginalized again [*tersisi kembali*]." Referring to Ispat's Indian ownership, Kyai Satibi continued, "If it was sold to India they would be nothing again [*jadi nul lagi*]." He feared that the underdevelopment that had plagued Cilegon until the massive state investment associated with the construction and operation of Krakatau Steel would return if the company was transferred to foreign ownership. Alluding to the fact that he had previously consented to moving Al-Khairiyah in the 1970s, he threatened to reclaim a still unpaid debt if the nationalized company was transferred to foreign ownership. With a menacing rap of his fist on the table he conjured up the possibility of an alliance between the two most formidable political networks in Banten: "This was my land before and if it is sold, I'll burn it all down…not for the interest of Indonesia, but for the interest of Cilegon first.…The people of Cilegon talk a lot, but if they are angered they will be united, the *ulama* with the *jawara,* and Krakatau Steel will be destroyed!"

The intimidation tactics that he deployed in the midst of Indonesia's political and economic crisis were apparently effective. Kyai Satibi said, "We brought three buses to Jakarta for the demonstration. There were hundreds of people. We wore turbans and the jawara wore their all-black clothing. Tanri Abeng was shaking in his boots!" Kyai Satibi confirmed accounts that suggested Krakatau Steel officials and local leaders had collaborated to scuttle the planned privatization. He said that the buses "were paid for by *oknum* [influential figures who use their power for disreputable purposes] within Krakatau Steel.…We *ulama* don't have any money you know." In response to local political outcry the national parliament began to inquire about the legitimacy of the proposed transfer. Furthermore, the controversy was taking place against the backdrop of tumultuous political events culminating in Suharto's resignation. Ultimately, as demonstrations and riots proliferated across the archipelago, Ispat decided that Indonesia was too politically unstable and pulled out of the deal, leaving Krakatau Steel without an international suitor.

In the years following the end of the New Order and the financial crisis a number of other proposals were put forward to privatize the company. However, during the period I was conducting research there was a lull in these plans for several reasons. First, influential political figures and corporate managers did not want to let loose what for years had been a cash cow. Between June 2003 and December 2004 global steel prices increased from $250 per ton to $600 per ton, reaching as high as $625 per ton in September 2004. Thus, the company was turning a tidy profit for the government. Second, political and company officials did not want a repeat of the tumult that had caused them to shelve their initial privatization proposal in 1998.

Religious leaders remained resolute in their opposition to privatization of Krakatau Steel even after the end of the New Order. Kyai Satibi thought that foreign ownership would mean that the new owners would bring outsiders to work at the company: "The people of the nation [*bangsa*] would only sit and watch, while the people they brought got all the jobs." He further invoked the historic debt that the state had incurred, explaining that the land for the factory was never "sold by the people, but only exchanged for compensation to build the factory. It's different from a sale!" In explaining his opposition to privatization Kyai Satibi argued that the agreement transferring the land that his school had held in the 1970s had been based on a gift logic (Mauss 1990) rather than the rationality of the market. In his eyes, local inhabitants had allowed the company to come to the region and operate undisturbed with the understanding that the sacrifice was for local and national development. They tolerated environmental pollution, growing inequality, and an influx of outsiders (many of whom were not Muslim) under the presumptions of faith in development. Furthermore, the leaders of Al-Khairiyah had consented to transferring ownership of the land on which the original school and its adjacent cemetery (with all its skeletal remains) sat based on the understanding that this was the cost of modernization. According to Kyai Satibi the exchange of land for development had not been conducted according to purely financial considerations but rather according to the understanding that the postcolonial state would remedy some of the disadvantages that the region had suffered as a result of colonialism (Moon 2009). In his eyes, the land on which Krakatau Steel sat had a history that could never be quantified in an accounting ledger.

Given these local and global political and economic considerations, by 2003 some senior managers at Krakatau Steel felt that the best opportunity to raise the capital needed for plant expansion and modernization would come through selling shares in the company to private investors through an initial public offering (IPO). However, others thought that going public would expose the company to the possibility of a hostile takeover and the uncertainty and whims of stock markets. By 2006 the company again decided to pursue a strategic investor. One joint venture that never materialized was a proposed deal with the Bank of China to develop a pelletizing process. This would have enabled Indonesia's domestic sources of low-grade iron ore from Kalimantan and Sumatra to be processed in the company's furnaces.[24] However, as the price for steel rose to record levels before the financial crisis of 2008, the government reconsidered and hoped to finish an IPO before commodity prices dropped again. The political obstacles to doing so appeared too great, though, and by the end of 2008 Krakatau Steel was again flirting with the idea of forming a partnership with either Australian-based BlueScope Steel or ArcelorMittal, one of Lakshmi Mittal's other companies (Krismantari 2008).

Debates over the future direction of the company were not merely conducted by corporate managers, government bureaucrats, and local religious and political leaders. Krakatau Steel employees heatedly debated the merits of privatization. On the one hand, those opposed to privatization expressed fear of job losses after the shift from state to private ownership. They often invoked a durable trope that had guided faith in development: that industrial modernization, the epitome of which was steelmaking, was essential to economic growth and national progress. Thus, their employment was justified by the centrality of steelmaking to national development. On the other hand, arguments in favor of privatization were motivated by the fear that the company could no longer rely on state investment for upgrades to aging production facilities and would thus go bankrupt due to an inability to compete in an increasingly global steel market. Furthermore, many were aware that privatization of state-owned enterprises was a condition of the IMF's bailout of the Indonesian government. Under the terms of this agreement, foreign companies would be the primary investors, and private ownership was expected to create "efficient and viable enterprises" (Government of Indonesia 2000).

In addition to calls for privatization, Krakatau Steel managers also had to address the reconfiguration of an economy that had previously been defined in national terms. The elimination of tariffs on imported steel posed another threat to the company's future prospects. Since the company's inception the central government had applied such tariffs to protect the growth of the domestic steel industry. Although the rate of these tariffs had declined over the three decades of Krakatau Steel's existence, they continued to ensure that the company enjoyed a favorable position in relation to transnational competitors. However, in April 2004 under pressure

---

24. All the ore processed at Krakatau Steel was imported because Indonesia's domestic sources were not of sufficient iron content to enable processing with the company's existing technology.

from downstream domestic consumers of steel the central government announced the complete elimination of these duties. One manager vowed to
take the company's fight against this new policy to the national parliament,
explaining, "We are going to run editorials in the newspaper about Krakatau Steel describing its function and position as a strategic industry. We
will show them how many downstream industries are dependent on our
raw materials. The best path to development is through production, not
trading. We will appeal to the nationalism of the legislators!" Thus, arguments similar to those that had been articulated against privatization were
mobilized to turn the tide against the elimination of import tariffs on steel;
namely, the modernist presumption that industrial production, especially
steelmaking, was crucial to national development.

These entreaties aside, the project of nationalist modernization that had
for so long been central to the New Order developmentalist project was in
the process of reformulation. The reliable infusions of state guarantees to
facilitate the expansion of steel production had reached their end. Import
tariffs would no longer shelter Krakatau Steel against competition from
steel behemoths in China, South Korea, Japan, and elsewhere. Perhaps
most ominously, the specter of privatization loomed on the horizon her-
alding an uncertain future. As debates over these wide-ranging changes
flared among factory employees, managers at Krakatau Steel turned to
Islamic spiritual reform as part of a strategy to create an "efficient and viable" enterprise. In so doing, they sought to create a spiritual economy in
which intensified Islamic practice would elicit the dispositions conducive
to corporate competiveness in an increasingly globalized economy.

Conclusion: A Tarnished Modernity

The financial crisis that afflicted Indonesia in the late 1990s called into
question the project of faith in development through massive state investment that had supported industrialization. In this respect, events in Indonesia resembled those depicted by James Ferguson in Zambia, where the
luster of metal also inspired faith in development. Zambian citizens once
held confidence that they were on the brink of joining the ranks of middle-
income countries, but by the late 1980s they had lost conviction in "the tele-
ological narratives of modernity" (Ferguson 1999, 14). Ferguson describes

how on Zambia's once-booming Copperbelt, in the wake of the economic crisis that led to diminishing living standards, "cynical skepticism replaced an earnest faith" (1999, 14). Ferguson suggests that the loss of faith in development that he found in Zambia may come to characterize much of the rest of the developing world. He argues that "something has happened in recent years to the taken-for-granted faith in development as a universal prescription for poverty and inequality. For Africa, at least, as for some other parts of the world, there is a real break with the certainties and expectations that made a development era possible" (1999, 247). Ferguson specifically invokes conditions in Indonesia after the Asian financial crisis to those that he encountered in Zambia, and suggests that it may be another example of a nation where "the modernist plot line of history seems to be running in reverse" (1999, 255).

When I was conducting fieldwork at Krakatau Steel it was clear that the company had not achieved many of the lofty expectations that development planners had envisioned. This was palpable not only in declarations that the political and economic crises were products of a deeper moral crisis but also in the dilapidated material condition of Krakatau Steel's factories, offices, and housing complex. It was further evident in the laments expressed by employees that facilities were not on par with those in European or North American countries, where a number had studied, trained, or travelled. Finally, it was evident that economic growth in the Cilegon region at large had not achieved the grandiose visions of modernist planners. The luster of modernity, like the luster of its metallic medium, had been tarnished.

This might suggest corroboration of Ferguson's conclusion that the assumptions of modernist developmentalism were being similarly questioned in Indonesia. However, as described in more detail in the following chapter, this was not the case. Rather those who had for so long held faith in development instead sought to develop faith. This project represented not so much a break in the modernist plot line of history as its reconstitution. In Indonesia the loss of faith in development did not precipitate the kind of hopelessness, anxiety, and sense of missed opportunities that characterized Zambia after the copper crash. Rather, Indonesians identified problems with the particular strategy of developmental nationalism that had been pursued in the country. In response, they sought to mobilize resources at their disposal to address those challenges. In practice what this entailed was not so much an abandonment of the developmentalist narrative but rather an attempt to revive it in different guise by developing faith among employees of state-owned enterprises, government institutions, and private firms. They did not call into question the conceptual foundations of developmentalism; they sought to reform how development was executed. Thus, this new project represented development's afterlife more than its ruin. Spiritual reform was posited as an antidote to the failure of state-directed development to bring about living standards characteristic of so-called developed countries. This involved a self-reflective approach to the political and economic crises in Indonesia insofar as these crises were taken to be the result of past misdeeds by those individuals who participated in spiritual reform. The creation of a spiritual economy sought to suture some of the divisions that characterized faith in development, such as the distinctions between spiritual and vocational knowledge, between religious practice and work, and between science and religion.

2

Developing Faith

During the Suharto era the Indonesian state aggressively sought to develop the nation through technocratic and technological interventions. Suharto drew a measure of his legitimacy from the fact that he had introduced fiscal stability and economic growth in contrast to the price shocks and financial disorder that had characterized the Sukarno years (Robison 1986, 120; Schwarz 1994, 43–44). The regime's success in improving the living standards of citizens served as a foil to justify authoritarian rule and political repression. The technocrats affiliated with the regime were responsible for enhancing Indonesia's industrial and technological capacity and ensuring that macroeconomic policies promoted fiscal growth. These experts took it as axiomatic that national development was the key to enhancing the living standards of the population (Thee 2003).

However, this faith in development was called into question by the economic turmoil and political crisis that occurred along with Suharto's downfall. The excesses of the Suharto regime were evident in the spectacular failure of several high profile and technologically intensive schemes, such as the state's quixotic forays into aircraft and automobile production. In addition, there was growing awareness that the country's lauded development success was in fact beleaguered by corruption, collusion, and nepotism (*kolusi, korupsi, dan nepotisme* or KKN). Furthermore, it was no longer obvious that the lives of Indonesian's citizens had improved, despite thirty years of the dogged pursuit of modernization. Adherents of Islamic spiritual reform concluded that the single-minded quest for economic development had been misguided and that the political and economic crises of the late 1990s and early 2000s were manifestations of what they considered a deeper "moral crisis." According to these Indonesians the turmoil and uncertainty that was a persistent feature of life after the New Order was due to the fact that the state and its subjects had embraced material development in contrast to moral development. In the rush to modernization, Indonesian citizens had lost sight of spiritual fulfillment and emotional connection.

Spiritual reform was a specific intervention designed to address the crisis precipitated by what some saw as a blind faith in development. It became apparent that schemes for Indonesian modernization had not achieved the effects expected. Thus, scientists and engineers previously committed to the principle that any worldly problem could be resolved through the proper application of technical knowledge turned to spiritual reform to address the apparent failures of development. The spiritual economy that emerged was a new formation in which faith itself was constituted as the object of development.

Designing Workers: The Logic of Spiritual Reform

Ary Ginanjar, the creator of ESQ, sought to elicit a new pattern of life through a meticulously designed training program in which he eventually hoped to enlist all Indonesian citizens. The program drew on ideas culled from human resources and personal growth training sessions in North America, Europe, and Asia.[1] I participated in or observed these three-day-

---

1. The program echoed not only the Seven Habits of Highly Effective People training offered at Krakatau Steel but also the "Ethics Retreat" described by Dorinne Kondo (Kondo 1990, 76–115).

long spiritual trainings over a dozen times between 2003 and 2008, both in Cilegon and in Jakarta. The training is a replicable form that has been delivered hundreds of times in Indonesia and, more recently, outside the country as well. The ESQ Leadership Center offers different versions of the training that are tailored for specific audiences, but the basic structure and principles of the program are the same. In addition to the three- and four-day "executive" and "professional" trainings, there are also two-day "regular" trainings, as well as sessions specifically for teens and younger children. At Krakatau Steel, most training sessions were three-day "professional" trainings, which were also regularly scheduled in numerous cities across Indonesia.

At Krakatau Steel the training sessions were held in the factory's education and training center. My participation in these trainings was initially as a trainee, as there was no other category into which an ethnographer could readily fit. Those admitted inside the training space were slotted into one of three categories: trainers, trainees, or alumni (the designation applied to those who completed the training). After completing the training I fit into the final category and was permitted to attend subsequent trainings as an observer. This status afforded me the opportunity to discuss the training with participants and alumni while the program was occurring. I was also able to get a behind-the-scenes view of the training. For example, as an observer I was able to see what happened to participants who were removed from the room after losing consciousness during particularly evocative moments. Many alumni from Krakatau Steel identified these episodes as cases of spirit possession (*kesurupan*).

One trainer, Zulfikir, gave me a schematic outline of what each day of the training was designed to achieve. He explained how the main activities undertaken were expected to elicit a specific kind of personal transformation. Thus, he referred to the first day as "ice breaking and conditioning," in which techniques were deployed to enable participants to open up to the possibility of "changing themselves" through the methods of ESQ. They were also introduced to the basic concepts on which the training is founded, such as the God spot, emotional quotient, and spiritual quotient. On the second day, after the participant has been "broken down" they were "reprogrammed" by being confronted with existential questions that they were obliged to answer to affirm their identity as Muslims. These included "Where are you from?" "Where are you now?" and "Where are you going?" He said that by posing these questions participants were encouraged to reflect on their own lives and recognize certain practices that were not compliant with Islam. Participants were instructed not to "worship" material things, property, their job positions, or their education. They were called on to atone for pursuing material concerns to the exclusion of living acceptably to Allah.

On the third day, Zulfikir told me that participants were "built back up anew." Techniques to practice self-control over material desire and emotional outbursts were introduced. Participants were encouraged to formulate a "vision and mission statement" for their own lives by creating life goals that are consistent with the moral requirements of Islam. Finally, the concept of "total action" was introduced through a *hajj* simulation. Total action referred to taking responsibility for one's acts and being "proactive" in one's work and home lives. This was a key lesson for employees of institutions that during the Suharto era were rigidly hierarchical and in which workers were expected to wait for orders from superiors rather than taking initiative of their own accord. Spiritual reform was designed to transform passive objects of the hierarchical system characteristic of the New Order into proactive subjects who made decisions based on their own judgment.

The basic structure of the training sessions I participated in and witnessed were essentially the same as the one I describe here, although there was some flexibility in the program. Ary Ginanjar and other ESQ employees continually integrated new ideas and activities that they had encountered into the training. The lead trainer at Krakatau Steel changed from Ary Ginanjar to his brother Rinaldi Agusyana in April 2004, about midway through the period during which I conducted the bulk of my fieldwork at the company. Ginanjar had designed the training to be a replicable form that anyone who had mastered the correct embodied dispositions could deliver. This was an important business technique, because it meant he did not have to deliver each ESQ training himself but could instead "license" others to give the training under the auspices of the ESQ Leadership Center. By December 2008, over eighty licensed ESQ trainers were regularly conducting sessions in Indonesia and Malaysia.

The primary vehicle for the training was a Microsoft PowerPoint presentation, a ubiquitous global form for conveying knowledge and producing truth (Rudnyckyj 2009). This highly sophisticated presentation

Figure 2.1. An overview of spiritual training in the Granada ballroom at the newly constructed ESQ convention center. Two of the projection screens display Ary Ginanjar's image. The other three screens have an image of the ESQ model. Note that the women (visible in headscarves) are separated on the left side from the men on the right. Copyright Ary Ginanjar Agustian, ESQ Leadership Center.

consisted of the customary slides with graphs, charts, tables, and a litany of bullet points, as well as video clips, colorful photographs, animated graphics, and popular music. The lead trainer deftly narrated this presentation in a range of oratorical styles, which variously resembled the enthusiastic rhetoric of a motivational coach, the contrived sincerity of a talk show host, the astute technical pronouncements of a corporate manager, and the fiery and evocatively emotive speech of a televangelist.

The sensory experience of the training was often remarked on by past participants and the environment was meticulously modified to elicit specific reactions. The sound in the hall was sometimes elevated to earsplitting volume, and huge speakers created vibrations that at times could be felt ominously oscillating through one's body. The lights in the room were manipulated to maximize the dramatic effects of points made. Interactive

Figure 2.2. Participants in an ESQ training session wearing 3D glasses. The training used sophisticated multimedia presentations to elicit affective dispositions. Copyright Ary Ginanjar Agustian, ESQ Leadership Center.

games and calisthenics were deployed to break up the monotony of sitting and listening. The air conditioning was turned to its lowest setting, creating a disconcerting chill in an otherwise sultry tropical climate. Cooler temperatures facilitated physical contact like embracing that was a key part of eliciting the affects deemed conducive to the personal transformation sought (see chapter 4). There were breaks for snacks and meals, and coffee and tea were dispensed at regular intervals, ensuring that the audience was alert, attentive, and enthusiastic.

At 7:00 a.m. on June 9, 2004, there was an air of eager anticipation as scores of employees milled about the large multipurpose room of Krakatau Steel's education and training center to begin their first day of ESQ training. The program was officially introduced by a manager in the human resources division who explained that the purpose of the training was to "uplift the motivation" (*bangkit semangat*) of company employees. Prior to introducing Rinaldi as the lead trainer, the authority of the method was constructed through slides projected on three huge screens at the front of the room that displayed photographs of previous groups that had participated in ESQ, including several branches of the military and a number of prestigious Indonesian companies.

The religious authority of the training was conveyed through a picture of and endorsement by Kyai Habib Adnan, a former member of the advisory board for the national Council of Islamic Scholars (Majelis Ulama Indonesia or MUI) and the person Ary Ginanjar identified as his chief mentor. Positive sanction from a representative of the MUI was critical, as it is an influential national organization that defines appropriate practice for many Indonesian Muslims.[2] Religious sanction for ESQ did not come only from members of institutions such as the MUI that are sometimes branded "conservative" or "traditional." Another prominent religious figure who had endorsed the program was Nurcholis Madjid, who during the years before and after the end of the New Order was widely regarded as Indonesia's foremost Islamic intellectual and a guiding force behind what became known as "liberal Islam" in Indonesia (Nurdin 2005). A quote from Madjid promoting ESQ was prominently displayed on the back cover of Ginanjar's first book (Ginanjar 2001).

After these endorsements were presented, the qualifications of Ary Ginanjar and Rinaldi were projected. These qualifications emphasized their previous positions as executives in successful Indonesian and multinational corporations. To an optimistic soundtrack of electronic music, many in the crowd were impressed by the fact that Ginanjar had authored two "best selling" books about ESQ. Participants were then invited to participate in a short prayer. Rinaldi announced that he would deliver the prayer in a "Muslim manner" but non-Muslim participants (of whom a handful usually attended trainings at the company) were encouraged to pray "in accordance with their own religions."

Over the course of the morning Rinaldi introduced a number of key concepts that Ginanjar had concocted or drawn from popular psychology,

2. The MUI is a national organization of Islamic scholars created by Suharto in part to neutralize possible political challenges framed in Islamic terms. For a discussion of the MUI and its increasingly prominent role as the dominant representative organization for Indonesian Muslims see Bowen 2003, 229–240. Bowen argues that the MUI has become the critical institution in Indonesia for defining appropriate conduct for Muslims.

life coaching, and business management principles. These concepts included emotional quotient, spiritual quotient, the zero mind process, and the God spot. The initial sessions of the training were dedicated to explicating these concepts and their relevance to spirituality as a foundation for action in the everyday lives of participants. Seven "rules" for participants were also conveyed at this time. Participants were instructed that to fully benefit from the training, one should "be an empty glass," "eliminate preconceptions" (*bersihkan persepsi*), "be focused," "express emotions," "not be a Mussolini,"[3] and "keep smiling." They were told that they did not need to worry about taking notes but instead should relax and view the material as if they were "watching a film."

After a short break for coffee and tea, Rinaldi launched into the key argument of the first morning—that religious practice was conducive to economic success. Evidence for this claim was drawn from a lengthy display of content downloaded from a webpage for an online story about a Harvard Business School seminar that was titled "Does Spirituality Drive Success in Business?" and was held April 11–12, 2002, in Cambridge, Massachusetts. Rinaldi used reports of this program to demonstrate that prominent business celebrities advocated spiritual practice as a key to commercial success. Participants were next presented with a lengthy critique of materialism in which executives from successful multinational corporations were invoked, such as the founder of the Honda Motor Company, Soichiro Honda. Although he was the president of a major global company, Honda was lauded for living a simple life with hobbies such as painting on silk. Rinaldi also asserted that Honda did not amass wealth for the sake of passing a fortune on to his children but rather encouraged them to seek their own worldly fortunes. This may have been a veiled critique of Suharto, who had allowed his children to use their father's political clout for gratuitous self-enrichment.

The critique of materialism was a major focus of the training, which may be understandable given that this is a relatively new issue in a country where the middle class has only in the last two decades grown to constitute

3. This meant that one should be open and receptive and not be arrogant and dismissive during the training. This point was graphically conveyed by using a World War II era photograph as a counterexample. The image depicted Benito Mussolini bearing a smug expression and crossed arms.

a sizable portion of the population. Secular materialism was represented as an obstacle to achieving real happiness and a major cause of stress. However, ESQ did not advocate complete abnegation of worldly possessions. Ginanjar told me, "Before I and my friends thought that money is everything. You know, money, houses, big cars…are everything! But now, I see that they are only a tool. It doesn't mean I don't drive a car. Now I have a bigger car, a better car, but it is not our value…not the goal, not the end." Instead, ESQ was designed to instill the principle that one's ultimate goal is to ensure otherworldly salvation.

After lunch, participants were invited to remove their shoes and sit on the thinly carpeted floor of the training hall. Moving from chairs to the floor created a more relaxed atmosphere and facilitated certain training activities in which chairs would have created obstacles. This transition evoked the embodied experience of participating in Islamic ritual activity, since a mosque likewise contains no chairs and worshippers remove their shoes before entering. Several times during the training the audience was exhorted to kneel in prayer toward the Kaaba,[4] which entailed participants turning over their right shoulders to face an angle roughly 150 degrees to the stage and kneeling in the direction of the *qibla*.[5] This pattern, in which participants sat in chairs initially but subsequently moved to the floor, was repeated on each of the three days.

The training further replicated the spatial arrangements of a mosque insofar as the physical separation of men and women was maintained. Although initially the small number of women participants were scattered throughout the audience, after the second break in the first day of training there was a clear gender division in the seating arrangements.[6] When I asked trainers and participants about this segregation, I was told that it was at the initiative of the participants themselves, occurring when they realized that the training was as much religious in orientation as it was dedicated to

---

4. This is the central shrine in the Al-Haram mosque in Mecca around which pilgrims circulate during the *hajj*.

5. The *qibla* indicates the direction toward the Kaaba which Muslims should face when performing prayers.

6. Although the vast majority of the workforce of Krakatau Steel was male, a small group of female employees were usually in attendance at spiritual training sessions. They were generally members of the company's clerical staff or employees of the company hospital, Krakatau Medika.

improving the human resources of the company. A pattern emerged over the three days whereby women congregated at the front of the room in the middle, and men sat around on the sides of the room and in the rear.

Three key events in the first afternoon set the stage for the rest of the training. These were intended to elicit the individual reflection of participants. First, an employee of Krakatau Steel, who had previously participated in ESQ training, provided a personal account of his or her experience. Referred to as "sharing," this testimonial entailed a description of the personal transformation that they had experienced as an effect of the training. This account lasted only about ten minutes, but it was emotionally powerful and the speaker wept openly. The story typically centered on a past history of personal inattention to Islam, a recitation of one's experience of renewal during ESQ and a rededication to Islam following it, and finally connecting this personal transformation to more widespread corporate success, with a plea that Krakatau Steel be "built up again" (*bangkit kembali*). Second, immediately following the sharing episode was the recitation of a long prayer in the darkened room in which participants were encouraged to "remember" their mothers and ask for forgiveness for past disobedience toward their parents. This collective paean of remembrance for one's mother resonated profoundly with the participants as it evoked the material and symbolic centrality of mothers in Indonesian domestic life (Koning 2000). This was the first time that there was widespread emotional expression in the room, as many broke into tears remembering improprieties against their mothers.

The juxtaposition of the sharing session in which employees were implored to return Krakatau Steel to "glory" with a session eliciting remembrance for past misbehavior to one's parents was not coincidental. In so doing, ESQ likened past disobedience to one's parents to disaffection toward the company in the present. By offering these two confessionals sequentially the training conveyed the message that just as employees had acted entitled to the care and material support once provided by their parents, they were now taking for granted the care and support provided by the company. Thus, the training sought to draw on metaphors of kinship, in which the factory was likened to a "big family" (*keluarga besar*) to cultivate employee solidarity (Shever 2008; Yanagisako 2002).

A central theme of ESQ training was that the origins of the twin pillars of Western modernity—science and capitalism—can be found in the

Qur'an and the *hadiths,* the collections of writings that relate the words and deeds of the Prophet Muhammad. The final key activity of the first day sought to prove that modern science had recently confirmed the truth of Islam. Rinaldi gave a history of astronomy in which he chronologically presented various theories for the structure and history of the universe. Thus, he began with Ptolemy's arguments against proponents of a flat earth and discussed Copernicus' arguments for a heliocentric solar system. He described how Galileo was persecuted by what he termed the "orthodox" Catholic Church for affirming Copernicus' teachings. He then discussed the ideas of Einstein, Hubble, and Hawking before delivering the day's climactic claim—that key developments in modern science were revealed to Muhammad in the seventh century and are evident in the Qur'an.

This astonishing argument was premised primarily on Edwin Hubble's formulation of the big bang to explain the origin of the universe and its subsequent "proof" (*dibuktikan*) by the Hubble telescope seven decades later. This lecture was a central feature of every ESQ training and culminated in a verse from the Qur'an, displayed in triplicate on the massive projection screens, that read: "Have not the unbelievers then beheld that the heavens and the earth were a mass all sewn up, and then We unstitched them and of water fashioned every living thing? Will they not believe?" (Qur'an 21, 30).[7] ESQ trainers provided a startling interpretation: that this passage referred to the big bang and that it "proved" Muhammad had received divine knowledge of the event thirteen centuries before it was encountered by modern science. Rinaldi asked the audience, "Is it possible [*apakah itu mungkin*] that Muhammad, a man, could have known of the big bang himself?" He paused theatrically and then answered the question emphatically of his own accord, "No! It is impossible!" The session quickly turned into a rousing collective prayer in which participants were incited to demonstrate their devotion to Allah. As many in the audience uttered vigorous protestations of faith, Rinaldi turned the microphone over to a participant who wailed an affirmation of his devotion to Allah. Nearly shouting, Rinaldi implored the speaker to declare that Allah was responsible for the creation of

---

7. Most Qur'anic passages are translated using the Arberry version, except where noted (Arberry 1955). The Arberry translation uses the Flügel numbering system, and the original quotations from ESQ training that I reproduce use the Cairo numbering system. Therefore, I have used the Arberry translation but kept the original Cairo numbering system.

the earth, the sky, and all humanity. He then grabbed the microphone back and roared at the audience, "Who has made you?" The assembly, many of whom were whimpering and wailing at this point, responded "Allah" in tortured unison. The potency of this point was reflected in the fact that it was often repeated to me by past participants of the program as evidence that the truths established by modern science were already contained in the Qur'an. ESQ used this argument to encourage the intensification of piety by affirming the commensurability of modern science and technical knowledge with Islamic doctrine.

The second day of the training again began at just after 7:00 a.m. with a prayer and a recapitulation of the climactic point of the previous day in which the truth of the Qur'an was affirmed through the fact that it anticipated modern scientific knowledge (and vice versa). After this, the participants collectively sang a *salawat,* a Middle Eastern musical form that praises the prophet Muhammad. This song, "Salaatuallah," was sung karaoke-style at high volume by everyone in the room multiple times during the last two days of the training, often immediately preceding breaks. After returning from a short coffee and tea break, the lead trainer gave an illustrated, interactive lecture in which the basic argument was that humans are all the same everywhere because they respond the same way to external stimuli. This claim was illustrated through an interactive session in which the audience was asked to describe its reactions first to images of bucolic landscapes and subsequently to photos depicting violence and destruction. The first set of images included serene lakes, shimmering streams, and grand mountains. The second set of images included photographs of emaciated World War II concentration camp victims and Eddie Adams's iconic Pulitzer Prize–winning photograph from the Vietnam War in which General Nguyễn Ngọc Loan holds a gun to the head of a Vietcong prisoner on a Saigon street. The near uniform revulsion among members of the audience to these images was invoked as evidence that Allah had imbued every human being with the same universal characteristics.

The notion of a universal humanity was also asserted through chiromancy. A graphic of two human hands was projected on the screens with the palm lines boldly accented. The three most prominent lines on each palm look something like ٨١ on the left hand and ١٨ on the right hand. These are the symbols used in the Eastern Arabic numeral system that correspond to the numbers 81 and 18. Surveying the room I saw most participants inspecting their own palms to verify this claim. Quickly a second graphic was projected that contained the equation $81 + 18 = 99$. Rinaldi told the audience that "Allah had inscribed these numbers" to remind humans of the *asmaul husna* (99 characteristics of Allah). He told the crowd these characteristics were inherent in all humans but were often "blocked" by negative influences. Immediately another set of slides reproduced "international business surveys" that showed that the top twenty most admired characteristics of businessmen around the world correspond with the *asmaul husna*. Thus, honesty, the most admired characteristic of managers according to these surveys, was likened to Al-Haqq, or the Most True. Visionary, which was second on the list, was asserted to be the same as Al-Bashir, or the All-Seeing. The *asmaul husna* were then invoked as qualities that employees should cultivate. Another slide was projected titled "The Culture of Work [*Budaya Kerja*] at Krakatau Steel" with four bullet-pointed attributes below: discipline (*disiplin*), openness (*keterbukaan*), mutual respect (*saling hormat*), working together (*kerja sama*). Rinaldi said that these were all "characteristics from the names of Allah" that employees should seek to develop in their everyday practices. Thus, participants could become better Muslims and better corporate employees by cultivating the characteristics with which Allah had endowed humanity.

The activities in the morning session of the second day essentially concluded the five central claims made during ESQ training. Most significant was the claim that enhanced spiritual practice yields business success. The second claim was that those who had benefited from New Order economic development (mostly middle- and upper-class citizens) had been too intent on material success and developing their technical knowledge but not focused enough on their emotional and spiritual development. Third, the training argued that the beneficiaries of development had been irresponsible. Just as trainees had acted entitled to parental love as children, their privileged place in Indonesian developmentalism under "Mister Development" Suharto had led them to feel entitled to corporate care. Fourth, ESQ asserted that Islam held eternal truths that were subsequently confirmed by modern science. Finally, the program affirmed that there was a universal set of human values that had been endowed by Allah in all humans and that these values were also conducive to business success.

Beginning in the afternoon of the second day participants in the program were led through a series of exercises intended to turn these theoretical

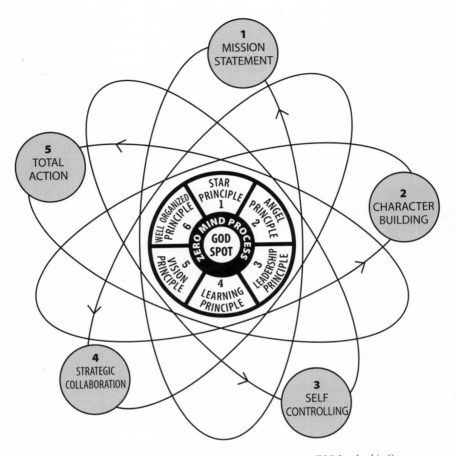

Figure 2.3. The ESQ model. Copyright Ary Ginanjar Agustian, ESQ Leadership Center.

claims into embodied practices. This involved interactive exercises in which participants were led through the principles and actions that make up Ginanjar's "ESQ model." The model consists of six core principles of ESQ that are based on the *aqidah* (six articles of the faith or *iman*) and five practices that are based on the five pillars of Islam. For example, the "star principle" is based on the first pillar of *aqidah,* monotheism. Ginanjar stated that this pillar of the faith, rebranded as the "star principle," implied that one should "possess an intrinsic feeling of calmness and security, high trust in oneself, strong integrity, a wise outlook, and possession of a high level of motivation, all based and built from a faith toward Allah" (Ginanjar 2001, 83). During the training, several stories were narrated to relate this principle, the most evocative of which was a dramatic rendition of the Old Testament story of Ibrahim and Ismail.[8] Ibrahim's readiness to sacrifice his son as a sign of his devotion to God was invoked as a model for the faith that a devout Muslim should practice. Participants in the training were rebuked for "forgetting" that their love for Allah should surpass love for any other thing or being, including their own children. The narration was delivered in such melodramatic tones, with Rinaldi himself weeping into the microphone, that by the end many in the audience also had tears streaming down their faces.

The stunning climax of the day only came later, immediately before *maghrib* prayers, when Rinaldi illustrated the "vision principle" which is based on the fifth pillar of *aqidah*—the conviction in life after death.[9] This principle echoes the second habit of Stephen Covey's Seven Habits of Highly Effective People program, "Begin with the end in mind," although it contains an explicitly salvific justification. The principle states that one should "always be oriented toward the final goal. Take every step in the most optimal manner and with conviction. Possess self-restraint and social restraint, because of the realization that there will be a 'Day After.' Possess certainty about the future and possess elevated spiritual composure out of the certainty that there will be a 'Judgment Day'" (Ginanjar 2001, 150). Proof for the afterlife was based on the research of Dr. Raymond Moody, a summary of which was projected on the giant video screens. The participants were told that Moody's research into near death experiences scientifically proved that a disembodied existence persisted after death.[10]

---

8. According to Islamic tradition Ibrahim took Ismail, his son with Hagar, to be sacrificed upon God's command (Qur'an 37, 101–113). This differs from Judaism and Christianity in which Abraham is called by God to sacrifice Isaac, Abraham's son with his wife, Sarah (Delaney 1998).

9. *Maghrib* is the first evening prayer for Muslims and occurs at sundown. It is a particularly important prayer for employees of Krakatau Steel because it represents the end of the workday for nonshift employees. The need to return home before *Maghrib* occasionally offered an excuse to leave work early.

10. Moody is a renowned American public intellectual, media presence, and best-selling author. A medical doctor, Moody also holds a PhD in philosophy and has conducted extensive research on near-death experiences, out of body experiences, and life after death (Moody 1976; Moody and Perry 1993). His website claims that *Life after Life*, his most well-known book, has sold over 13 million copies.

Immediately thereafter participants were confronted with their fate in the afterlife and instructed that they must take responsibility for their religious practice if they wanted to avoid damnation. The room was pitch black, the sound system was elevated to a thunderous volume, and the air conditioning appeared to be turned to its coldest setting, creating an almost refrigerator-like chill. Two film clips were juxtaposed with a voice-over by the lead trainer in which he narrated the agony of death and the horrors of hell. The first film clip was from one of the climactic scenes in the Hollywood blockbuster *Titanic* in which hundreds of near lifeless bodies surround the sinking vessel, freezing to death in the icy waters of the North Atlantic. This clip was immediately succeeded by one from a Harun Yahya film called *Kehidupan Alam Barzakh* (Life in purgatory).[11] The clip depicted a visual representation of a corpse being called to account for worldly sins in the afterlife as hellacious fires burn the corpse's body. In dramatic tones trainees were ominously reminded that they too will be called to account for their sins in the afterlife. These graphic depictions brought to a dramatic close the second day of training. Many left in tears, and several told me that they found this portion of the training the most disconcerting but also the strongest in inciting them to question the way in which they live.

In contrast to the agonizing conclusion of the second day, the third day began in much calmer fashion. The audience was instructed in techniques to memorize the *asmaul husna* to facilitate their salvation. Then participants took part in an extended prayer, and a child, who had successfully memorized the *asmaul husna*, recited the 99 names standing at the front of the room. Rinaldi reproached the crowd, saying, "If a small child nine years of age can memorize these 99 names, then certainly all of you can too." Participants in the training told me that there was a strong incentive to memorize the names because doing so was understood to ensure direct admittance to heaven on Judgment Day. For trainees, who had been confronted with a graphic video depiction of the misery of hell on

---

11. Harun Yahya is the pen name of Adnan Oktar, a Turkish public intellectual and a critic of Darwinian theories of evolution. His series of DVDs and books critiquing atheism, communism, and Darwinism are dubbed into Indonesian and circulate widely in contemporary Indonesia. See www.harunyahya.com.

the preceding day, memorizing the *asmaul husna* offered the possibility of otherworldly redemption.

Rinaldi then explicitly connected Islamic history to business leadership in a lecture on the "leadership principle," which drew on the second pillar of *aqidah* commanding faith in prophets. This principle was illustrated with a graph drawn from an article titled "Pygmalion in Management" published in the *Harvard Business Review* (Livingston 1988). The graph represented the relation of employee motivation to business success. The y-axis was labeled "strength of motivation" and the x-axis was labeled "probability of success." The x-axis had three equidistantly spaced numbers: 0.0 at the y-axis, 0.5 in the middle, and 1.0 at the far right. Above the numbers was a smooth bell curve that peaked above 0.5. To those in the audience, most of whom had degrees in engineering and other technical fields, the graph demonstrated that motivating employees was most effective when they were led to believe that any undertaking had only a 50 percent chance of success. If they felt there was little chance of reaching a goal, or a too easy possibility of success, motivation would decline. The lesson was that managers had to consistently convey to their subordinates that corporate goals had only a 50-50 possibility of realization. The leadership principle was also illustrated in film clips from *The Message,* a 1976 film about the life of Muhammad that stars Anthony Quinn as Hamza, the prophet's uncle, and Irene Papas as Hind, the leading antagonist of Muhammad in Mecca. Muhammad was invoked as a visionary leader and a model for a modern CEO because he had inspired the first Muslims in the face of persecution and the possible destruction of the faith. Drawing on the preceding lesson from the Harvard journal, Rinaldi asserted that the rapid expansion of Islam during the religion's early years was attributable to the fact that early Muslims did not know they would be successful, but their leaders were able to convince them that their struggles were not lost causes either.

Next Rinaldi delivered a spirited motivational lecture likening work to a form of religious worship. "Never forget, we all work for Allah," Rinaldi shouted while a series of quotes from the Qur'an flashed on the screen. He exhorted company employees to "become representatives of Allah at Krakatau Steel" and consider their labor "a vehicle to meet Allah." Drawing on evidence from the Qur'an and the *hadiths,* Rinaldi declared that by working hard one could insure otherworldly salvation. Following this explicit link between work and worship the most fantastic event of the training took place. This was a simulation of the traditional Islamic practice of *talqin,* which was described as the "climax" (*puncak*) of ESQ training.[12] *Talqin* is a funerary practice that consists of instructions offered to a corpse on how to respond to the questions of the angels of death, who will visit the recently deceased after the last mourner has departed from the grave. Over the public address system an assistant trainer recommended that "people with high blood pressure or heart conditions and pregnant women" not participate.

In the dimly lit hall over two hundred participants sat in pairs embracing each other while heavy metal music roared at ear-splitting decibel levels. One, playing the role of the angels of death, Mungkar and Nakir, yelled "Who are you? Who is your God? Who is your prophet? What is your book?" while the other, playing the role of his or her own corpse, wept tearful declarations of repentance. Two assistant trainers dressed in dark business suits paced frantically about the room, guiding the participants in the simulation. They screamed into microphones in an animated call and response. One repeatedly shouted, "Who are you?" while the other offered answers at equal volume. These responses varied: "*Laa ilaa ha illallah* (There is no God but Allah).... Wealth can lie.... Children can die.... Allah is my flesh.... Allah is my destination.... Put Him into your heart.... Put Him in your body.... Put Him into your marrow.... My God is not property.... My God is not money.... *Laa ilaa ha illallah.*" By framing this traumatic simulation of their own future burials with exhortations that work is a means of ensuring salvation, participants were encouraged to conclude that work was a form of worship.

As the training program moved toward its culmination the message changed from repentance to becoming proactive. Thus, participants worked through five practices contained in the ESQ model over a period of about eight hours. These practices were based on the five pillars of Islam and were called 1) "mission statement" based on the *syahadat* or Muslim

---

12. The *talqin* ceremony is well documented in accounts of Islamic practice in Indonesia. Geertz provides an account of the *talqin* in eastern Java (Geertz 1960, 71) and Bowen describes a similar ceremony in the Gayo highlands (Bowen 1984, 24–25). However, the accounts of Geertz and Bowen both describe an actual funeral ceremony, whereas during ESQ the *talqin* was a simulation intended to prepare participants for the afterlife. Thus, no actual corpse was present.

confession of the faith, 2) "character building" founded on the requirement to pray five times a day, 3) "developing self-control" derived from the
requirement to fast from sunup to sundown during Ramadan, 4) "strategic
collaboration" developed out of the requirement of each Muslim to pay
zakat or 2.5 percent of their income to charity, and 5) "total action" based
on the requirement that each Muslim make the pilgrimage to Mecca at
least once during their lifetime, if they can afford to do so. Interactive exercises were devised to illustrate each of the practices. Thus, for "strategic
collaboration" each participant paired up with another, shined his or her
shoes, and then reciprocally paid the other for the service. The funds were
then collected for donation to charity. A common criticism of employees of
state-owned enterprises was their poor customer service, and the exercise
was intended to illustrate that it "feels better" to serve than to be served.

As day stretched into night, Rinaldi gave an impassioned motivational
speech about how the employees had to "Remember the greatness of God"
and "Raise up [*bangkit*] Krakatau Steel!" He continued in resounding fashion for several minutes and people in the back of the room gradually began
to take to their feet. Before long, all the participants were standing and
moved to the front of the room, where a succession of company employees
took turns standing on a chair and giving emphatic motivational speeches
exhorting their colleagues to return Krakatau Steel to greatness. The common refrain was "Raise up KS!" shouted at peak volume alternated with
yells of "*Allahuakbar!*" (God is great). This combination was repeated frequently and interchangeably. Thus, developing faith by recognizing the
greatness of God through enhanced Islamic practice was equated with returning the company to its earlier glory under faith in development.

The concluding exercise of ESQ was intended to illustrate how hard
work and devoted worship were mutually constitutive. While music with
a pulsating beat and histrionic melody played loudly, the participants
simulated three well-known stages of the *hajj* pilgrimage. These included
tawaf, the circumambulation of the Kaaba; the *sa'i,* a ritual that consists of
running seven times back and forth between the hills of Safa and Marwah
in Mecca;[13] and, the stoning of Jamrat Al-Aqabah, in which pilgrims hurl

---

13. The *sa'i* ritual consists of running or rapidly walking seven times back and forth between
the hills of Safa and Marwah in Mecca. This is a reenactment of Hagar's anxious search for water,
before the well of Zamzam was revealed to her by Allah.

rocks at three representations of the devil.[14] The chairs at the edges of the room were stacked neatly to maximize the usable space in the hall, and the women and men were divided into two groups on opposite sides of the room. Three successive representations of the devil drawn on big flip charts were displayed. The participants were given little balls of paper that were vehemently hurled at the pictures. The motivational music reached a crescendo when the *sa'i* was enacted by running back and forth across the room. Each participant completed seven cycles, while a dramatic historical video glorifying Krakatau Steel was projected on the screens.

Finally, an impressive replica of the Kaaba was introduced into the center of the room. Participants walked around it singing, "*Laa ilaa ha illallah*" (There is no God but Allah), while two different videos were juxtaposed on the projection screens. The first showed pilgrims circling the actual Kaaba in Mecca, and the second contained a live feed of the simulated circumambulation taking place in the room. The video juxtaposition blurred the distinction between the actual ritual and the simulated one. The line was further rendered vague at the conclusion of the simulation when the trainers saluted the participants with chants of "Hey *haji, haji, haji.*" The trainers and alumni went around the room miming the act of cutting a lock of hair of those that had "just completed the *hajj*." This was modeled after one of the activities that pilgrims undertake during the actual *hajj*, when one's hair is shorn to symbolize the personal transformation that one is expected to experience during the pilgrimage. The subjective change expected during spiritual training was thus likened to the transformation that one is said to experience during the actual *hajj*.

The mood brightened considerably when the lights were brought up to full illumination. Rinaldi spoke about the need for employees to remember their mission in life was to ensure their salvation and said that "the training was intended to achieve a transformation" conducive to enabling this. A video of Ary Ginanjar was projected in which he saluted the participants for completing the training. Rinaldi said that the "training was given by Allah and was based on the five pillars of Islam" and, in customary Indonesian fashion, asked for forgiveness for any mistakes that he or his staff had

---

14. The stoning ritual takes place in Mina just outside of Mecca and represents rebuking of the devil. This requires collecting a number of pebbles from the ground on the plain of Muzdalifah and hurling the pebbles at the three pillars at Mina, which represent the devil.

made. After a series of speeches and exchanges of gifts between the ESQ trainers and representatives from Krakatau Steel, the event was brought to a close. Each participant filed out of the assembly hall into the foyer, where they received a certificate testifying to the fact that they had completed the training, and then into the darkness of an already advanced evening.

Managing Indonesian Muslims: The Scale of Spiritual Reform

ESQ training was one manifestation of the emergence of a broader formation in Indonesia during the years following the end of the Suharto regime. This spiritual economy, as I describe in detail in the next chapter, entailed combining personal growth, life-coaching, and human resources principles with Islamic practice to provide a design for middle-class Muslim lives. In addition to the emergence and dramatic growth of ESQ a number of similar initiatives sought to combine management knowledge and Islamic practice.

When I participated and observed this training in 2004, ESQ still operated on a relatively modest scale. Although Ary Ginanjar had attracted some influential Indonesians to the program, it was just beginning to expand rapidly (see table 2.1). By the end of 2004, 45,000 people had completed ESQ training, but shortly thereafter the program exploded in popularity as Indonesians were attracted to the program in ever-increasing numbers. Although I found ESQ's brazen attempt to represent Islamic ethics as conducive to corporate success intellectually fascinating, I had no inkling that I had encountered merely the early stages of the program's tremendous growth. When I returned to Indonesia in 2008, over 616,000 people had

TABLE 2.1. Cumulative Number of Participants in ESQ (at Year End)

2001	43
2002	1,700
2003	15,000
2004	45,000
2005	138,000
2006	269,000
2007	465,000
2008	616,000

Sources: http://www.esqway165.com, http://www.esqkepri.com/joomla

gone through the training, thousands more were enrolling in the training program each week, and the company was expanding aggressively elsewhere in Southeast Asia.

Although Krakatau Steel was one of the first large companies to embrace ESQ, the program quickly spread across Indonesia to more of the country's most prominent governmental institutions. By early 2006 Ary Ginanjar had decided that his greatest growth would come from what were called "public" trainings, in which people paid up to $350 out of their own pockets to participate. By 2007 ESQ had met its goal of becoming a national movement by establishing branch offices in thirty out of thirty-three Indonesian provinces.[15] ESQ seeks not only to enable Indonesian companies to cultivate practices conducive to competitiveness in an increasingly transnational economy but also to globalize in its own right. In April 2006 ESQ realized its ambition to "go global" by holding the first overseas ESQ training in Kuala Lumpur. In praising the program, Mahathir Mohamad, the former Malaysian prime minister, suggested that ESQ built upon his Look East Policy. He endorsed the program, saying, "This is the first time I have met Ary Ginanjar, but I believe that my thinking converges with the aspirations of ESQ" (Sutan 2008). In addition, full ESQ training sessions have been held in Singapore and Brunei, and smaller events have been organized for Indonesian expatriates in the Netherlands, Australia, and the United States.

In 2005 the ESQ Leadership Center initiated construction of a new office tower and convention center in south Jakarta, which was partly funded through investment shares sold to past participants. The bottom seven stories of the building replicated the exterior of the Kaaba. Cubic in shape, it is clad in black marble with a wide, golden-colored band of stone surrounding the section about two-thirds of the way up the sides. By May 2008 the opulent convention center had been completed, and ESQ trainings were regularly held in a facility specifically designed for it. The company planned to lease the still under construction office space above to multinational corporations.

---

15. The only three Indonesian provinces in which ESQ had not conducted activities were Gorontalo, Maluku Utara, and Nusa Tenggara Timur. By 2009 ESQ had consolidated its focus on Malaysia, Singapore, and thirteen of Indonesia's most wealthy provinces: East Java, Central Java, West Java, Bali, Riau, East Kalimantan, Papua, Riau, South Sulawesi, West Sumatra, South Sumatra, North Sumatra, and the Jakarta capital region.

In addition to ESQ, there were multiple other manifestations spiritual reform, several of which used the term "management" (*manajemen*) in their title. "Management" had become a common catchword in Indonesia in the aftermath of the New Order, because the economic crisis was attributed in part to a failure of management. At state-owned enterprises "good corporate governance" had become one rubric under which corporate executives sought to reform the past practices of their institutions. The financial difficulties that their companies faced were represented as due to administrative failure and corruption. While many efforts to promote better management were secular and technocratic in nature, a number of initiatives, including ESQ, sought to find precedent for better administrative practice in Islamic history and texts. These programs commonly invoked the English loanword *manajemen* in their official names and included programs such as Manajemen Qolbu, Celestial Management, and Manajemen Syariah.

The Manajemen Qolbu Corporation was another widely popular initiative to merge Islamic practice with management principles (Hoesterey 2008; Watson 2005). This Islamic services conglomerate used first an English-derived term (*manajemen*) and then an Arabic word (*qolbu*) to yield a name that translates as "Management of the Heart Corporation." The company was founded by the charismatic engineer-turned-television preacher Abdullah Gymnastiar, widely known as Aa Gym. Until his star dimmed after his decision to marry a second wife in December 2006, he was one of the most recognizable public figures in Indonesia and appeared regularly on several national television channels.

Aa Gym developed a training program similar to ESQ, called Management by Conscience (Manajemen Suara Hati). This program also drew on principles from life-coaching and human resources management literature. Over forty state-owned and a few private companies sent staff to the Aa Gym's headquarters in Bandung for training, including Garuda, PT Perusahaan Listrik Negara (the state electrical utility), and PT Telkom (the national telecommunications company). Employees of government bureaucracies such as the Ministry of Finance and the Directorate General of Taxation also participated in Management by Conscience. Managers at Krakatau Steel had considered contracting Manajemen Qolbu to execute spiritual reform at their company. Ultimately they chose ESQ instead because the latter offered in-house training at the factory complex, whereas

Management by Conscience training would have required that all employees be bused to Aa Gym's headquarters in Bandung.

Another high-profile business guru who sought to merge Islamic practice with management knowledge was Riawan Amin, the CEO of Bank Muamalat Indonesia. Bank Muamalat is Indonesia's first Islamic bank and was founded after Suharto embraced Islam and supported the establishment of ICMI (Hefner 1996). In 2004 Amin published *The Celestial Management* (Amin 2004), which provides another model of how enhanced Islamic practice could improve corporate human resources. A former vice president for human resources at Bank Muamalat, Amin was deeply familiar with the self-help and human resources management literatures on which he, Ary Ginanjar, and Aa Gym drew. He also developed a training program based on his Celestial Management model that was similar in substance to ESQ, but was directed mainly toward employees of Bank Muamalat. Thus, this training program was not marketed to a broader audience in the same way that ESQ and Manajemen Qolbu were.

Efforts to produce a spiritual economy did not only involve businessmen such as Ary Ginanjar, Aa Gym, and Riawan Amin who looked to Islam to promote better business management practices. In the opposite direction, Islamic intellectuals saw management knowledge as a means of achieving their social and political objectives. Even groups that were labeled conservative or fundamentalist sought to combine Islam and management knowledge. Ismail Yusanto, a leader of Hizbut Tahrir's Indonesian branch, coauthored several books on what he termed "*syariah* management" (Yusanto and Widjajakusuma 2002, 2003).[16] Hizbut Tahrir seeks the introduction of *syariah* law in Indonesia, and Yusanto wanted to develop principles for modern corporate management that were compatible with Islamic law.

Toward this end Yusanto developed his own management training program, which he called Establishing Individual Will (Pembinaan Pribadi Amanah or PPA). The program consisted of several modules, such as one on "self-control and improvement training." He told me that his training program was dedicated to unifying "work ethics" (*ethos kerja*) and Islamic "ethics" (*ethika*). The central message advocated in the program is

---

16. Hizbut Tahrir is a global network that seeks the reestablishment of a unitary Islamic caliphate consisting of all majority Muslim countries.

that according to Islamic doctrine work is not simply an act of material improvement but of spiritual improvement as well. Yusanto said that, according to the *hadiths,* a person who works hard will have a portion of their sins forgiven (*terampuni*). He explained to me that "if a person understands work ethics in Islam there is no reason to be lazy. We see in Indonesia although most are Muslim, there are problems. So we offer the training as a solution to those problems."

The difference between ESQ and PPA had to do with how they respectively treated individual agency. Yusanto was a strong advocate of the implementation of *syariah* law in Indonesia and likened it to a "code of conduct...that all businesses have [*bisnis semua punya*]." This insistence on the introduction of a code to regulate the lives of Indonesian citizens differed from Ginanjar's vision. ESQ was pessimistic about the viability of external interventions into individual life. This conviction emerged out of Ginanjar's belief that efforts to deploy the coercive force of the state to govern the comportment of Muslim citizens would fail, just as the heavy reliance on violence had sown seeds leading to the ultimate demise of the Suharto regime. In contrast, Yusanto argued that citizens needed a guide (*petunjuk*), in the form of a state or state-like authority, to ensure compliance with Islamic principles. ESQ advocated a universal humanism in which the central tenet was that each human had the same innate sense of morality. Hizbut Tahrir was less sanguine about human nature. Yusanto did not consider all Muslims as imbued with the values prescribed by Islam. Indeed, the central political goals of Hizbut Tahrir position the group's leaders as the arbiters of moral behavior.

Yusanto feared that corporate interests and business practices led to behavior incompatible with Islamic teachings. In his eyes, to ensure correct moral practice, Islamic scholars needed not only the coercive force of the state but also the ability to ensure that commerce too complied with *syariah* principles. Yusanto considered ESQ ineffective because it was only a first step insofar as it made ethics a personal matter. In contrast, the goal of PPA was to reorganize companies according to *syariah* principles. He saw Islamic practice not as a matter of personal ethics; instead, he insisted that *syariah* should be used as a roadmap for organizing entire institutions.

In addition to efforts such as ESQ, Manajemen Qolbu, Celestial Management, and PPA, forms of management knowledge that were not explicitly religious were extremely popular in Indonesia. Bookstores in the country were replete with translations of self-help and life-coaching best-sellers of both domestic and foreign origin. Indonesia was the first country in the world outside the United States in which a licensed version of the Seven Habits of Highly Effective People training program was offered. In addition, dozens of authors such as Ginanjar have adapted ideas from books published in Europe, North America, or elsewhere in Asia to develop their own interpretations of management knowledge.

The popularity of management knowledge is so widespread in Indonesia that when Stephen Covey came to Indonesia in November 2005 to launch the Indonesian translation of his book *The Eighth Habit: From Effectiveness to Greatness,* he was introduced by the country's president, Susilo Bambang Yudhoyono. President Yudhoyono lamented the fact that Indonesia was "still lacking the kind of national dynamism that have [*sic*] propelled other nations to true greatness" (Yudhoyono 2006, 21). He then spoke of the potential that Covey's principles held for reviving Indonesia's development aspirations, saying, "It is my hope...that the words of wisdom that you will hear from Stephen Covey will bring us a step closer to awakening this culture of excellence" (Yudhoyono 2006, 25). Although he did not seek to combine it with Islamic practice, the Indonesian president too looked to management knowledge to resolve Indonesia's crisis of faith in development.

Simulating the Development of Faith

The scale of the emergent spiritual economy in Indonesia was further evident in the many unofficial simulations of ESQ training that proliferated across the country. These simulations involved replicating various aspects of the training. Around Cilegon, they were held in both private and public spaces. I spoke with a number of Krakatau Steel employees who engaged in various adaptations of ESQ, and I was told that they were a common occurrence at other sites where the training had been held. The extensive interest in new ways of practicing Islam is a reflection of the widespread resurgence of Islam apparent among Indonesia's growing middle classes and noted by Suzanne Brenner. She showed how this resurgence was evident in the broad circulation of books, magazines, newspaper articles, and other printed material that addressed correct Islamic practice and discussed what was entailed in a modern Muslim lifestyle (Brenner 1996). Others have noted the emergence of similar debates and discussions across the Muslim world (Deeb 2006; Hirschkind 2006; Mahmood 2005; Ong 1990). The ad hoc simulations of ESQ training were another means by which Muslims in contemporary Indonesia sought to formulate a way of life that was simultaneously modern and Muslim; a practice that was compatible with religious imperatives and the norms entailed in industrial, bureaucratic, and corporate labor.

Given that many in Southeast Asia do not treat intellectual property with the same reverence that it is accorded in Europe and North America (Aragon and Leach 2008; Vann 2006), those organizing facsimiles of ESQ training found no fault in their execution. However, in spite of the fact that ESQ overtly draws on the intellectual work of others (Goleman 1995; Zohar and Marshall 2000), Ary Ginanjar, Rinaldi, and others affiliated with the ESQ Leadership Center expressed increasing consternation over the imitations of the training that mushroomed across Indonesia. For example, an ESQ trainer told me about a particularly enthusiastic alumnus in Jombang, East Java, who had been caught videotaping a training without permission. He was asked to stop and complied willingly, explaining that he merely wanted to spread the message of ESQ to others who were unable to attend. However, several weeks later the exact same person was caught videotaping the training a second time. The proliferation of facsimiles had progressed to the point that by 2005 ESQ hired a prominent Jakarta law firm, HKGM Partners, to protect its franchise.

Policing facsimiles of ESQ training presented a paradox for Ary Ginanjar. On the one hand, the growth of corporate revenues was predicated on maintaining control over the exclusive right to distribute his intellectual property. On the other hand, expansion of his growing business was dependent on building a network of subordinate trainers who could effectively deliver the training. Ary Ginanjar sought to make ESQ an effective institution and not one that was dependent on his personal charisma. This required introducing technologies of seriality (Anderson 1998) to cultivate trainers who could deliver the ESQ training on a scale far larger than Ginanjar could achieve working on his own. Only through building a cadre of dedicated trainers could he both deliver the message on a scale large enough to achieve the national transformation he sought and increase his business revenue. Thus, the ESQ Leadership Center invested quite heavily in training trainers to master the embodied dispositions that were deemed most effective in eliciting the desired subjective transformation.

One new ESQ trainer, Haidar, who had previously worked as a Seven Habits of Highly Effective People trainer, was surprised at the differences between the two types of training. He said that the Seven Habits trainers simply learned on the job and then reviewed their experience with colleagues afterward. There was no formal period of apprenticeship. In contrast, Ginanjar had created an elaborate training for trainers. Haidar told me he was extremely surprised when he was hired by ESQ at how much more difficult it was to give ESQ training compared to Seven Habits training. He said that the first time he delivered the resounding religious lectures, "my voice was cracking.... I didn't know how to stand, they were constantly correcting me." Furthermore, Haidar told me that someone could become a "licensed" ESQ trainer only after he or she had served as an assistant to Ary during one of the executive level trainings.[17]

In December 2008 I visited the room at the ESQ Leadership Center where the training for trainers took place. Before these apprentices had an opportunity to perform the training in front of a live audience, they were trained to master it through repeatedly mimicking the vocal dispositions replicated in videos taken of Ary Ginanjar delivering the training. In the long, narrow room fourteen computers lined the walls, seven to a side. Prospective trainers sat attached to headphones and a microphone and studiously mimicked the vocal inflections and embodied dispositions that Ginanjar used to deliver the training. The scene was evocative of long established techniques of Islamic education in Indonesia, although with a decidedly different twist. In *pesantren* and other settings for Islamic instruction students sit in orderly rows engaged in rote memorization of the Qur'an in Arabic (Dhofier 1999; Gade 2004). However, rather than long hours spent in textual recitation, to achieve the status of ESQ trainers students were disciplined through a decidedly more interactive technological medium, Microsoft Windows.

The ESQ Center deployed another disciplinary technology to monitor the effectiveness of those who had completed the computerized training. On the third floor, above the main staircase, was a video monitor in which

---

17. Although most officially licensed ESQ trainers were men, there were also a smaller number of female trainers.

the performance of each of the roughly eighty ESQ trainers was projected. In succession, a photo of each trainer was displayed with supplementary information about their performance. This included the trainer's name, the number of trainings they had delivered in the two previous months, a numerical category called "points," and a rating. The rating was either "satisfactory" or "unsatisfactory." It was a bit disconcerting to see a smiling face next to "unsatisfactory" in large, red block letters projected for roughly ten seconds on the monitor, before the next hopeful visage was displayed. Rinaldi explained the trainers were responsible for not only delivering ESQ but also finding institutions that would pay for the training. Each trainer was expected to sell a set number of trainings each month. The category called "points" referred to the number of training programs that each trainer had sold.[18] By making these rankings public, the ESQ Center relied on the affective sense of shame to motivate employees deemed unsatisfactory.[19]

While Ginanjar sought to protect his intellectual property through his licensing scheme, he was also conveying skills that were increasingly valuable in the emerging spiritual economy. The tension between spreading the message and training potential business competitors was reflected in one notable change that took place on the ESQ website in mid-2009. Prior to that time notification of upcoming trainings had always included the name of the trainer delivering the future program in addition to the date and location at which the training would be held. However, in 2009 the name of the licensed trainer delivering each training was no longer listed. Instead, the listing reflected only one of two options: either "Ary Ginanjar" for the executive trainings at ESQ's new convention center in Jakarta or "Licensed by Ary Ginanjar." I was unable to confirm why this change was made, but it may have been due to the fact that Ary had become concerned about the prospect that some of the subordinate trainers would cultivate charismatic authority rivaling his own. Were one of these trainers sufficiently popular and ambitious enough to create their own method of integrating Islamic

18. A means of simultaneously surveilling and disciplining employees, the monitor evoked the huge production board that recorded worker productivity and hung above the floor of the silk factory where Lisa Rofel conducted ethnographic research in southern China (Rofel 1997)

19. As others have shown, shame is an important motivating affect in Indonesia (Anderson 1999; Lindquist 2008).

practice and management knowledge it could conceivably create direct competition with Ginanjar's program. Such concerns illustrate the tension between charismatic and bureaucratic authority inherent in the emerging spiritual economy (Weber 1958a).

Ginanjar's concern about restricting the dissemination of the knowledge over which he claimed ownership was not unfounded. At Krakatau Steel I heard about several instances in which unlicensed versions of the training were reproduced. One particularly enthusiastic group of employees organized what they termed the "Krakatau Steel ESQ committee." They sought to propagate the practices entailed in the training on a more widespread basis, both among company employees and among inhabitants in the community of Cilegon and beyond. The group used a well-organized PowerPoint training session that they had independently created to deliver the training free of charge to individuals who had received small business development loans and grants and in-kind donations from Krakatau Steel. Due in part to the fact that state-owned enterprises were not "pure business" but also had a "social mission," Krakatau Steel had established a unit to sponsor local community development called the Community Partnership and Development Program (Program Kemitraan dan Bina Lingkungan or PKBL). The PKBL provided development assistance to small businesses in north Banten, including in the cities of Cilegon and Serang, and in the Bandung area.[20]

In June 2004 I attended the fifth (unlicensed) training that the Krakatau Steel ESQ committee organized to disseminate the lessons of ESQ to individuals who had received those grants. Although this simulacrum of the training was executed in the same space where the official trainings were carried out, it was done on a decidedly less impressive scale. The hall was populated with only about 130 people, whereas the regular trainings often packed the space with more than double that number. The imitation

---

20. Bandung was the capital of West Java province, in which Krakatau Steel had formerly been located before Banten became an independent province, and therefore the company historically had sponsored community development in the Bandung region as well. Additionally, many employees at all levels of the company hierarchy originally came from the Bandung region, a fact that may have also ensured the persistence of community development initiatives in Bandung. Bandung is quite distant from Cilegon and required an automobile trip of at least six hours during the period when I conducted research for this book. The completion of a toll road in 2005 has since reduced that time.

training lasted only one day rather than three. The lights were not manipulated with nearly as much skill. In the official trainings varying degrees of darkness were used to great effect to elicit embodied practices, such
as weeping and hugging. Furthermore, the sound system was not nearly
as powerful. Although the audio was projected at what appeared to be
equal volume, the bass did not shake the bodies of participants as it did during the official trainings. The staging was not nearly as elaborate, leaving
gaps during some of the transitions. There were awkward pauses at the end
of religious lectures before the music for subsequent group activities was
cued. Audience members looked around tiredly, unsure of what was coming next. The PowerPoint presentation, although demonstrating considerable aplomb, was not nearly as polished as the official ESQ presentation.

In spite of some of the formal shortcomings the training was delivered
with no less enthusiasm and sincerity than trainings offered by the official ESQ Leadership Center. The committee consisted of five individuals
who rotated in leading the participants in the same lessons and activities
that were contained in the original training. Like the trainers officially employed by ESQ, they wore slick black business suits with dark purple, blue,
or black collared shirts. While the images used in the PowerPoint presentation differed from those used in the actual ESQ training, the Krakatau
Steel committee had done an impressive job tracking down images from
the Internet that resembled those in the official trainings. The committee
had clearly spent quite a bit of time to produce a replica of the training that
was as faithful as possible to the original, albeit one that operated under a
set of different constraints. Because it compressed three days of material
into one, the simulated training only touched on the main concepts and
themes that the original introduced. Although they had not benefited from
the elaborate training for trainers that ESQ had developed, for the most
part those members of the factory's committee who delivered the training did a passable job at reproducing the vocal inflections and physical
gestures that made the trainings delivered by Ary Ginanjar and Rinaldi
so powerful.

In delivering the simulated training, the Krakatau Steel committee made careful effort to recognize Ginanjar as the inspiration behind
their work. In reverential terms they described the history of ESQ while
an image displayed a smiling Ginanjar above his date of birth (March 24,
1965) and the words "Master ESQ Trainer" in English. The content of

these local trainings, however, had more humble aspirations. Fajri, who played a leading role in the Krakatau Steel ESQ committee, told the audience that the goal of the session was to "to discuss spirituality, but also to show how through the development of small business... we can make Cilegon prosperous and successful." Thus, whereas Ary Ginanjar saw one of his chief goals as increasing the prosperity of the nation (and after that the world), those involved in delivering the replica trainings held decidedly more local aspirations.

In spite of the considerable efforts the committee dedicated to creating their own simulated version of the training, it did not appear to reach quite the same impact among members of this group as the official, licensed trainings had achieved with Krakatau Steel employees. For the most part, the audience gazed deadpan at the lectures and interactive sessions. When music was played and the crowd was exhorted to embodied action through either dance or calisthenics, only a handful complied and those who did appeared self-conscious under the glaring lights of the hall. During the renditions of remembrance for one's mother and the retelling of the story of Ibrahim's aborted sacrifice of Ismail there was no effusive weeping. There were no episodes of spirit possession or people entering into trance states, as commonly occurred during the climactic sessions of the official training. Perhaps most notably, those in the audience did not seem to quite grasp the central argument that enhancing spiritual practice would create greater commercial success. In conversations with several of the participants during breaks they said that they viewed the experience as a religious lesson that offered techniques to enhance their Islamic faith.

In addition to some of the significant differences between the two versions of ESQ that I describe above, a further reason explains their more modest success. The participants in the simulated programs by and large did not work for massive industrial or commercial firms and thus were likely not exposed to the discursive practices of human resources training programs. This meant that they were not familiar with the *habitus* expected of participants in this genre of employee training program (Bourdieu 1990). Activities such as clapping in unison or cheering on command are acquired behaviors, and it was apparent that many in the group were unfamiliar with the techniques of collective management deployed to elicit these responses.

When I asked one of the members of the Krakatau Steel ESQ committee why the training they presented elicited only a tepid response compared with the certified version delivered to company employees, he invoked relative educational levels. This was a common way in which Krakatau Steel employees distinguished themselves from those who did not work at the factory and were indigenous (*pribumi*) to Banten. He told me that fully comprehending ESQ required education and that those in the audience did not possess the requisite background to understand some of the key points, particularly the lessons that invoked psychological concepts and the history of science.

By late 2004 the ESQ Leadership Center had begun to crack down on the unauthorized versions of the training that had proliferated across Indonesia. Of particular concern were the training programs offered by groups such as the Krakatau Steel ESQ committee, which provided the training for free to people who might have otherwise paid to attend public versions of the official training. Although Ary Ginanjar did offer some versions of the training for which participants could attend without payment, these sessions were often strategically directed toward groups that could advance his goal of national spiritual reform, such as public school teachers. For example, in February 2004 ESQ organized the ESQ Cares for Education (ESQ Peduli Pendidikan) program, which provided the training at no cost to public school teachers in provinces across Indonesia. By July 2007 over fifty thousand teachers had gone through the training (*Republika* 2008). Complementary trainings further appeared to be executed in situations that would lend positive publicity to ESQ. In contrast, unauthorized trainings had little public relations value. The ESQ legal representative told me that he had called the Krakatau Steel committee to request that they cease conducting their version of the training. They complied with the request and, in exchange, were given quasi-official status as the ESQ representatives for Banten province.

Simulations of ESQ were not restricted to the semiformal efforts of groups such as the Krakatau Steel ESQ committee. Stories circulated among trainers and others about instances in which alumni of the program reenacted some of the more dramatic events in the training on their own. For example, one day I visited Umar at his home to interview this veteran of the hot strip mill about his participation in the Team of Five political movement described in chapter 6. He was often asked to help organize participants during the official ESQ training sessions at Krakatau Steel. When I arrived, after some introductory pleasantries, he said to me somewhat dismissively, "You missed it last night."

"Missed what?" I replied.

"ESQ! We did it here, at my house," he said gruffly.

Umar went on to explain that several of his colleagues from the mill had gathered together to reenact some portions of the training. He had purchased a CD containing the music of the new age artist Kitaro, which figured prominently in ESQ training. In addition they had watched several VCDs distributed by the ESQ Leadership Center that featured lectures by Ary Ginanjar.[21] Finally they had tried to elicit some spiritual experiences by reenacting some of the activities that had occurred during the training. "It was very spiritual," he told me with a cryptic smile.

In both Cilegon and Jakarta, I heard stories about groups of alumni who gathered together to recreate portions of the training. When I asked Haidar about it, he told me that a participant in one of these events had gone insane during an unlicensed training in Banten. He said, "When they were with Ary they had a spiritual experience during the angel of death (*malaikat kubur*) session and they wanted to repeat it.... They thought it would be more powerful if they actually went live, so they reenacted it in a real cemetery." Haidar said that the participants had taken turns occupying an actual grave in a local cemetery while the others delivered the interrogation. Haidar said one of the participants in this feral version went into a fit when he faced this interrogation from inside an actual grave and attributed the madness to the overexuberance of the group. "You see, Ary builds in stages. He only discusses the afterlife on the third day when people have been prepared for it.... This is why he always starts a session with a motivational exercise, to make sure that trainees are in the right frame of mind. Those people doing the unlicensed trainings don't know how to prepare people adequately in advance."

Demigods and Demagogues: Critiques of Spiritual Reform

For the most part employees of Krakatau Steel and other Indonesians responded positively to ESQ training. However, some were critical of the training, a number that grew as its popularity increased. Four objections

---

21. VCD or View Compact Disk is a digital video standard common throughout East and Southeast Asia.

were raised, both among Krakatau Steel employees and by others I spoke with in Jakarta: 1) ESQ encouraged people to act in ways that were contrary to either "true" Islamic teaching or to Indonesian "culture"; 2) alumni treated Ary Ginanjar like a deity (*mendewakan*) or saint; 3) Islam was fundamentally opposed to material engagements such as commerce; and 4) ESQ was a form of propaganda or brainwashing.

Two stories illustrate the criticism that ESQ caused people to act in ways contrary to either Islam or Indonesian norms. Adit, a senior manager at Krakatau Steel who was an influential advisor to the newly installed CEO, was steadfastly opposed to ESQ. He told me in animated terms that the training had precipitated two divorces between company employees. In both cases, after attending ESQ training, two female employees claimed to have found themselves and come to the conclusion that their unhappy marriages were the biggest obstacles to finding worldly contentment. Shortly after attending ESQ they demanded divorces from their husbands. Although ESQ did not sanction divorce and Ginanjar may very well have counseled against such action, the program did emphasize that people should take responsibility for their lives by becoming proactive. It is not improbable that some could have interpreted this as a lesson to change one's marital status if one concluded that it was personally unsuitable.

A second story I heard in Jakarta also involved ESQ inciting people to act in ways that were incommensurable with Islamic kinship traditions. It concerned an event that took place in 2005 on the island of Batam, a prosperous economic development zone that is part of the Singapore-Johor-Riau growth triangle. A Malaysian couple with six children attended ESQ training with their newborn son, Farrabi. After hearing the account of Ibrahim's willingness to sacrifice his son, the mother decided that she too should surrender her infant as a sign of her devotion to Allah. During a break in the training another woman passed by the Malaysian couple and commented on the infant. The mother, who already had five children, took the flattering remarks as a sign that she should give her baby to the woman. As it turned out the passerby was unable to have children herself. The story became "proof" of the power of ESQ to bring about profound instances of personal sacrifice. The child became known among ESQ alumni as "the Ismail of Indonesia." Some former devotees, however, soured on ESQ after the event because they asserted that Islam did not recognize adoption. Thus, they turned against the program because they felt it was encouraging people to act in ways that were contrary to Islamic practice.

Some also criticized ESQ because they asserted past participants in the program "worshipped" and "deified" Ary Ginanjar. Adit said he became suspicious of ESQ after he had heard that people had begun to regard Ginanjar as the bearer of supernatural qualities. Some of his most ardent devotees would ask him whether specific days were auspicious for undertaking certain activities, such as travel. He told me, "People send Ary text messages asking whether it is OK to go to Jakarta on a certain date.... This is not acceptable according to Islam!" Adit was displeased because, although he did not think that Ginanjar intentionally cultivated these representations, by answering the text messages he did not dispel them either.

Adit also expressed frustration that some of Krakatau Steel's most senior managers accepted Ginanjar's claims as divine injunctions. One example was the notion of the "universal *tawaf*" that was conveyed during ESQ training. This referred to the notion that all of Allah's creations rotated in the same direction. Thus, on the third day of the ESQ training, participants were instructed that the entire universe from the "macrocosmos" (cosmic) to the "microcosmos" (microscopic) turns in a counterclockwise direction. A Qur'anic verse depicted on the projection screens read "Hast thou not seen how to God bow all who are in the heavens and all who are in the earth, the sun and the moon, the stars and the mountains, the trees and the beasts, and many of mankind?" (Qur'an 22, 18). This projection was followed by three videos exhibited in rapid succession. First was an astronomy video that gradually panned out from the solar system to the Milky Way galaxy to the entire universe and showed all three rotating in a counterclockwise direction. The next video showed electrons orbiting the nucleus of an atom in the same direction. This was immediately followed by the final video, which depicted a circulating throng of *hajj* pilgrims also moving counterclockwise around the Kaaba in Mecca.

The apparent ubiquity of counterclockwise rotation was invoked as proof of Allah's grand design for the universe. Several Krakatau Steel employees invoked this as evidence that ESQ represented unassailable truths about how one should live. Suwono, an influential manager who had graduated from ITB and referred to himself as a "cultural engineer," cited further examples that he thought confirmed the universal *tawaf.* These included the fact that a bolt turned counterclockwise rose up, in the direction of heaven. When I asked him why the hands of a clock turn in the opposite direction, he attributed it to the fact that it was "made by man," and thus did not conform to the universal laws of God.

Adit, on the other hand, was skeptical of these claims and declared that the way they were interpreted at Krakatau Steel led managers to make changes that he found "irrational." Adit gave an example that matched something I experienced in early 2004. I had become briefly confused when I was driving to a meeting at the company's central administrative building. Upon passing through the checkpoint leading to the front of the building, I began to turn left as I had done since arriving in Cilegon five months earlier. However, the security guards patrolling the gate quickly stopped me and informed me that the direction of the one-way road that encircled the building had been reversed and that all traffic was forthwith to proceed in a counterclockwise direction. Several months after the incident Adit revealed to me that this change in traffic pattern came after a high-ranking director had attended ESQ and decided that traffic around the building should proceed in the direction of the universal *tawaf,* the same direction that pilgrims circulated around the Kaaba.

Others had concluded that ESQ was nothing less than a cult dedicated to Ary Ginanjar. Abdul was a former devotee of ESQ who, by the time I returned to Indonesia in 2006, had become a staunch critic of the program. He had downloaded articles about cults from social science journals on the Internet and read a definition of a cult to me to demonstrate the point. He said that shortly after ESQ began organizing *umroh*[22] tours to the Middle East in 2005, a tour group member took a photo of Ginanjar on the Jabar an-Nur.[23] Apparently there were "colored balls" in the photo that some of Ginanjar's most ardent followers took to be planets. They saw the photo as evidence of his supernatural abilities and interpreted this to mean that he was a "sun" around which planets revolve. Abdul saw this as

22. *Umroh* refers to a pilgrimage to Saudi Arabia that resembles the *hajj* but does not take place during the official *hajj* season. This pilgrimage involves many of the same rituals that are conducted during the *hajj* but unlike the *hajj* does not have to be undertaken during the month of Dhu al-Hijjah. Although *umroh* is recommended, it is not obligatory. The *hajj* is required of every Muslim who can afford it.

23. The mountain that holds the cave in which Muhammad received many of his initial revelations.

evidence that he was "becoming a demigod," which he found contrary to Islamic teachings that clearly distinguished mortals from those with divine prowess.

Another critique of ESQ had to do with the argument that enhanced Islamic practice was conducive to business success. Several people I spoke with believed this was a corruption of Islamic teaching, as religion was purely a "spiritual" affair and to "tarnish" it with "materialism" was a disgrace. This criticism of the larger phenomena of spiritual reform in Indonesia was energetically articulated by Kyai Haji Syafiq, a sprightly man who had mastered the cultivated eccentricity that was shared by several of the *kyai* I met in the area around Cilegon. Although he did not invoke Ary Ginanjar specifically, he was highly critical of the broader formation of which ESQ was a manifestation. He said:

> No one knows true Islam anymore. They only build mosques for show. Sure they pray a lot, but only for themselves.... These new *kyai* are nothing but soy sauce peddlers [*penjual kecap*]! Damn them all! Who is that one? Zainuddin MZ.[24] He is nothing but a big clown. Aa Gym is the same. The good ones are not heard. Those *kyai sontoloyo*[25] talk big but do nothing. They all have a bunch of big mouths.... Religion is just a commodity now.... Islam has become just a tool to sell commodities.

Syafiq's critique of the new breed of spiritual reformers such as Aa Gym, Ary Ginanjar, and Zainuddin MZ represents a broader shift in Islamic authority that is taking place in Indonesia and in many Muslim communities around the world. Older religious leaders such as Syafiq, whose authority lies in their command of vast patron-client networks based in Islamic schools (*pesantren*), are threatened by upstart proselytizers who adroitly use mass media and technology to convey Islamic teaching but are not graduates of *pesantren* and rarely have any formal religious education

---

24. Zainuddin MZ is a well-known Islamic preacher who rose to popularity in the 1980s based on his cassette sermons and television roles before becoming involved in party politics (Hoesterey 2009). Zainuddin had presidential aspirations in the 2004 elections and was the leader of one remnant of the United Development Party (Partai Persatuan Pembangunan), which was created during the New Order as an amalgamation of Islamic political parties. Ultimately, he was disqualified because his party did not reach the necessary threshold of support in parliamentary elections to place a presidential candidate.

25. *Sontoloyo* is an exclamation of derision.

(Eickelman and Anderson 2003; Hirschkind 2006). In response they crit-
icize the upstarts as concerned with money and material things and cor-
rupting Islam for a message that is not true to the religion.

Some former adherents of ESQ who later became disenchanted with
the program also accused ESQ of prioritizing material concerns over spiritual ones. Abdul claimed that he became disillusioned with the program
when he came to the conclusion that the paramount objective of ESQ was
to make money, not to improve Indonesia or expand Islam. In 2006 Abdul
told me that ESQ was run as a private company with all the profits going
directly into Ary Ginanjar's personal bank account. I asked him about the
foundation (*yayasan*) that ESQ had established and the relief aid that the
company had contributed to assist victims of natural disasters, including
floods in Jakarta, the 2004 tsunami in Aceh, and earthquakes in Beng-
kulu and West Sumatra. Abdul dismissively likened this charitable work
to the foundations that Suharto had established during the New Order as
mechanisms to support his authoritarian regime. He negatively compared
ESQ to Manajemen Qolbu, which he said "makes all of its financial records public...but there are no public records and no audits of ESQ."

The final common critique of ESQ was that it was a "propaganda
tool" (*alat propaganda*) that sought to "brainwash" (*cuci otak*) and manipulate employees into doing what the company wanted. Muliadi, who had
worked for over twenty years at Krakatau Steel, said that ESQ was "a tool
to suppress [*menundukkan*]...employees, so that they don't rebel [*beron-
tak*]...so that they don't protest [*protes*]." He told me, "According to the
ESQ staff, employees should be proud of their work. They think it helps
other people if they understand the meaning of life—that they work for
Allah, not for their family or money." However, he did not think that these
efforts to domesticate the workforce were effective, explaining that it only
lasted "two months, maybe three months. After that it will be back [to the
old ways] again!"

Allegations that ESQ was a tool to brainwash employees were not always uttered disapprovingly. I spoke with one senior professor who was in
line to become the chief administrator of Jakarta's State Islamic University
and was also part of the circle of influential people who supported Ary
Ginanjar's efforts. Nazaruddin had studied in the United States and spoke
English fluently. To my surprise he spontaneously used the term "brainwashing" to refer to the program. He said, "It is a little brainwashing...but

in the good sense. It is based on the Qur'an, so it is good for people!...It doesn't destroy anything. They feel it can even enhance their quality of life....So people become more religious, more humble, more productive, and more tolerant." Like other elites who embraced ESQ, Nazaruddin viewed the program as a means of social engineering that held open the possibility of resolving some of the problems that afflicted Indonesia in the wake of the Suharto years.

Some Indonesian intellectuals in the humanities and social sciences were also dismissive of ESQ. They referred to it as "pseudo-science" and as "Islam light." One prominent Indonesian scholar who held a PhD from an Ivy League university explained that "proving" Islam by showing how its truth claims were evident in science ignored the distinguished history of Islamic reasoning. He said, "If I were asked by a company to give a lecture on Islam, I would pick a topic like piety [*takwa*] and then show how different Islamic scholars had treated the topic throughout history." He also objected to arguments that purported to show Islam and science were complementary through analogical reasoning. Although he admitted that ESQ was convincing because of its sophisticated use of technology, he thought the methods deployed were improperly suited to the existential questions that were being posed. He continued, "They are trying to suggest that science offers answers to questions, which, in fact, most scientists would avoid." Furthermore, he objected to the exuberant displays of emotion in ESQ, which he viewed as an innovation foreign to "traditional" practices. A similar argument was presented in less acerbic fashion by a younger intellectual who had won a Fulbright scholarship to study in the United States. He referred to programs such as ESQ as "chicken soup" Islam, alluding to the *Chicken Soup for the Soul* series of self-help books that have been translated into Indonesian and are available in bookstores throughout the country.

Engineering Islam: Reconciling Secular and Spiritual Reason

Although these negative evaluations are perhaps predictable, it is harder to explain the appeal of spiritual reform. Most employees of Krakatau Steel and many more people across Indonesia and, more recently, Malaysia found ESQ training compelling. As in Europe, North America, and

Asia, life-coaching and self-help programs have proliferated across Southeast Asia in recent years. Three major reasons account for the proliferation of efforts to develop faith in contemporary Indonesia. They speak not only to the appeal of ESQ but also to the formation of the wider spiritual economy of which it is a part. First, these efforts appeared to reconcile Islam with the twin pillars of modernity: science and capitalism. This was an attractive message for people who had been educated in technical and scientific fields in a secular school system but who identified as Muslims by family and personal practice. Second, they offered a forum in which Indonesians who had benefited from Suharto's authoritarian regime, only to see the New Order collapse, could find atonement for their complicity in what later was considered a corrupt and morally bankrupt system. Third, after the events of September 11, 2001, ESQ offered participants a means to proclaim a devout Muslim identity but not one that was automatically positioned against the West. Rather, it was an identity that was in more nuanced dialogue with it. In the wake of those events and the subsequent reactions to them, many Indonesian periodicals recapitulated versions of the "Clash of Civilizations" thesis (Huntington 1993). Islamic spiritual reform provided a way of being in the world that contrasted with these oversimplified accounts of post–Cold War geopolitics.

The aspect of ESQ that resonated most persuasively with employees of Krakatau Steel was that it configured a mode of Islamic practice that was commensurable with the twin mainstays of modernity: science and capitalism. This entailed the creation of a spiritual economy and a set of equivalences between Islam and scientific practice and technical knowledge, which I refer to as engineering Islam.[26] Engineering Islam refers to the introduction of Islam into spaces from which it was previously absent by making it appear compatible with scientific expression and technical knowledge. Prior to the introduction of ESQ, many employees explained that there had been a separation of religious practice from the spaces of work. Industrial production was understood to be a secular practice, and the spaces appropriate to religious practice were the home and the mosque. Furthermore, engineering Islam refers to the practice of representing modern scientific achievements as presaged in Qur'anic revelation. Finally,

---

26. This approach to Islam resonates with the role of engineering in Indonesia's colonial modernity (Mrázek 2002).

it captures how formal equivalences were made between Islam and engineering insofar as religious principles were expressed in mathematical form. Analogies between science and engineering on the one hand and Qur'anic citations and Islamic history on the other created compatibility between two modes of knowledge that were previously taken to be opposed. Engineering Islam illustrates that developing faith is not a complete break with faith in development, insofar as they both presume a similar technocratic outlook in which any worldly problem is capable of being solved. Engineering Islam held tremendous appeal to well-educated employees of state-owned enterprises, many of whom held advanced degrees in scientific fields and other technical specializations ranging from metallurgy to chemical and industrial engineering to business.

Many Krakatau Steel employees attributed their enthusiasm for ESQ to the fact that it demonstrated certain scientific achievements were anticipated in the Qur'an. This was a particularly compelling means of affirming the truth of the Qur'an and representing Islam in such a way that it appeared compatible with the engineering knowledge in which they had been inculcated. When I asked employees why they found ESQ convincing they most often invoked the argument made during the training that the Qur'an anticipates the use of big bang theory to explain the origins of the universe. This was expressed in variations of the question, "Did you know that the Qur'an actually revealed the big bang before scientists knew of it?" The question revealed a strong desire of employees schooled in modernization, insofar as the technical fields in which they were educated are ensconced in secular reason, to reconcile their vocational identities with the Islamic practice to which many had been exposed to in their youth. Employees also frequently invoked another example from the training in which a scarlet-colored nebula that resembled the form of a rose was projected.[27] This image was overlaid with a Qur'anic citation that read, "When the heavens shall be cleft asunder, and become rose red, like stained leather. Which then of the bounties of your Lord will ye twain deny?" (Qur'an 55, 37–38). The fact that astronomers had recorded an image that resembled something suggested in the Qur'an was invoked as further proof that the revealed knowledge of Islam anticipated modern science.

---

27. This nebula was featured by NASA as the Astronomy Picture of the Day and can be viewed at http://antwrp.gsfc.nasa.gov/apod/ap991031.html (accessed June 8, 2009).

To employees at Krakatau Steel and other state-owned enterprises, ESQ appeared to offer a resolution to the apparent incommensurability between Islam and the mainly secular project of technological development. Gusniarto, a chemical engineer in the department of planning and technology, explained that the goal of ESQ was to explain verses of the Qur'an that people had not yet understood. As we sat in his office in the building that housed offices for administering steel production processes, he said, "The Qur'an challenges us to prove what [of its contents] are true and what are not.... There are actually two kinds of verses, written verses and unwritten verses. The first are in the Qur'an and the second include everything around us, all natural phenomena." He said that traditional Islamic education in Indonesia focused on the former. It was dedicated to "ritual activity" such as the correct way to perform prayers (*sholat*) and how to read the Qur'an in Arabic.

ESQ, in contrast, was dedicated "to exploring the greatness of God from a scientific point of view. It explores the foundation of the universe, the foundation of life, like the fact that all the material in the universe moves counterclockwise. This is a scientific fact, everything moves to the left. Electrons move around the atom. Planets move counterclockwise around the sun." When he invoked the universal *tawaf* as evidence that science had confirmed Allah's grand design, I pointed out that whether these orbits move clockwise or counterclockwise depended on one's perspective. But Gusniarto was indifferent. To him it was self-evident that the proper perspective to observe these orbits was from above, from the perspective of Allah.[28]

He further marked the distinctiveness of ESQ by contrasting it with a Qur'anic study group (*pengajian*) that he attended weekly. He explained, "ESQ is different because at *pengajian* we discuss different Qur'anic verses. The emphasis is on discussing the rules, about our relationship with God and other human beings, about do's and don'ts, about how to pray, what is the correct way to fast. But in ESQ we look at science and the relationship between science and religion." He asserted that this search for knowledge outside the text was consistent with what Allah had demanded of human beings. To illustrate the point he opened a Qur'an to show me the famous

---

28. Donna Haraway has referred to the adoption of this subject position as the "god trick" (Haraway 1991).

first few verses of the al-Alaq *surah,* which declare "Read: In the name of thy Lord Who createth, / Createth man from a clot. / Read: And thy Lord is the Most Bounteous, / Who teacheth by the pen, / Teacheth man that which he knew not" (Qur'an 96, 1–5).[29] Gusniarto explained that "these verses ask Muslims to think, not just to follow. . . . ESQ shows how religion and science match each other."

Krakatau Steel employees carried efforts to reconcile Islam and science beyond the training, to the actual production of steel. Ibnu, a manager at the hot strip mill, invoked a passage in the al-Hadid *surah,* which reads, "We sent down iron, wherein is great might, and many uses for men, and so that God might know who helps Him, and His Messengers, in the Unseen" (Qur'an 57, 25). He explained this passage did not mean that steel was something that had been given to human beings but rather that Allah had endowed humans with the capacity, in the form of knowledge, to make steel. Ibnu jotted down the chemical symbols for iron (Fe) and carbon (C) in my notebook, explaining that in their pure state these were nothing like steel. Iron is "soft" (*lunak*) and carbon is "brittle" (*rapuh*) but when combined they could make a "strong, hardened" (*kuat keras*) material that "we call steel." This material was not directly given by Allah, as he provides only "raw materials and knowledge" (*unsur-unsur dan ilmu*). It was dependent on humans to figure out how to use them productively.

Ibnu then connected this lesson to the goal of ESQ, which he understood was to "develop faith" (*membangun iman*) of participants by showing that "the discoveries of Westerners (*orang barat*) are concordant (*sesuai*) with the Islamic religion." Echoing the astronomy lectures during the training, he said that ESQ demonstrated that the truth of the Qur'an was "proven" by modern science. "All the verses of the Qur'an can be uncovered using technology, such as medicine or astronomy." He had come to this conclusion through his personal experience studying metallurgy. He told me that as a student he had used a microscope to examine crystal structures and told me that the intricate designs showed "the great creative power of Allah." He then invoked the furnace in the adjacent hot strip mill that scorched steel slabs to over one thousand degrees to further illustrate this power. "Imagine," he said with a smile while leaning forward as if to share a piece

---

29. Here the Pickthall translation of the Qur'an best captures the point that Gusniarto sought to convey (Pickthall 2000).

of life-altering information, "if humans can make something that hot, how about the power of Allah? Hell must certainly be far hotter!" According to this tautological circle of reasoning the technical achievements of human beings were offered as proof that one must hold faith in God because God had made humans and endowed them with the knowledge to produce steel out of iron, carbon, and heat.

Calculating Life

Another aspect of engineering Islam was evident in the widespread use of mathematical formulas to affirm the truth of the religion. Thus, it was not just the content of ESQ but also the form through which it was represented that was designed to appeal to those whom Ary Ginanjar sought to reform. Not only did he endeavor to prove the compatibility of religion and science, but he also used the language of science to construct the truth of the program.

One formula was central to both the training and the broader self-improvement philosophy developed by Ary Ginanjar: the zero mind process (ZMP). This formula was based on the answer to the question that many primary school students ask shortly after they are first exposed to long division, "What happens when a number is divided by zero?" The zero mind process was derived from the answer to this question: any number divided by zero is equal to infinity. The formula for the zero mind process was displayed boldly on the projection screens as $1/0 = \sim$. In the equation, 1 symbolized an individual, 0 represented the individual's ego, and infinity referred to Allah. The lesson that participants were to draw from this formula was that by reducing one's ego one could, according to Ginanjar, "get closer to Allah."

A formula was also used to show how participants could embody the *asmaul husna,* the characteristics of Allah, and was based on slightly more advanced algebra. This formula was based on the algebraic axiom that any number to the power of zero is equal to one and was represented on the projection screens and in printed material as $a^0 = 1$. Like the zero mind process, it was intended to demonstrate the virtue of humility. In this formula the symbols were rearranged, with "a" standing for the individual and 0 representing "those who do not feel self-important, but rather only as servants of Allah." One represented Allah, the one and only God. Thus, during the training Rinaldi explained, "One represents the characteristics (*sifat-sifat*) of Allah. When we are zero the characteristics of Allah will emerge!" These formulas were just two examples of the numerous formulas that Ary Ginanjar had devised to represent religious principles in scientific form.

These formulas were part of the larger spiritual economy, insofar as they presented Islamic practices in terms familiar to educated Indonesians. These engineers and scientists had obtained their technological knowledge as part of the New Order regime's faith in development. In this sense they were children of Suharto, "Mister Development." Thus, these formulas illustrated the broader formation in which those well-educated in technical fields used the representational schema of mathematics and engineering to illustrate religious principles. During one ESQ training in Jakarta in October 2004, I spent the better part of the afternoon with Karnawan, a mechanical engineer who was on the aircraft maintenance staff for Garuda, Indonesia's national airline. He had graduated from two of Indonesia's foremost universities but had never formally studied Islam. However, he explained that after he had worked at Garuda for several years he became interested in the religion. Although he was well compensated and enjoyed a comfortable life by even North American standards, he told me that previously he was unfulfilled. He said, "The trigger for my interest in Islam came from an aircraft engine." He explained that for years his work had been guided by the notion of "air worthiness," in which he had to evaluate whether an aircraft engine was capable of flying safely. He told me that the general criteria for evaluating aircraft engines could be applied to human life: "It is similar to the principle that should guide a life. What kind of life is worthy of living?" Thus, his job maintaining engines for the fleet of Indonesia's largest airline had led him to the profound existential question that has confronted human beings for millennia. After he was exposed to ESQ during an in-house training that Garuda had contracted, he became convinced that Islam offered the answer to this question.

Karnawan referred to himself as a "religineer" or religious engineer. His experience during ESQ encouraged him to develop something he called "spiritual engineering," by which he sought to reflexively apply engineering principles to Islam and apply the practices of Islam to engineering. As an example he said, "Whatever Muhammad does is certain and should be followed. Whatever he told us not to do, we should not do. It is just like a digital system." By this he meant that, in binary fashion, every human action either conformed to or contrasted with the examples provided by the prophet Muhammad. In trying to decide how to act, Muslims could look to the prophet to decide which actions were commensurable with Islam and modify their practices accordingly. He explained that spiritual engineering meant "spiritualizing through digital theology and engineering by digital technology." As an example of spiritual engineering, he showed me several formulas he had concocted to represent religious principles in mathematical form. He told me he had compiled forty separate notebooks with such formulas.

One formula that Karnawan was particularly enthusiastic about was the "equation of human sin (*rumus dosa manusia*)," which is based on a triangle labeled with three angles: A, H, and U. As he drew the triangle in my notebook he told me that each of the three angles stood for something, with A indexing Allah, U referring to the universe, and H representing human beings. He then worked through the following series of geometric equations:

$$\text{Eq. } \Delta = AU/Sin \, \Delta \, H = AH/Sin \, \Delta \, U = HU/Sin \, \Delta \, A = 2r$$
$$Sin \, \Delta \, H = 2r/AU$$
$$\text{Or, } Sin \, H \equiv AU$$

As I desperately tried to recall the rules for sine and cosine equations that I had last been exposed to in secondary school, he concluded grandly, "The sins of humans [Sin H] are identical to Allah [A] multiplied by the universe [U]!"

Those engaged in the project of engineering Islam were indifferent to the contention that science and religion offered fundamentally different ways of knowing. I argued that science was an ongoing, unstable process of human understanding (Kuhn 1962), whereas religion proclaims a set of eternal, unchanging truths. Science starts with the premise that its mode of knowing is incomplete and always subject to the possibility that more data and new thought might yield better explanations. Religion, in contrast, is far more stable insofar as it contains revealed principles that cannot be subject to revision. For example, I asked Rinaldi what the implications for ESQ would be if physicists decided that the big bang theory was incorrect and came up with a new explanation for the origins of the universe. He responded with indifference as if the answer were self-evident, "If there is a new theory, it only means that our interpretation of the Qur'an was wrong. It didn't say what we thought it did. So we have to go back and read it again—to find a new explanation…but [an explanation] will surely be there."

In sum, engineering Islam resolved a sense of contradiction that many of those who had come of age during Indonesia's New Order had experienced. They had grown up in families where Islam, in varying degrees, was part of everyday life. In some cases religious practice was more strongly emphasized than in others, but for all of them it had been, to some extent, a part of how they defined themselves and were defined. However, Islamic practice was downplayed during the 1970s and 1980s as the New Order had thrown itself headlong into the project of national development. It was taken as axiomatic that development and modernization were unconnected to Islam. In part, this was a strategic calculation intended to diminish the influence of political groups that had threatened the viability of the new nation-state in the 1950s and 60s. In this political and economic context New Order modernization had proceeded under the assumption of a separation between a secular workplace and a domestic life in which one was able, although by no means obligated, to practice religion. Many employees expressed that before ESQ they had felt split and internally conflicted between their home lives in which Islam was an important orienting activity and their careers in which religion played no part. They reported to me that ESQ had "made them feel whole again." A major part of the resolution to what they referred to as a "split personality" was that ESQ provided them with evidence that Islam and science were compatible.

Furthermore, engineering Islam appealed to middle-class and upper-middle-class professionals in technical and applied fields. This cohort was steeped in the conviction that the appropriate deployment of human knowledge could solve any problem that presented itself. Their educational background was in disciplines such as engineering, medicine, architecture, plant and fisheries science, and business. These disciplines share the modernist presumption that worldly problems can be solved through the application of reason. Social scientific and humanities disciplines focus more on asking better questions rather than posing specific solutions. In contrast, adherents of Islamic spiritual reform in Indonesia were inculcated in an educational milieu in which it was presupposed that worldly challenges could be resolved through the application of knowledge. ESQ and other manifestations of spiritual reform, such as life-coaching and self-help genres in North America, approached living a life as a technical problem that could be addressed through rational intervention. Thus, for many participants in these programs living a correct life could be approached much as one might build a bridge or enhance the production of a steel mill, through subjecting it to the cold light of reason.

Making Moderate Muslims: Reconfiguring Religious Identity

In addition to appearing to resolve what some saw as a conflict between science, technology, and development on the one hand, and Islam and spirituality on the other, ESQ also provided members of Indonesia's middle class with an identity commensurate with contemporary political and ethical concerns. The pivotal events that framed this assemblage were the end of the Suharto regime and the events of September 11, 2001, and their aftermath.

The end of the New Order is without a doubt one of the two most significant events in Indonesia's postcolonial history, alongside the bloody transfer of power that took place following the aborted coup of 1965 (Anderson, McVey, and Bunnell 1971; Robinson 1995; Roosa 2006). Suharto's resignation as president of Indonesia in 1998 following a thirty-two-year period in which he held a virtual stranglehold on political power was a momentous event in the lives of virtually every Indonesian citizen. It was particularly significant for the middle-class and upper-middle-class citizens who make up much of the workforce at state-owned enterprises such as Krakatau Steel who had benefited from the tremendous bureaucratic expansion that took place during the Suharto years. Employees at these institutions had profited more than most Indonesians from the New Order state's developmentalist objectives and thus found themselves awkwardly positioned at the end of the Suharto regime.

This group had benefited because many of those who obtained positions at state-owned firms did so as a direct result of the state's simultaneous embrace of technological development and affirmative action policies. As noted in chapter 1, Muslim Indonesians had enjoyed preferential hiring and promotion policies at state-owned firms as the government sought to redress what it perceived as historical discrimination against so-called *pribumi* Indonesians. Thus, they had been among the greatest beneficiaries of the billions of dollars that Suharto had poured into programs intended to enhance Indonesia's technological and industrial capacity.

When the regime collapsed this cohort was uncomfortably positioned vis-à-vis Indonesia's democratic transition. Blame for the economic crash that occurred concurrently with the political crisis was in part attributed to the state's unproductive investment in technological development but also to the fact that funds earmarked for development had been misappropriated or siphoned off in practices that later came to be classified as corrupt. At Krakatau Steel upper-level and mid-level managers who held the authority to sign off on purchase orders established independent shell companies that served as suppliers for everything from spare parts to office computers. They paid for the supplies at a substantial premium over the actual price of the goods and pocketed the surplus funds. These practices were alluded to during the overview of the ESQ session I described earlier in this chapter when Rinaldi declared that participants had taken the company's beneficence for granted in the same way that they had taken motherly love for granted. A substantial number of employees of state-owned firms were doubly implicated in the now discredited Suharto regime: on the one hand because they owed their livelihoods to the regime and on the other because they had engaged in some of the very practices that were later understood to have brought down the regime.

ESQ training did not explicitly invoke these practices but implicitly alluded to the complicity of many trainees with the earlier regime. Thus, in sessions in which the trainers led the participants in collective pleas for atonement from Allah, these pleas were usually articulated either in metaphorical fashion or in vague and general terms. ESQ trainers told me that a central goal of the training was to eliminate corruption, which they took to be a foremost manifestation of the "moral crisis" in the country. However, corruption was seldom explicitly mentioned during the training. When I asked Rinaldi about this he said, "Yes, it is true. We rarely mention corruption specifically, but the effect [of the training] is to reduce corruption." He said that although eliminating corruption was seldom overtly invoked, those who participated in the training understood that this was in fact a primary objective.

Indeed, a prevailing message was that participants in the training had become too materialistic, worshipping meaningless material things, and forgetting that Allah should be the sole subject of their devotion. Thus, several sessions over the course of the training involved distressed collective prayers when the trainers led participants in tearful pleas in which everyone in the room "asked for forgiveness" (*mohon ampun*) from Allah. In asking for forgiveness from Allah and recommitting themselves to Islam, participants in ESQ training could absolve themselves of their complicity with the New Order and adopt new subjectivities that were compatible with the post-Suharto present. This was a present in which they were no longer dependent on the state to ensure their well-being but ready to compete in an increasingly global economy.

In one of the few instances in which corruption was overtly mentioned, Rinaldi argued that it was just that those who were dishonest would face damnation. He said:

> Allah…is the one who implanted honesty in the heart of human beings. Is it appropriate that people who are dishonest, people who manipulate and engage in corruption, should go to hell? Is Allah cruel? In fact he is not cruel at all, he is caring! Allah provides plenty of reminders. Imagine, because of corruption, because of dishonesty, what happens? Destruction, deprivation, degeneration! Take Krakatau Steel. The price of steel has become expensive, isn't that true? Yes! If we can't compete, who loses? Every employee, their families, the nation as a whole will lose! Thus, is it appropriate that people who are dishonest go to hell? Yes, it is very appropriate that they go to hell!

Thus, employees who engaged in corruption were ultimately hurting themselves and their families because they were making it more difficult for the company to compete against outside companies that were being granted increasing access to the Indonesian steel market. For this they deserved the ultimate otherworldly punishment. Because this cohort had benefited from a regime now widely discredited and viewed as corrupt, the message of ESQ proved attractive.

In contrast, lower-level employees who had not done as well were not as receptive to the training. The common explanation for this was that they were less educated and thus could not understand all the arguments that were presented. However, another reason for the failure of ESQ to provoke powerful effects among those at lower levels of the company hierarchy may have been because they had less for which to atone. They had not benefited from the largesse of the New Order state to the same degree.

While they had been given decent jobs, they had never had the opportunity to obtain education or training overseas under company sponsorship. Lower-level employees were not provided with as many company benefits and had fewer opportunities for promotion. Finally, they were never in a position to personally profit from company activities by setting up shell companies with privileged access to purchase orders. Appeals to plea for collective forgiveness may have rang hollow for this group because they had much less for which to forgive.

A degree of the popularity of spiritual reform initiatives such as ESQ can also be attributed to political conditions outside Indonesia, specifically the events of September 11, 2001. Ary Ginanjar had been developing the concepts and ideas that led to the ESQ training during the late 1990s and published his first ESQ book, which later sold over a hundred thousand copies in Indonesia, in May 2001. His mother told me he had submitted the proposal to more than half a dozen Indonesian publishers, including the widely respected houses Mizan and Gramedia. However, none of those presses thought the book was worthy of publication, so he financed the book himself under his own imprint, Penerbit Arga.[30] Shortly after the publication of the book the events of September 11, 2001, occurred and dominated the news in Indonesia for months (if not years) afterwards. The destruction of the World Trade Center and subsequent invasions of first Afghanistan and then Iraq caused many in the press and on the streets to conclude that Samuel Huntington's apocalyptic vision of post–Cold War geopolitics had come to pass.

While many in Indonesia were focusing on the apparently unbridgeable differences between Islam and the West, Ginanjar argued that the West embraced ideas such as hard work, self-discipline, responsibility, and personal accountability that were practices intrinsic to Islam as well. In the early days of ESQ, Ginanjar presented some of his core ideas at religious events and other meetings in the area around Jakarta. These presentations provided the foundation for the formal ESQ training program that debuted in 2002. At points the training program invoked the West as a negative counterexample, for instance when talking about the epidemics of suicide, drug abuse, and adultery that were depicted as characteristic of life in the United States and Europe. However, during the training scientific

---

30. Arga is an abbreviation for Ary Ginajar Agustian.

contributions from Europe and the United States were also invoked to provide authoritative evidence for one of the general points that Ginanjar sought to make. For example, the fact that Harvard Business School had organized a seminar on the relationship between spirituality and business success gave justification to Ginanjar's own theories about the relationship between these two domains.

In the aftermath of the attacks and counterattacks that escalated between those who claimed to represent Muslims and those who claimed to stand for Western values, ESQ offered an appealing moderate, middle ground. The rapid expansion of ESQ training after its introduction likely can be attributed, at least in part, to the fact that the message of the training, focusing on individual growth, personal self-help, and the applied principles conducive to commercial success appealed to those who were concerned with the way that Islam was represented in the Western media after 2001. Ginanjar suggested as much. At the end of a conversation we had in May 2004 he said to me, "Mr. Daromir, please explain to the people of Europe and America that…they don't need to worry about the Muslims. That what we do here is the real one.… There is no difference between…Christians and Muslims." For some adherents it was no doubt this message that marked the greatest appeal of ESQ training.

Furthermore, programs of spiritual reform in contemporary Indonesia are moderate insofar as they do not advocate rejection of the West. Spiritual reformers such as Ary Ginanjar emphasize a universal humanity premised on the fact that all humans contain a "God spot." Thus, they do not see Islam as locked into an inevitable conflict with the West. As one Krakatau Steel manager and ESQ advocate remarked, "We have a saying, Americans are not Muslim, but they are Islam-like" (*bukan Islam, tapi Islami*). By this he meant that, like Muslims, Americans "keep their commitments and are attentive to time and cleanliness." Developing Islamic practice was not a stance against the West but a way of enhancing the transnational competitiveness of Indonesian workers.

Conclusion: Developing Faith

In response to what he described as a "moral crisis" Ary Ginanjar reconfigured the relationship between faith and development in Indonesia so that faith itself became an object of development. During the New Order, development was the raison d'être of government policy and practice. However, after Suharto's spectacular collapse, the logic of enhancement and growth that underlay the project of modernization was applied to the religious practices of the industrial employees who were supposed to be the purveyors of development. This was a fundamental premise of the various moderate Islamic spiritual reform initiatives that emerged and grew rapidly in popularity in the years following Suharto's resignation. Islamic practice, long subordinated in Indonesia, was seen as a means to revive economic growth.

Developing faith did not represent the end of faith in development but rather a reconfiguration of its logic. The very same modernist logic that had guided the project of Indonesian development was still at work in initiatives to develop faith. Implicit was the assumption that worldly problems could be addressed through technical intervention and the application of human knowledge. Thus, faith was not viewed as a mystical or irrational practice but as something that could be instilled through design and calculation. Developing faith and, in so doing, creating new patterns of human life, was executed according to the same logic that earlier justified building bridges, toll roads, and factories. Religious practice was something to be enhanced through a series of technical interventions. Thus, participants in the training were exposed to a highly rationalized set of practices that had been reliably tested for their effectiveness at eliciting the desired sensory responses.

Furthermore, for many citizens in contemporary Indonesia who had come of age during the apex of state-led developmentalism, Islamic spiritual reform appeared to resolve a number of oppositions that had plagued the project of national development. ESQ spiritual training offered a recipe for living that was simultaneously Muslim and modern. Thus, one could simultaneously be an engineer and a devout adherent of Islam. The message was particularly effective because it was delivered in idioms, such as mathematical formulas, which participants recognized as tools that provided transparent, true representations of the world.

The spectacular growth of moderate Islamic spiritual reform movements after the end of the Suharto regime demonstrates a change from an order characterized by faith in development to a new configuration in which religious faith was simultaneously an object to be developed and a means of reviving the economic growth that had characterized much of the Suharto regime. Initiatives such as ESQ sought to enhance religious faith for two reasons. First, as demonstrated in this chapter, many believed that Islam had been separated from the everyday life of the purveyors of development during the Suharto era. In response ESQ enacted the reconciliation of Islamic knowledge and scientific practice. Second, spiritual reformers interpreted Islamic practice as conducive to success in an emerging global economic order. I now turn to this second aspect of developing faith to illustrate how ESQ and similar phenomena represented the emergence of a spiritual economy.

Part II

INTERVENTION

3

SPIRITUAL ECONOMIES

In addition to engineering Islam by contending that Islam was compatible with scientific knowledge, ESQ training sought to configure a mode of Islamic practice that was conducive to corporate success in an economy no longer defined in national terms. This chapter describes an empirical manifestation of what are termed spiritual economies.[1] Spiritual economies elucidate how economic reform is conceived of and enacted as a matter of religious piety and spiritual virtue. The concept consists of three primary components: 1) reconfiguring work as a form of worship and religious

---

1. Two anthropologists have used the phrase *spiritual economies* in passing (Brenner 1998, 171; Klima 2002, 153, 282–286). Although related, my development of the concept differs in important ways. For example, Brenner uses the concept to refer to the way in which many Javanese believe that through mastering "desires they can accumulate both material wealth and spiritual merit" (Brenner 1998, 171). My use of spiritual economies refers to how spirituality is produced as an object of self-management and intervention to instill economic reason. Thus, my focus is not on the economic benefit of accumulating spiritual merit but rather on inculcating ascetic values to produce new types of laboring subjects.

duty; 2) objectifying spirituality as a site of management and intervention; and 3) inculcating ethics of individual accountability that are deemed commensurable with norms of transparency, productivity, and rationalization for purposes of profit.

As described in the introduction, the proponents of spiritual reform considered the separation of religious ethics from economic practice as the root of Indonesia's financial crisis. In their eyes, this disjunction resulted in rampant corruption, a lack of accountability, and labor indiscipline. Spiritual economies illuminate these efforts to inculcate dispositions deemed conducive to both pious religious practice and productive labor. The concept of spiritual economies captures how reformers in Indonesia combine the asceticism and rationalization intrinsic to both Islam and neoliberalism to produce a new configuration of being in the world. Islam is not merely a vehicle in this process, as spiritual reform is taken to both enable Islamic virtue and effect dispositions that enhance corporate productivity and competitiveness in an increasingly transnational economy. Self-discipline, accountability, and entrepreneurial action are represented as Islamic virtues that should inform conduct both within and beyond the workplace. The concept of spiritual economies captures an aspect of the afterlife of development, insofar as it sheds light on the ways Indonesians sought to mobilize Islamic practice to meet the predicament posed by economic integration across national borders.

The concept of spiritual economies is what Max Weber called an "ideal type": an abstract composite designed to enhance understanding of interconnected phenomena in the world.[2] Thus, it is intended to enable analysis of a convergence of diverse influences.[3] However, it is a conceptual tool

---

2. According to Weber an ideal type does not refer to something that exists empirically but rather is devised by an analyst as a means of explanation through comparative analysis. He writes "an ideal type is formed by the one-sided accentuation of one or more points of view and by the synthesis of a great many diffuse, discrete, more or less present and occasionally absent concrete individual phenomena, which are arranged according to those one-sidedly emphasized viewpoints into a unified analytical construct. In its conceptual purity, this mental construct cannot be found empirically anywhere in reality" (Weber 1949, 90).

3. In this book I refer both to the concept of spiritual economies (in the plural) and a specific spiritual economy (in the singular). The former usage refers to the general assemblage of the afterlife of development, religious resurgence, and transnational economic integration in which work is reconfigured as worship, spirituality becomes a site of government, and the individual ethics of accountability commensurable with neoliberal norms are inculcated. The latter usage refers to the specific ethnographic conjuncture from which the concept emerged empirically.

that is created by the analyst and not an existing thing in the world. Furthermore, the concept does not entail a unified theory of the relationship between capitalism and religion. Rather, my intent in formulating the notion of spiritual economies is to enable research and analysis of analogous formations occurring elsewhere in the world.

The concept of spiritual economies is directed toward phenomena similar to those addressed by the notion of occult economies but is intended to elucidate an articulation between religious resurgence and economic globalization that is not quite captured by the latter. Comaroff and Comaroff define occult economies as "the deployment of magical means for material ends or, more expansively, the conjuring of wealth by resort to inherently mysterious techniques, techniques whose principles of operation are neither transparent nor explicable in conventional terms. These techniques, moreover, often involve the destruction of others and their capacity to create value" (Comaroff and Comaroff 1999, 297n231). In their eyes, the crisis of faith in development has led to a resurgence of occult practices as a refuge from the dislocations precipitated by structural adjustment and other neoliberal reforms. Comaroff and Comaroff center their arguments on sensationalist accounts of mystification and fetishism, including witchcraft and the killing of accused witches, the resurgence of zombies, pyramid schemes, and the illicit sale of body parts for occult ends. While occult economies may be useful in understanding some phenomena, it is not so useful in comprehending Islamic reform in contemporary Indonesia and other instances where religious practices are combined with corporate norms. In contrast, spiritual economies emerge from analysis of the practices mobilized inside key sites of industrial production to address the challenge posed by the failure of development and increasing integration into transnational markets.

Whereas occult economies treat capitalism as premised on mystification and fetishism, spiritual economies focus on the process of rationalization inherent in capitalism. Occult economies emerge out of the proliferation of two kinds of irrationality. On one hand, those subject to neoliberal reforms comprehend these transformations in irrational ways—those who have seen their lives disrupted in dramatic ways have no other recourse but magic and mystery to comprehend these changes. On the other hand, neoliberal policies are disseminated with religious fervor by those who succumb to their spell. In contrast, spiritual economies point to a set of ascetic practices that involve individual ethical reform conducive to neoliberal values, such as transparency and accountability. This is not blind ascription to a totalizing gospel; instead, it is the mobilization of a particular set of religious techniques to address specific challenges. Thus, I do not treat religious practice as a retreat into magic and mystery but rather as the deployment of a set of ascetic practices designed to make humans into specific types of beings (Asad 1993; Weber 1990). Thus, occult economies treat capitalism as based on illusion and mystification through the processes of fetishization, whereas spiritual economies focus on how capitalism entails the rationalization of practice to create greater efficiency, transparency, and productivity.

The distinction between rationalization and mystification points to an important methodological difference inherent in these two concepts. Occult economies presume that those subjected to the "culture of neoliberalism" (Comaroff and Comaroff 2000) do not fully comprehend the changes in which they are enmeshed, leading them to account for these changes in mystical and occult terms. In contrast, and in keeping with the methodological approach of para-ethnography I outlined in the introduction, subjects in a spiritual economy comprehend the challenges they face, although they may not be in complete control of the means to remedy them. Unlike occult economies, spiritual economies do not presume that the ethnographer possesses a more privileged insight into the predicaments faced than those under analysis. Thus, rather than resorting to religion and magic as a reaction to the dislocations and ruptures brought about by economic changes, those enmeshed in a spiritual economy look to religion as a means of developing the ascetic practices and applied techniques commensurable with demands toward greater productivity, efficiency, and transparency. A different perspective of agency is inherent in these two concepts. Occult economies, like many Marxian approaches, suggest that capitalism can be separated from modern subjects. It acts on those subjects from the outside through deception, mystification, and fetishization. In contrast, in spiritual economies capitalism does not act so much *on* the subject as *through* the subject by effecting practices and ethical dispositions.

Finally, those most enmeshed in the particular spiritual economy I describe were more often supervisory-level employees rather than those at the bottom of the corporate hierarchy. As I spent more time at training sessions in Cilegon and subsequently Jakarta, it became increasingly apparent that the managers and other elites involved in ESQ were at least as, if not more, interested in cultivating their own religious practice than they were in enhancing the religious practice of those whom they supervised or employed. Spiritual training was directed at—and resonated more profoundly with—well-educated senior and midlevel managers at Krakatau Steel as opposed to operators and line workers. In contrast, occult economies refer to the mystification of the marginal and dispossessed that turn to supernatural explanation and intervention to resolve quandaries that they find otherwise incomprehensible. The concept of spiritual economies captures the self-disciplinary aspects of the articulation between religious resurgence and economic globalization in a way that is not adequately addressed by occult economies. Thus, spiritual economies shed light on globalization as entailing a specific type of practice insofar as it captures the proliferation of an ethical regime in which hard work is a morally sanctioned activity. As such it shows how asceticism is "carried out of monastic cells and into everyday life" (Weber 1990, 181).

Spiritual economies involve efforts to connect individual religious piety to broader projects of economic transformation and development. In asserting the social character of economic relations, the concept builds on James Scott's notion of "moral economy" (Scott 1976) that demonstrates how certain economic relations are embedded in social relations and characterized by reciprocity among patrons and clients.[4] In Scott's formulation, clients accept outwardly exploitative economic arrangements because of an implicit understanding that patrons will provide for them in the event of hardship. However, there are some important differences. Whereas a moral economy is dependent on a relation of reciprocity, in a spiritual economy this ethic is replaced by an ethic of individual accountability to God. Thus, those enmeshed in a spiritual economy make judgments about such factors as time, productivity, and corruption based on a particular understanding of religious duty. The increasing emphasis on individual accountability as part of the broader ongoing reconfiguration of the company's position was a common topic of discussion among factory employees.

---

4. Scott drew on an earlier formulation of moral economy by E. P. Thompson, who demonstrated how bread riots in eighteenth-century England were not functional responses to historical events but rather political and cultural claims based on notions of traditional rights and customs (Thompson 1971).

Like the concept of moral economy, spiritual economies are attentive to the extension of economic rationality into domains from which it was previously absent. Scott describes situations in which exchanges do not conform to an economic logic but rather to a social one. He shows how the introduction of economic rationalization through colonial capitalism precipitates the breakdown of this system. Similarly, the concept of a spiritual economy illuminates the proliferation of economic rationality into sites, practices, and institutions from which it was previously limited. One foreman in the slab steel plant at Krakatau Steel explained to me that prior to the mid-1990s "the social was the most important and profit was secondary," but "now profit is number one and the social mission [*misi sosial*] is number two." Employees said that this "social mission" was premised on "*padat karya,*" which literally translates as "dense work" and refers to the past pattern of hiring more workers than necessary to operate a business. This pattern is common at many Indonesian businesses, including both state-owned enterprises and private corporations. At Krakatau Steel, a thinly veiled debate pitted those who saw the company's mission as "supporting the livelihoods of the masses" (*hajat hidup orang banyak*) against those that sought to make the company competitive in an increasingly global steel market by reducing its labor costs.

The values that characterized the "social mission" were similar to those outlined by Clifford Geertz in his studies of village Java. The notions of *padat karya* and *hajat hidup orang banyak* evoke patterns of "work spreading" that Geertz observed as characteristic of rural Indonesia during the 1950s and 1960s (Geertz 1963a). Geertz argued that peasant culture in Java was premised on an ethic of "shared poverty" in which Javanese peasants accepted their station in life and lacked the motivation and entrepreneurial ambition to improve their livelihoods.[5] Geertz interpreted the ethics of shared poverty as the primary obstacle to economic development, or "takeoff" in the parlance of modernization theory (Rostow 1960). In the years following the end of the Suharto regime the problem for state technocrats, development agencies, and corporate managers was not so much overcoming cultural barriers to enable Indonesia to proceed along the track toward modernity. Rather they sought to emphasize how cultural values could

---

5. Geertz's notion of "shared poverty" was widely criticized by subsequent scholars for his failure to acknowledge rural hierarchy and stratification (Hart 1986; White 1983).

be made conducive to the extension of economic rationality into domains from which it had previously been constrained.

Labor rationalized according to social principles (providing more comparatively good-paying factory jobs and distributing particularly strenuous activities), as opposed to economic principles (avoiding redundancy and maximizing efficiency), evokes the ethical formation identified by Geertz. However, Krakatau Steel managers made the decision that, in the long run, this formation was not compatible with the new economic arrangement in which the state no longer guaranteed the viability of the company. At Krakatau Steel, patterns of institutionalized work spreading were evident in one especially intensive portion of the production process where molten steel is cast into solid slabs, weighing ten to thirty tons each. Other company employees explained that workers in the slab steel plant were more "hot-headed" and attributed their emotional volatility to the dusty, deafening, sweltering climate of the plant. Hariyanto had the arduous task of ensuring the smooth exchange of molten steel from giant ladles into the massive casting machine. He took turns with a coworker in half-hour blocks to monitor this transfer. The heat and noise generated in this portion of the steelmaking process made it a physically demanding job, but Hariyanto said that rotating the job with another employee made it tolerable because the hardship was "divided in two" (*dibagi dua*). Although the work was difficult and undercompensated, he told me that it was better than anything else he could find. He was aware, however, that the job could likely be performed by a single employee and feared that his position, a single task performed by two people, would be made redundant should privatization occur.

At stake in privatizing Krakatau Steel was the rationalization of a latter-day incarnation of practices of work spreading. Displaced from the agrarian countryside, practices similar to those observed by Geertz were introduced into industrial production as a development strategy, as this displacement enabled the creation of a vast number of well-paid employment positions. In the aftermath of Suharto's downfall, the formation of a spiritual economy represented the reconfiguration of the earlier social logic of nationalist development. Efforts to merge religious practice and market norms stood in stark contrast to the rationality that characterized state-owned enterprises during the New Order. The tension between the company's social mission and its business mission was acute. One general manager told me that a 1995 Booz, Allen, and Hamilton management consulting audit of the company advocated releasing one-quarter of the company's total workforce, corresponding to at least fifteen hundred permanent, full-time positions. Managers often cited the latter-day practice of work spreading as a rationale for poor job performance at the company, claiming that employees at the company lacked motivation because they knew they were superfluous. Spiritual training sessions were one means through which managers hoped to transform lackluster job performance, by making it a matter of religious duty. The concept of spiritual economies illuminates this new economic ethic of individual productivity and accountability that stands in contrast to the social mission characteristic of state-owned enterprises during the Suharto regime.

Managing Spirits

The concept of spiritual economies draws on approaches that treat economy not as an autonomous realm of production, exchange, and consumption but rather as a technology for eliciting certain types of subjects and practices (Callon 1998; Mitchell 2002, 80–119; Mitchell 2005). These approaches build on Foucault's argument that the concept of "economy" was central to the emergence of a distinctly modern form of political rationality he called governmentality (Foucault 1991). Governmentality links management of the self, the family, and the state (Barry, Osborne and Rose 1996; Ong 1999; Rose 1999). Foucault writes, "In an upwards direction the sovereign must first learn how to govern himself, his goods, and his patrimony after which he will be successful governing the state. Downwards continuity means that when a state is well run, the head of the family will know how to look after his family, his goods and his patrimony, and consequently individuals will behave. The central term of this continuity is the management of individuals, goods and wealth within the family: *economy*" (1991, 92). Foucault chronicles the resignification of the compound word economy, which in ancient Greek had referred to the management (*nomos*) of the household (*oikos*). Later the term *economy* came to denote a domain for the production and administration of subjects. This occurs through the application of an unprecedented mode of knowledge (statistics) on a new object (a population). Drawing on this approach, I argue that in contemporary Indonesia, Islam is invoked to elicit subjects complicit with norms of efficiency, productivity, and transparency. In diagramming this spiritual economy, I show how Islam serves as a medium through which subjects of spiritual reform are made accountable to themselves, their families, their work, and the nation at large.

The formation I refer to as a spiritual economy entitled a total way of life within which the population was represented at a number of different scales. At the most elementary scale it involved a set of ethical practices of individual transformation intended to link personal spirituality to a broader project of national economic reform. These included things such as repenting for past sins to become more honest in the future. It also involved work on the self that sought to inculcate techniques to manage one's emotions and relate better to coworkers. Thus, spiritual economies capture efforts to link self-government to the government of the family and the nation.

Spiritual reformers posed self-government as an alternative to ongoing efforts to implement Islamic *syariah* law in Indonesia (Bowen 2003, 173–199). In early 2004 Rinaldi told me that spiritual reform was not simply a matter of "more rules." He said, "We already have enough rules...but if you touch them here [gesturing to his chest] they don't need rules. They won't accept a commission, even without more rules."[6] In the years following the end of the Suharto regime, a number of groups advocated the implementation of *syariah* law in Indonesia. These included groups such as Hizbut Tahrir and branches of the MUI (Indonesian Council of Islamic Scholars), both discussed in the previous chapter. However, spiritual reformers explicitly contrasted their project with these efforts. The program was intended to inculcate an ethic of individual self-policing based in Islamic practice in contrast to calls for the state to enforce Islamic law. The spiritual economy did not consist of rules and regulations but rather an ethic of self-management, which was referred to as "built-in control" and is described in detail below.

---

6. "Commission" (*komisi*) was a widely deployed euphemism for kickbacks on sales in which the salesperson would individually benefit at the expense of the firm for which he or she worked.

This spiritual economy likewise operated on the household. Family relations were a frequent topic of ESQ training, and participants often encouraged other family members to enroll in the training. During spiritual training, participants were constantly admonished to remember their obligations toward family members. As described in the previous chapter, participants were repeatedly called on to remember and ask for forgiveness for improprieties against their parents. In addition, relationships between parents and children were a recurring theme. After being admonished to atone for the way in which participants treated their mothers in the past, they were reminded not to love their children as much as they love God, because children can be "taken away tomorrow," whereas Allah is "everlasting." Furthermore, kinship networks provided a means for the dissemination of ESQ. At training venues ESQ staff circulated promotional material advertising shorter one- and two-day long sessions designed for younger audiences, such as ESQ Teens and ESQ Kids. I met several adherents who proudly told me that every member of their family had attended ESQ training. In 2009 a new training called ESQ Parenting was launched, which was designed to provide techniques to become more effective parents.

The population constituted in a spiritual economy entails not only selves and families but also Indonesia as a whole. One of the objectives of ESQ is to strengthen the human resources of the entire professional population of Indonesia. In 2005 Ginanjar launched a program called Developing a Golden Indonesia 2020 (Membangun Indonesia Emas 2020), which is premised on the idea that spiritual reform can enhance national development. Echoing former prime minister Mahathir Mohamad's developmentalist Vision 2020 project in neighboring Malaysia (Bunnell 2004; Chin 1998), Ginanjar saw ESQ as a means of training a new generation of Indonesian business and corporate leaders who will improve the economic fortunes of the country by the year 2020.

Worshipping Work and Balancing Seraphic Accounts

Above the cavernous half-kilometer-long floor of Krakatau Steel's hot strip mill, where twenty-ton slabs were heated to over one thousand degrees and thunderously flattened into smooth sheets of coiled steel, a huge

Figure 3.1. A sign in hot strip mill reading "HARD WORK IS PART OF OUR WORSHIP" above a glowing strip of steel.

banner read HARD WORK IS PART OF OUR WORSHIP.[7] Similar signs were posted in other mills as well. Making work into religious worship was not merely an Orwellian slogan inscribed on various factory edifices. Spiritual reformers sought to make this slogan an embodied practice through transforming work into religious worship. In their eyes such a transformation offered a solution to the end of faith in development. Whereas previously in Indonesia economic development was posed first and foremost as a technical problem (Amir 2007a; Thee 2003), movements for spiritual reform active in state-owned enterprises suggest that after the end of the New Order development was being posed as an ethical one.

---

7. KERJA KERAS MERUPAKAN SEBAGIAN AMAL IBADAH KITA.

The first component of a spiritual economy involves inculcating the ethical maxim that work in the world demonstrated one's devotion to God. According to one human resources manager, Sukrono, this intervention was the result of an updated reading of the Qur'an. He explained:

> When we were a small developing country in the 1970s we thought that worship [*ibadah*] meant praying [*sholat*], giving alms [*zakat*], or going on the *hajj*, but this is not true. In fact, from studying the Qur'an we know that passages dealing with these things are only about 20 percent of the content, the rest of the Qur'an is about human relations. The crucial thing is that in everyday activity—waking up and going to work, doing family errands, and so forth—one's intentions [*niat*] are toward worship....In the *hadiths* there is the story of Muhammad and the stone maker. Muhammad saw two people. One was always at the mosque, engaged in ritual. The other was working so hard, providing for his family, that he didn't have time for ritual. Yet, it was he who went to heaven while the former did not.

Here Sukrono illustrates how Islamic worship had been interpreted as a form of worldly motivation. He focuses on three of the five pillars of Islam: praying, giving alms, and going on the *hajj* pilgrimage. The faith in development that had guided Indonesian modernization during the New Order had proceeded under the assumption of a separation of religion from the economy. In contrast, the afterlife of development entailed recasting the Qur'an as a human resources manual. In so doing Sukrono echoed Ary Ginanjar's transformation of the five pillars of Islam into recipes for corporate success, for example, by rebranding *zakat* as "strategic collaboration." In fact, Sukrono finds evidence for what Max Weber called "worldly asceticism" in the *hadiths* (Weber 1990, 154). Fulfilling one's duty to God is not restricted to following the five pillars of Islam, or what Ary Ginanjar called mere "ritual" activity. Rather, following the principles that Muhammad illustrated during his life, everyday practices such as working and supporting one's family constitute religious activity equal to observing the required rituals.

Krakatau Steel employees who had participated in ESQ had similar interpretations about what work as worship meant. Yanto, who worked in the Krakatau Steel credit union, made the connection between religious practice and labor through time and discipline. He said that a good Muslim must be constantly attentive to time because of the Islamic requirement to pray five times each day at predetermined hours. Likewise, work at the company required constant attention to the clock. Yanto said, "I have to be sure to wake up on time, be to work on time, take my breaks at the right time....It is the same with prayer, it has to be done at the right time. One has to be disciplined in both religion and work." Yanto's interpretation of the relationship between time, work, and discipline echoes Weber's characterization of this relationship as a central component of "the spirit of capitalism" (Weber 1990, 47–78).

Proponents of ESQ represented worshipping work as capable of resolving the challenge posed by the end of state-directed, nationalist development. Haidar, who was discussed in chapter 2, was passionate about improving economic conditions in Indonesia. I had originally met him when he was working as an instructor for the Seven Habits of Highly Effective People training at Krakatau Steel. He had done a master's degree in human resources at a European university and expressed interest in moving to the United States to write a PhD dissertation on the central tenet of ESQ training: that religious practice enhances work motivation. He had become very interested in ESQ, and several months after I first met him, he was hired by Ary Ginanjar to be an ESQ trainer.

While Haidar was still working as a Seven Habits trainer, he expressed frustration at the routines exhibited by employees at state-owned companies. He had formerly worked for a major multinational corporation in Jakarta. Haidar was disconsolate that he had heard employees joking that KS (the acronym for Krakatau Steel by which the company was known across Indonesia) actually stood for *kerja santai* or "relaxed work." He found it appalling that one day, after he had concluded a day of Seven Habits training, a Krakatau Steel employee commented as they were leaving the training facility that it was "almost dark...as if he thought it was unusual to leave work so late. But in Jakarta it is totally normal. No one leaves work until after dark!" He was likewise aghast at how lackadaisical Krakatau Steel employees were when it came to reporting for work: "They show no embarrassment at arriving ten, fifteen, even twenty minutes late! And they do it over and over! They have no shame about it!" Haidar became convinced that ESQ was more effective in increasing the motivation of Indonesian workers than other forms of applied management knowledge, such as the Seven Habits of Highly Effective People training. His comments illustrate how proponents of spiritual reform contracted by state-owned enterprises sought to turn work into worship by instilling greater self-discipline among corporate employees. He attributed the greater effectiveness of ESQ to the fact that it is grounded in Islamic principles and would resonate more widely with the predominantly Muslim population of Indonesia. He contrasted ESQ with Seven Habits training programs, explaining that ESQ "puts people back on the right track of Islam, by using the five pillars of Islam and six pillars of the faith. It enhances integrity, but in the language of corporate Indonesia....It helps people make a new commitment to religion." Although at the time he was still working as a Seven Habits trainer, he revealed that he thought ESQ was more effective, "to be honest, I am not so sure how effective the Seven Habits are. We trainers have a joke. Do you know what the eighth habit is?" Realizing that he was now addressing me, I responded that I did not, to which he replied with a smile, "To forget the first seven!"

There are similarities and differences between the Protestant ethic described by Weber and the efforts of Indonesian spiritual reformers to make work a form of worship. They are similar insofar as ESQ sought to inspire an ethic of self-confidence similar to that which the doctrine of predestination precipitated. Weber argued that Protestants could only tolerate living with the overwhelming odds that most human beings would ultimately be damned was by convincing themselves that they were exceptional. Thus, followers of Calvin had "an absolute duty to consider oneself chosen, and to combat all doubts as temptations of the devil, since lack of self-confidence is the result of insufficient faith, hence of imperfect grace" (Weber 1990, 111). In the act of convincing themselves of their salvation they attained an ethic of overwhelming self-confidence. Weber shows how this ethic was common to both Calvinists and the titans of commerce of the industrial age, arguing that "those self-confident saints" can be "rediscover[ed] in the hard Puritan merchants of the heroic age of capitalism" (Weber 1990, 112). Similarly, self-confidence is perhaps the signature expression of contemporary titans of the post-industrial economy.

ESQ sought to inspire an ethic similar to that held by the "self-confident saints" described by Weber. It did so by rigorously preparing participants through simulations of what they believed they would face in the afterlife and offering them formulas for living an upstanding Muslim life. Participants gained the confidence that they could meet the criteria for admission to the celestial paradise. Thus, existence was approached as a technical problem and formulas for living were roundly disseminated. By mastering these formulas and conforming to them, one could attain confidence in one's own salvation. Participants in ESQ were often marked by their buoyant and outgoing dispositions, perhaps a product of their conviction.

However, there are also some important differences between the spirit of capitalism and spiritual economies. For Weber, the ethical orientation that emerged from the doctrinal revisions made by Protestant theologians later precipitated an austerely rationalized, capitalist way of life. This relationship was historical and thus contingent and unintentional. In contrast, for spiritual reformers in contemporary Indonesia, the link between corporate success and religious piety is calculated by design. They are convinced that developing faith will bring Indonesia prosperity.

In another difference from Weber's Protestants, the participants in Indonesian spiritual reform are confronted by a God who exercises meticulous surveillance through proxies rather than a distant God operating at great remove from the solitary individual. Participants in ESQ explained that two of Allah's angels, named Rokib and Atid, kept a watchful eye over each individual by constantly recording one's merits and sins. For example, Kustowo, who worked in the billet steel plant, described how these two angels, "maintain a database" (*mencatat database*) of all human actions to determine whether an individual will be saved. Using the English words "reward" and "punishment" he said that these two angels compile an inventory of the positive and negative actions of each human. The balance of this inventory determines the fate of the deceased in the afterlife. An individual with a surplus of merits would gain access to heaven while a surfeit of sins would consign one to the fires of damnation. "Only the individual, God, and the two angels know about our behavior," Kustowo told me. "If we do something *halal* [lawful] we get a reward. If we do something *haram* [forbidden] we get a demerit." This account of seraphic surveillance was also related during the ESQ training and resonated deeply with many participants.

These notions of Islamic accountability mirror the elements that Marilyn Strathern finds characteristic of "audit cultures." These protocols of finance are increasingly ubiquitous in a wide range of contemporary institutions and compose the "taken-for-granted process of neoliberal government" (Strathern 2000, 3). Spiritual reformers thus draw on a common concept in Islamic eschatology and transform accountability at work into a matter of religious worship (Maurer 2002). The report compiled by the two angels is filed away for Judgment Day to await a final decision on one's celestial qualifications. In this dimension of a spiritual economy, Islamic audit practices converge with norms designed to ensure conformity to economic rationality. Thus, treating work as a form of worship involves cultivating an ethics of individual accountability that is latent in both Islam and neoliberalism.

"Unshackling the God Spot" to Unleash a Universal Spirit

The second component of a spiritual economy involves the creation of spirituality as a site of management, intervention, and manipulation. Rendered in English, *spirituality* was likely a term with which participants in ESQ previously had only passing familiarity, if that. Consequently, it had to be created and understood as located within individual human bodies, before it could be activated and acted on. Spirituality was invoked as something that had been lost due to the regime's faith in development during the New Order. Ary Ginanjar lamented "for too long Indonesian companies have emphasized science and technical knowledge" but neglected spirituality. This meant that Intellectual Quotient (IQ) was prioritized as the index of one's qualifications and capabilities. In contrast, Ginanjar saw his mission as enhancing the spiritual knowledge (which he termed Spiritual Quotient or SQ) of Indonesians through spiritual training.

The notion that the failures and excesses of Indonesian developmentalism had resulted from prioritizing intellectual and technical knowledge over spiritual knowledge and emotional connection was compelling to employees of Krakatau Steel. Kusmanto, a technical expert in the public relations department, said that ESQ training had called into question some of the long-held presumptions under which the company had operated.[8]

---

8. Technical expert (*ahli teknik*) was an official job title at Krakatau Steel. There were three levels of technical expert: elementary technical expert, midlevel technical expert, and principal technical expert (*ahli teknik pertama, ahli teknik madya,* and *ahli teknik utama*). The speaker in this case was a midlevel technical expert. According to the corporate structure of Krakatau Steel, technical experts generally held university degrees, but were part of the functional (as opposed to the structural) hierarchy. This meant that they usually handled advanced engineering or administrative tasks but did not manage other employees. Thus, unlike structural employees, they had no subordinates.

He explained, "Krakatau Steel no longer uses IQ as the only measure of an employee's competence, but now we also emphasize the spiritual and emotional development of employees as well." He reasoned that a productive business needed employees who were not just technically capable but who acted in a morally and socially exemplary manner as well.

ESQ training represented the discovery of SQ and EQ and their ultimate combination by Ary Ginanjar as revolutionary advances in a history of progressive scientific achievement. On the first morning of ESQ training, before Rinaldi recounted the history of astronomy to show that the Qur'an predicts the big bang, he provided a similar historical chronology of the "discovery" of the concepts of IQ, EQ, and SQ. The latter two were drawn primarily from the work of North American and European management trainers and life-coaching gurus. Most influential were Danah Zohar and Daniel Goleman, whose academic affiliation with Harvard University accorded them authoritative status as producers of truth. Goleman, who received a PhD from Talcott Parsons' Department of Social Relations at Harvard, is credited with "discovering" emotional quotient, EQ (Goleman 1995; Stein and Book 2000). Zohar, who undertook PhD studies in the Department of Psychology at Harvard and has taught at several business schools, is described as identifying the spiritual quotient, SQ (Zohar and Marshall 2000). ESQ represents these two objects as inherent in all human beings. The shift from faith in development to developing faith did not indicate the abandonment of the assumptions on which modernization had been premised. Rather the project of faith in development was based on incomplete knowledge because it had privileged technical knowledge (IQ) to the exclusion of spiritual and emotional knowledge (SQ and EQ).

The emphasis on spirituality, however, was not a rejection of science in favor of mysticism. Ary Ginanjar saw his project as compatible with scientific knowledge and drew on the most recent developments in psychology, psychiatry, and neuroscience. During ESQ training, spirituality was represented as simultaneously general and particular: a universal human attribute that was physically isolated in the individual bodies of every human being.[9] For evidence Ginanjar drew on the scientific work of the University of California San Diego neuroscientist V. S. Ramachandran who "found

---

9. Paul Rabinow similarly observes that spirituality is simultaneously particular and general in contemporary France, insofar as "the spiritual lives in the person, it forms the 'general part' of

the existence of the God spot in the human brain" (Ginanjar 2001, xxxix).
Ramachandran's work, which shows a certain region of the brain becoming more active during religious activity, received widespread attention in
North America (Connor 1997; Hotz 1997). As described in the previous
chapter, Ginanjar argued that the center of spirituality in most humans, the
God spot, is "shackled" (*terbelenggu*) by preconceptions and prejudices that
lead people to behave immorally, ignore work duties, and engage in corruption. Further, spirituality was represented as universal because specific
religious traditions were merely surface manifestations of the same underlying global spirituality. An important goal of the training was to eliminate
obstacles to unshackle the natural propensity for spirituality, believed to be
an innate characteristic of every human being, to guide daily practice.

The English term spirituality conveyed further authority to Ginanjar's
project. When I asked him why he used an English term as opposed to an
Indonesian or Arabic term like *rohani* as the central object of the training program, he responded that it lent universal authority to his project
of spiritual reform. He said, "If I use Indonesian [in the training] they will
think that it is about religion. But if I talk in English, they will think that
it is universal. That it is science, not religion."

The formation and mobilization of spirituality was designed to have profound effects. The training equated the asceticism of spiritual practice with
a disciplined work ethic. Thus, opening one's God spot enabled the emergence
of the inherent human work ethic to emerge. During the training Rinaldi
invoked a locally specific cultural example, the Sultan of Yogyakarta's palace
servants (*abdi dalam*), whom he claimed worked not for money but rather
for the pride of working for the divine sultan (Woodward 1989). This ascetic ethic served as verification that these servants had opened their God
spots.

Later Rinaldi told me the contemporary crisis in Indonesia was a result
of the fact that most citizens in Indonesia "don't know why they work,"
in contrast to the palace servants who based their worldly action on ascetic
values. Thus, they needed to be reminded that "they work for God." He
said that working for God meant "unshackling the God spot." I asked him
what this meant and he continued, "Every human being is already honest,

the particular" (Rabinow 1999, 11). The fact that spirituality can be flexibly located both in the individual and in a social group is part of what makes it powerful.

just, and accountable. But they don't always act this way. Why? Because their God spot is blocked! It is blocked because of all the negative influences in the world. What they need is to return to spiritual values. ESQ opens up the God spot and allows the goodness that is already inside people to come out." He contended that knowledge of right and wrong is already intrinsic to human beings: "Conscience exists in humans. No one has to teach them to not do corruption, because people already know that it is wrong.... These things are not taught by men but given by God." Participants are thus instructed that through unshackling their spiritual center, the God spot, they can renounce degenerate pasts and become better workers, kin, and Muslims.

The formation of a spiritual economy entailed constituting spirituality as a means and site of both self-discipline and government "at a distance" (Miller and Rose 1992). Cultivating spirituality within subjects of spiritual reform was intended to make participants more amenable to managerial norms, but it was also intended to make participants more effective at self-management by transforming their work performance into a matter of religious piety. Thus, the development of faith through inculcating spirituality was designed to achieve a more effective mode of self-governing. Living a virtuous religious life was likened to being a virtuous laborer and vice versa. A spiritual economy involves the creation of spirituality as an object, represented in this case as the God spot, which is understood to be located within the body and represents the truth of the subject (Dumit 2004). Spirituality is activated and acted on to elicit specific dispositions in those who participate in spiritual reform. These dispositions include the next component of a spiritual economy: cultivating an ethics of individual accountability through what was called "built-in control."

Developing Built-In Control

The third component of a spiritual economy entails inculcating ethics of individual accountability that are commensurable with transparency and efficiency. ESQ was intended not just to develop a work ethic grounded in Islamic practice but also as a tool to eliminate rampant corruption at Krakatau Steel. Proponents believed that the initiative would transform what one employee described as a "culture of corruption" at the company.

As described earlier, since its inception Krakatau Steel was widely conceived of as a vehicle for social development in addition to economic growth. Political leaders sought to elevate living standards for educated Indonesians by creating middle-class livelihoods through well-paid salaried jobs. However, this system did not promote either individual accountability or entrepreneurial behavior. Anthropologists working in China report an analogous tension between the collectivism of the Cultural Revolution and the individualizing techniques implemented during economic reforms in post-Mao China (Kohrman 2005; Rofel 1999; Yan 2009). In Indonesia, this tension was exacerbated by the fact that social development created opportunities for the personal enrichment of managers that later became defined as corruption.

Corruption has long been a concern in Southeast Asia (Jackson and Pye 1978; Sutherland 1979), but although countries such as Singapore have taken dramatic steps to increase transparency in their governments, in Indonesia corruption is viewed as a persistent problem by both Indonesians and transnational organizations. Many Indonesians are suspicious of elites and widely assume they use their positions to their personal advantage, whether evidence for this exists or not (Butt 2005; Schrauwers 2003). Further, the discourse on corruption, circulated by transnational institutions has had far-reaching effects on how Indonesians see themselves and their place in the world. Transparency International routinely ranks the country at the bottom of its global Corruption Perception Index survey. Multilateral institutions such as the World Bank have stated that "Indonesia remains the most corrupt country in East Asia" (World Bank 2003). These surveys, reports, and press releases are widely reported in the Indonesian press and are frequently the subject of public discussion and outrage. Overlooked in these negative appraisals is the fact that activities classified as corrupt may in fact draw on patron-client relations that do not conform to a logic of transparency and rational choice (Scott and Kerkvliet 1977; Lomnitz-Adler 1992, 253). In such arrangements rights and responsibilities are not premised on the actions of liberal subjects, the autonomous and rationally maximizing individuals who are a specific effect of Western European history (Mehta 1999; Povinelli 2002).

State-owned companies have been long regarded as sites of some of the most egregious corruption. This was an effect of the fact that faith in development entailed reliable, consistent infusions of cash from the central government under import substitution industrialization policies (Heryanto

1988; Hill 2000). Suharto's Golkar party had used state-owned enterprises to distribute patronage during the New Order. Systems of audit and accounting existed in the administrative structure but were scantly enforced. For example, Kadiono, an employee of Krakatau Steel's internal audit department, told me that members of his department had trouble confronting those suspected of corruption, particularly in cases where the accused was a long-time acquaintance of those employees charged with enforcing the audits.

Krakatau Steel employees and outside observers (such as journalists, academics, and NGO activists) thought the company was rife with rampant corruption. Systematic collection of information on corruption obviously presents methodological challenges, but anecdotal evidence was overwhelming. Employees routinely regaled me with stories about people at all levels of the company hierarchy who were complicit with, if not direct participants in, activities that were branded corrupt (*korupsi*). At lower levels these were small scale. For example, employees reported that company security guards routinely accepted bribes from thieves removing stolen materials from factory grounds. In response the company mandated that every vehicle leaving the plant was subject to an inspection of the trunk to ensure that no one left the grounds with valuable materials. This policy was the source of recurrent consternation among plant employees who lamented the long traffic backups that often occurred at the exit to the factory zone, particularly during shift changes. One common practice among factory workers was referred to as "time corruption" (*korupsi waktu*). This involved an employee leaving work early but giving his or her company-issued identity badge to a colleague so that the offender would be clocked out at the apportioned time, thus receiving the wages to which they were entitled and evading disciplinary action. This problem was serious enough that the company's labor union had posted brusque notices on bulletin boards in a number of different buildings that cited a passage from the collective bargaining agreement. The announcement read, "To all Krakatau Steel employees. With the implementation of the 2004–2006 collective bargaining agreement you are hereby informed not too leave your badge with anyone because it will have FATAL results for employees."[10]

---

10. "Kepada seluruh karyawan PT Krakatau Steel. Dengan telah berlakuanya KKB periode 2004–06 di mohon kesadaranya untuk tidak menitipkan badge kepada siapapun karena akan berakibat FATAL bagi karyawan."

At higher levels of the corporate hierarchy were more serious incidents of collusion in the procurement and marketing divisions. They involved arrangements in which kickbacks were paid on various company purchases. Employees at the level of division head or manager had the authority to approve purchase orders that were negotiated with outside parties. It was common practice to take a kickback, or what was referred to as "commission" (*komisi*) on these agreements. The orders involved commodities the company regularly purchased, including oil, computers for an office, or spare parts for the giant machines that melt and form raw steel. Hadi, an operator in the hot strip mill, elucidated some examples of collusion and corruption in his plant, telling me that "sometimes we received goods from suppliers. They were supposed to send first-class products (*spek kelas satu*), but what was received was fourth class. The first-class materials will last for several months, but the fourth class maybe only two weeks.... A piece of equipment that only cost 140,000 rupiah[11] would be sold to the company for 14 million!"[12] He said that oil pipes for many of the hydraulic systems in the hot strip mill had leaks, but no one ever bothered to fix them because certain managers were receiving kickbacks on purchase orders for the oil. These managers had agreements to procure oil from specific suppliers at a premium over market value. The suppliers would then return a portion of the premium to the manager who had signed off on the purchase order. Hadi contended that costs for wasted oil "could be as high as 1 billion rupiah per month"[13] at the hot strip mill.

The reliable infusions of development funds that characterized faith in development meant that seepages from company accounts could be willfully dismissed. However, given the end of government guarantees and increasing international competition due to the deregulation of the formerly nationalized steel market, such drains were increasingly subject to transnational norms of audit and accounting. After the end of the Suharto regime, the central government exerted increasing pressure on state-owned enterprises to operate at a profit. They were no longer justified on their strategic value, as they had been in the past. Furthermore, the impetus to privatization meant that Krakatau Steel increasingly had to look to outside

---

11. Equivalent to roughly $15.
12. Equivalent to roughly $1500.
13. Equivalent to roughly $100,000.

investors, and these foreign creditors demanded market-oriented norms of accounting, audit, and fiscal control.

Proponents of spiritual reform sought to inculcate an ethic of self-management, which they termed "built-in control," to eliminate corruption and facilitate privatization by making the company more attractive to outside investment. Djohan, a senior manager at Krakatau Steel who had attended graduate school in the United States, connected the practices of spiritual reform to new economic norms. He gave a personal account of his spiritual awakening and its effect on his attitude toward his job. In somewhat stiff English he poignantly confided:

> ESQ helped me communicate with God.... You can manage your heart through the methods of ESQ.... When someone asks for a bribe,[14] if they have already managed their heart well, their heart will urge them, "Please don't do that!"... That is built-in control. If you can manage your heart well, you can develop your built-in control [then] the employees don't do corruption. Not because they are afraid of their superiors, not because they are afraid of their leaders, not because they are afraid of regulations that will have them sent to jail. But I am afraid. Why? Because I have already seen how someone who does corruption is tortured in hell!

Djohan illustrates a spiritual economy by asserting that enhanced Islamic piety is a method of inculcating an ethic of personal responsibility (Rose 1999). He evoked the climactic moment at the end of the second day of the training, when a corpse is called to account amid the fires of hell, in explaining how he came to the conclusion that corruption was contrary to Allah's design. Cultivating an ethics of personal responsibility comes out of remembrance of one's individual relationship with God (Luhrmann 2004).

This focus on individual accountability and self-management through Islam has further significance. In 1981 a key Indonesian Special Forces (Kopassus) military base housing three battalions was relocated to a site adjacent to the west Serang toll road entrance, a fifteen-minute drive from the main gates of Krakatau Steel. As the region was becoming a strategic site of industrial production, the state located a prominent military installation

---

14. Djohan actually used the acronym "KKN" (see chapter 1), which is commonly used to refer to a bribe and this is how I have translated it here.

a short drive away to ensure the preservation of order. During the Suharto era the state's monopoly on coercive violence and occasional willingness to use it produced a brutally effective check on collective political action by workers. Furthermore, James Siegel has shown how fear and state violence shrouded in secrecy were a central means through which the New Order state was able to hold on to power in Indonesia for thirty-two years (Siegel 1998, 2006). The end of the Suharto regime and increasing international pressure on the Indonesian military to conform to human rights regimes meant that the state could no longer act with impunity. Given the reduced repressive capacity of the Indonesian state and the precarious position of Krakatau Steel, which had to compete in an increasingly globalized steel market, managers such as Djohan saw self-management and individual accountability as values that were indispensable to the survival of the company.

Developing faith was designed as a remedy to the problem of chronic corruption. ESQ training was premised on both the renunciation of the ethics of materialism to which corruption was attributed and atonement for these past sins. Extreme reactions to the training were interpreted as proof that those so afflicted had committed particularly egregious acts of corruption in the past. By inculcating an ethic of individual accountability based in Islam, managers sought to eradicate such improprieties at the factory.

Conclusion: A New Mode of Government

Spiritual economies elucidate how religion and neoliberalism are combined to enlist subjects in governing themselves. In making spirituality a site of intervention and action, subjects are inculcated with norms conducive to what the architects of this spiritual economy referred to as "built-in control." By interpreting work as a form of worship, everyday work is reconfigured as a means of achieving otherworldly salvation. Religious practices are reconfigured according to norms of maximum economy insofar as principles such as transparency, productivity, and rationalization are represented as ethics intrinsic to Islam. Spiritual economies further illuminate how audits enable the assemblage of religion and neoliberalism. These constant, detailed reflections on individual practice to ensure compliance with abstract norms are common to neoliberal practice and the practice of Islam configured in ESQ training.

The combination of Islamic ethics and business management and life-coaching practices entailed a new mode governing selves, families, and the nation at large. Thus, proponents of ESQ saw the program in opposition to recent calls for the implementation of *syariah* law in Indonesia. They viewed such calls as demanding more rules whereas ESQ offered the possibility of eliminating ills such as corruption through more effective self-government. Further, by finding precedent for business management knowledge in Qur'anic injunctions and events in the history of Islam, spiritual reformers designed a mode of Islamic practice conducive to commercial success. The extension of built-in control is both particular and general because it entails individual ethical reflection that can be replicated throughout the population at large.

In contemporary Indonesia the economy is increasingly defined in transnational, rather than domestic, terms given that state-owned companies can no longer depend on protective tariffs and government subsidies. The intensification of Islamic practice is represented as a means to address these challenges as it offers the possibility of increasing the productivity and competitiveness of Indonesian workers. By 2009 the massive job loss that many feared had not yet transpired. However, Indonesian government officials and Krakatau Steel managers still see privatization as the key to future viability. In September 2008 the national parliament finally consented to the sale of a 30 percent stake in Krakatau Steel through an initial public offering (Suharmoko 2008). Whether privatization will require corporate restructuring and job losses, as many at the company feared, remains to be seen.

The success of ESQ in Indonesia stemmed from the fact that it could be simultaneously universal and particular. Those who took part in the program became self-confident in their own individual religious values and practices. In addition, they could be made receptive to the argument that Islam was a manifestation of underlying universal values. This flexibility is part of what makes ESQ neoliberal (Harvey 1989; Ong 1999). At the same time that Ary Ginanjar promoted ESQ as grounded in the five pillars of Islam and the six pillars of *iman,* he also asserted that it was universal because it was grounded in scientific knowledge. He envisioned spiritual reform as a remedy to Indonesia's crisis of development but also worked actively to introduce it to non-Muslims both within the country and overseas. He drew inspiration for the training from Islam but argued that Islam was an outward manifestation of an underlying universal spirituality. Ary Ginanjar and other proponents of ESQ stressed either the program's universality or its particularity with different audiences at different times. This flexibility was in part responsible for the program's popularity and spectacular growth.

The creation of this spiritual economy in Indonesia was neither a wholesale translation of Weber's spirit of capitalism, nor was it a strict interpretation of Islamic texts and practices. Spiritual reformers connected Indonesia's economic development to its spiritual development, because they saw the cultivation of Islamic practice as conducive to the introduction of economic rationality into a domain previously organized according to a social logic. From their perspective this involved the cultivation of ethics that were already intrinsic to Islam. Indonesia's earlier New Order push to modernization through supporting primary industries such as steel production was characterized by an unyielding faith in development. Post-Suharto efforts to enlist the nation's workers in a spiritual economy show how faith itself was being recast as development.

4

Governing through Affect

After an exhausting session in which ESQ participants were exposed to the climactic scene of the hit Hollywood blockbuster *Titanic,* Rinaldi Agusyana dramatically brought to a close the second day of an ESQ training session. He exclaimed:

> Let the tears spill as a sign of your longing for Allah, of your repentance to Allah. Ya Allah, ya Allah, chill the fire of your hell with these tears, ya Allah! Forgive all our mistakes, ya Allah! Have mercy, ya Allah! Wipe it clean, ya Allah! Wipe everything clean, ya Allah! You promised that you would wipe clean every sin, you would forgive every sin, and this day, ya Allah, we swear that we will wash away every one of our past sins, ya Allah!

The hall was still shrouded in darkness and illuminated only by an ESQ logo in the shape of an atom with five electrons glowing ominously from three huge projection screens. Before leaving the room and heading off to perform the dusk prayer, employees embraced the coworkers sitting closest to them. Many still had wet tears grimly staining their cheeks and quickly drying in the parched air of the room's cooling system. They exchanged embraces with forlorn expressions after experiencing a deeply moving collective prayer and multimedia presentation that had lasted for over two hours and purported to represent the experience of death. It was the culmination of an eleven-hour day of training that seemed to fatigue even the most enthusiastic employees. Among the most notable aspects of the scene was the way in which the room had been tailored to elicit intense affective displays, visible in collective embraces, damp eyes, and plaintive wails of penitence.

Such displays during ESQ training sessions at Krakatau Steel illuminate how proponents of spiritual reform sought to govern through affect. Affect served as a medium through which the subjects of the new spiritual economy were realized. My attention to this formation stems from the realization that the potent deployment of affect during ESQ training distinguished it from other employee training programs at Krakatau Steel, such as the Seven Habits of Highly Effective People. Whereas both ESQ and the Seven Habits sought to increase the productivity and effectiveness of company employees, the latter program was executed in a dry, sober timbre. ESQ, in contrast, was punctuated with intensely affective displays, which were instrumental to achieving an enhanced sense of Islamic devotion and, ultimately, the personal transformations sought by proponents and participants.

Affect and Spiritual Reform

Governing through affect involved three components. First, what spiritual trainers referred to as "opening the heart" involved making participants receptive to the message of ESQ through recourse to Islamic tradition. Second, what I refer to as "the circulation of tears" refers to deep collective weeping that both represented and physically enacted becoming a new type of person. The final stage is "management of the heart," the ultimate goal of spiritual training, represented as a form of self-management in which one exercised "built-in control" and acted in ways that were deemed simultaneously conducive to global corporate competitiveness and individual otherworldly salvation. Thus, the personal change sought through the mobilization of affect during ESQ was designed to harmonize self-interest with collective interest, analogous to the early modern projects to transform passions into interests and described by Albert Hirschman (1977). The affective dimensions of ESQ were designed in part as a panacea to the effects of the crisis of faith in Indonesian development.

The dramatic affective enactments were characteristic of projects of spiritual reform that inculcated ethical dispositions common to both Muslim and neoliberal practice. While most work on neoliberalism depicts it as creating detached subjects, I argue that the mobilization of affects was critical to facilitating neoliberal reform in Indonesia. Building on the work of Nikolas Rose, I term this mobilization governing through affect. Rose has demonstrated how what he calls "advanced liberalism" is premised on "governing through freedom," which entails managing populations not through constraining human conduct but through incitement to action (Rose 1999, 84). Thus, people are not compelled to behave in certain ways but rather do as they please with the caveat that they are accountable for the consequences of their actions. The concept of governing through affect builds on Rose's notion of governing through freedom in that I focus on the medium through which a new subject of government could be realized. However, a focus on affect contains some differences from a focus on freedom. An important distinction is that governing through freedom is premised on an ethics of individual autonomy, whereas governing through affect involves the creation of an ethics of shared sentiment. This ethics of shared sentiment was critical to creating a spiritual economy. Furthermore, governing through freedom involves subjecting freedom to rationalization and calculation. Affect, however, can be subjected to rationalization and calculation but also constantly threatens to exceed them.

Harmonizing Interests: Regimes of Affect

My attention to the relationship between affect and economic change draws on the insights of the political economist Albert Hirschman. Hirschman demonstrates how affect became an object of reflection at the dawn of European modernity (Hirschman 1977). A recurrent problem for sixteenth- and seventeenth-century theorists of statecraft was that the passions of the sovereign threatened order and stability. These theorists sought a new order that would harness passions toward some productive end and align the self-interest of those who govern with the collective interests of the governed. Those involved in spiritual reform in contemporary Indonesia undertook a project that resembled converting passions into interests in similar conditions of political tumult. They sought to "open hearts" through various affective enactments and ultimately achieve what they termed "management of the heart."[1]

Hirschman's account of the conversion of passion into interest, which he argues enabled the formation of both capitalism and the modern state, contains striking parallels with the Foucaultian approach to the emergence of governmentality deployed in the previous chapter. Hirschman's account of the relationship between affect and capitalist transformation offers insight into the emergence of modern forms of government of the self. Hirschman details efforts by the eighteenth-century physiocrats who "wanted to motivate [the sovereign] to act correctly … of his own free will. In other words, they were looking for a political order in which the power holders are impelled, *for reasons of self-interest,* to promote the general interest" (Hirschman 1977, 97). Similarly, Foucault writes that a constitutive feature of governmentality is the emergence of the principle that "a sovereign who wishes to govern the state well must first learn how to govern himself, his goods and his patrimony, after which he will be successful in governing the state" (Foucault 1991, 90). Thus, for both Hirschman and Foucault a characteristic feature of modernity is that the sovereign no longer exists in a relation of externality to the state or society. In Hirschman's account, the rationalization of government is characterized by a search for "more effective ways of shaping the pattern of human actions" (Hirschman 1977, 15). In Foucault's it is represented by the liberal maxim of "frugal government" where the most effective government is that which governs least (Foucault 2008, 28–29). Modern states are characterized by the harmonization of the interests of those who govern with the interests of the governed. Thus, government of the self and government of the collectivity become part of a single order. The problem of aligning self-government

---

1. As Andrea Muehlebach has shown, Adam Smith's corpus demonstrates that a concern with affect was constitutive of liberalism from its inception (Muehlebach 2007). Muehlebach shows how Smith's reflections on "moral sentiments" (Smith 2002) were intimately connected with his prescriptions for market freedom (Smith 1976).

with government of the collectivity was what was at stake in ESQ training. Spiritual reformers sought to inculcate what they termed "built-in control" through management of the heart. Affect played a critical role in achieving self-management and collective government.

Configuring Selves: From Emotion to Affect

When I participated in and observed ESQ training I was astonished at how participants were so effectively moved to collective weeping and other affective enactments. These displays were critical to the project of developing faith to redress the crisis of faith in development and to confront the challenges of globalization. However, existing anthropological approaches to emotion did not quite illuminate the contours of the phenomenon that I sought to comprehend. Thus, in focusing on affect, I build on previous anthropological work on emotion, but I find affect a more powerful concept to understand these phenomena.[2]

Whereas most previous anthropological treatments of affect have been pursued through the concept of emotion, affect offers more analytically productive insights (Boellstorff and Lindquist 2004; Lutz and Abu-Lughod 1990; Lutz and White 1986; Rosaldo 1980).[3] Affect refers to relations practiced *between* individuals rather than experiences borne by sole individuals. The transitive qualities of affect are apparent in words derived from the same root such as affection, a "favourable or kindly disposition towards a person or thing; fondness, tenderness; goodwill, warmth of attachment" (*Oxford English Dictionary* 2008). It is this transitive quality that simultaneously creates its progenitor as well as its recipient that is analytically valuable. The verb form of emotion, *to emote,* is an intransitive verb and thus does not necessarily take (and make) an object. Unlike the noun *emotion,*

---

2. This section builds on arguments initially developed in Richard and Rudnyckyj 2009.

3. The anthropology of emotion sought to seize analytical terrain from the discipline of psychology by demonstrating that emotions are inherently social (Abu-Lughod and Lutz 1990, 2). In contrast to psychological approaches, anthropologists showed how emotions are historically constructed and locally meaningful (Hollan and Throop 2008). This work tends to use the term *emotion* interchangeably with the term *affect*. This tendency has persisted. In an introduction to an edited collection of articles on emotion in Southeast Asia, affect and emotion are deployed synonymously (Boellstorff and Lindquist 2004, 439).

affect is both a noun and a transitive verb. Thus, grammatically it necessarily takes an object, pointing to its inherently reflexive capacity.

Building on the approach in the previous chapter, affect is useful because it contains the transitive qualities of what Foucault referred to as "conduct" (Foucault 1983, 220–221). The transitive verb form of *affect* is defined as "to have an effect on" (*Oxford English Dictionary* 2008). Affect as a form of conduct can be a means through which people conduct themselves or conduct others by making certain avenues of action possible and foreclosing other potential courses. As will become apparent in the subsequent chapter, however, affects and the forms of conduct elicited through affect are never completely determined and may also give rise to unintended consequences (Sedgwick 2003).

Furthermore, affect is a powerful form of communicative action that is visible both within and outside language. During fieldwork I found that affective enactments were communicated not only through emotional discourse but also in embodied practices. For example, I was told that certain forms of religious speech were thought to be more effective if they were articulated through tears. Practices such as crying and embracing were critical means through which subjects worked on themselves and others, formed new collectivities, and adopted new configurations of personhood.

Previous anthropological studies of emotion have focused heavily on language as the primary means through which to understand emotion as an object within cultures (Lutz and Abu-Lughod 1990). This attention to the critical role of language in studies of affect has yielded important results. However, it is important to note both discourses about affect as well as what might be termed extra discursive affect. Although affective discourse was central to governing through affect, affect is not limited only to language. Affect is also visible (and perhaps most effective) when mobilized in embodied practices. The materiality of affect is evident in the multiple sensory experiences with which it is associated, such as sight, sound, touch, and feel (Sedgwick 2003). Eve Sedgwick suggests that while affect is expressed in language, it is sometimes even more powerfully expressed outside language. In governing through affect communicative acts exercised through the body play a central role. Mutual embraces and the circulation of bodily fluids, such as tears, are critical to the production of personhood and relations between subjects (Strathern 1988). This is to suggest that practices such as contact between bodies, the release of bodily fluids, and paralinguistic enunciations, such as wails and sobs or cheers and squeals of delight, are powerful techniques through which subjects and relations between subjects are enacted, acted on, and manipulated.

Governing through Affect

During ESQ training sessions intense displays of affect (such as shame, grief, joy, compassion, and fear) were notable because, according to prevailing anthropological accounts, such overt displays are rare in Southeast Asia. The mobilization of affect during spiritual training sessions did not fit either of the two dominant themes in anthropological attention to emotion in Southeast Asia. On the one hand, anthropologists have focused on the way in which great emphasis is placed on concealing emotions and, on the other, on periodic instances in which individuals and groups violate this normal state of affairs and run amok. Conventional anthropological representations of "inner" Indonesians (inhabitants of the islands of Java and Bali) hold that tremendous personal pride is placed on the exercise of *halus* (refined) behavior. Thus, visible displays of affect are often constrained in Indonesia (Geertz 1961, 110–118). More recently anthropologists have argued that a personal ethics of restraint often masks inward states of discord and turbulence for many Indonesians (Lindquist 2004; Wikan 1990). The converse of the norm of emotional restraint is amok—the infrequent but highly visible instances in which individuals or groups violate the normal focus on concealing emotion and launch into mad frenzy (Kresman, Hadin, and Sumarni 1989; Siegel 2001; Winzeler 1990). Whereas Kathleen Stewart has drawn anthropological attention to ordinary affects, what drew me to the affective displays in spiritual reform was their *extraordinary* character (Stewart 2008).

Management of the heart did not refer to concealing affects but instead to more effectively administering them for the goal of spiritual reform. This involved enacting affects in public settings at specific times. These affective displays were not the ecstatic states of amok but rather involved employees of huge industrial operations enmeshed in distinctly modern techniques of proselytization that included digitally reproduced images and sound. At the same time that participants were enlisted in the management of their own affects, they themselves were entangled in a new regime of governing through affect; affective modulation was a step toward eliciting different configurations of personhood. Extensive planning to elicit desired affective states had clearly gone in to the development of these programs. This planning involved careful manipulation of sound, light, temperature, and other sensations in order that participants would achieve the desired spiritual and emotional states. Participants quickly learned (or already knew) the appropriate responses to the affective cues that were deployed. Furthermore, the emphasis was not so much on concealing affect as on mobilizing its transformative capacities. The circulation of tears and mutual embraces took place in collective, public sessions in which these affects would be visible to coworkers, friends, and other colleagues. As part of an emerging spiritual economy, affect was conducive to political and economic change. My focus is on the mobilization, modulation, and manipulation of affect to elicit a new subject—the worshipping worker described in the previous chapter. Thus, governing through affect refers both to the government of selves through affect and the ways in which selves seek to govern their own affect.

Opening Hardened Hearts

Spiritual reform took the heart as the central object of individual transformation. The initial step in achieving personal transformation entailed what was referred to as "opening the heart" (*membuka hati*). Both proponents of and participants in ESQ considered opening the heart a primary goal of the training. By this they meant enhancing one's Islamic practice to enhance one's moral virtue and become more disciplined in everyday activities, including work. Many of those who professed spiritual transformations averred that they knew that their heart had been opened because they were able to cry during religious practices such as prayer (*sholat*) only after they had attended ESQ sessions. An indication of the transformation of one's heart was expressing grief through crying.

This metaphor of opening the heart circulates in a wider Indonesian discursive frame in which, like English, the heart is viewed as an individual's emotional center. However, translated literally the heart refers to a different organ. As Boellstorff and Lindquist note "the key Indonesian term *hati,* which means both 'liver' and 'seat of the emotions' is thus sometimes rendered as 'heart'" (Boellstorff and Lindquist 2004, 438). The word for a physical heart is *jantung*. Some adherents of ESQ, such as Arief, a veteran employee of the hot strip mill, connected the two signifiers by explaining that one's physical heart (*jantung*) "beating more quickly is a sign of the transformation" of one's emotional center (*hati*).

Before a participant in ESQ could be immersed in the circulation of tears and achieve management of the heart, the heart had to be opened. The association between opening one's heart and crying was repeated throughout spiritual training. This process was illustrated though a dramatic rendition of the story of Umar bin Khattab in the morning of the second day of ESQ training. Umar, the second caliph, had initially refused Muhammad's revelations but ultimately became one of his staunchest devotees. Participants were reminded that crying during religious worship followed in the footsteps of Umar.

Umar's heart was described as the site in which he experienced personal transformation. Initially he was a fierce warrior with a "hard heart" (*hati keras*) who had denigrated Muhammad's teachings during the period when Muslims were being persecuted in Mecca. However, after hearing the recitation of Qur'anic verses, Umar was moved to tears and converted to Islam. Rinaldi invoked Umar as an example of one who was physically powerful and "arrogant" (*sombong*) because of his worldly prowess but upon hearing the "beauty of the Qur'an" his heart was opened. Rinaldi further related the story of Umar's conversion:

> He allowed the light to enter and what a light it was that entered!...So his heart became pure; it purified his feelings.... That is what is called the forty Hertz oscillation. That is what is known as divine guidance [*hidayat*]. That is what happens when someone says, "This is what I am seeking! This is what I am seeking! This is what I am seeking!" At that moment Umar was not able [*mampu*] to hold back the tears. These are the signs [*ciri-ciri*] that Allah gives to those who attain divine guidance.

Umar's tears, visible signs that he was affected and his heart had been opened, were an oft-cited model for ESQ participants. They were invited to follow Umar not so much in the sense of converting to Islam but rather in returning to Islam, enhancing individual spiritual practice, and transforming themselves. This was metaphorically represented when his previously closed heart was unblocked, allowing it to be filled with the "light" of divine instruction. Participants were enjoined to make themselves more than mere "ritual" subjects of Islam. Becoming immersed in the circulation of tears, an embodied state and a material symbol of personal transformation, was how subjects of spiritual reform convinced themselves and demonstrated to others that their hearts were opened.

The Circulation of Tears

Effusive weeping was the embodied practice through which the metaphorical project of opening the heart was achieved. I refer to these tearful expressions of grief as the circulation of tears. At key moments of spiritual training and in other public practices of Islam in contemporary Indonesia, participants engage in *qolbun salim,* which James Fox has described as "ritual weeping for one's sins in a concentrated effort to achieve purity of heart" (Fox 2004). This weeping, often elicited by a particularly moving collective prayer or lecture on a religious topic, is central to the project of spiritual reform. Tears are a material representation of the transformation of the heart that is the object of spiritual reform. At key moments of the training tears rolled down the cheeks of those affected and were often accompanied by mournful wails. The act of crying circulated through the audience during ESQ training sessions. What began as a small number of people weeping during particularly evocative lectures, collective prayers, or moving videos, effectively elicited tears from others in an escalating crescendo. The weeping typically began with one or two isolated individuals but steadily spread to others. By the end of some sessions it felt as if almost everyone in the room was in tears.

Indeed, the circulation of tears had the greatest impact on past participants in the program. For example, whenever I brought up ESQ with Kusmanto, the technical expert mentioned in chapter 3, he focused on the fact that many participants wept during the training program. This had made an overwhelming impression on him. He had never seen coworkers cry and he had never himself wept during religious worship. He took the manner in which he and many other ESQ participants were dramatically affected as a testament of the profound transformation that the program was capable of eliciting. His astonishment may be attributable to the fact that, although he had lived in Banten for over twenty years, he was born in the central Javanese court center of Solo whose inhabitants are reputed to be some of the most refined (*halus*) in the archipelago. The ability to effectively mask one's emotional states is considered to be an outward manifestation of this refinement. It was only during his participation in ESQ that he found himself acting contrary to these dispositions.

Kusmanto first attended ESQ in 2002 and expressed amazement to me that his attendance marked the first time he was able to cry during religious activity. He took a Qur'anic verse as textual justification for feeling moved in one's heart when the verses of the holy book are recited. This verse reads, "Those only are believers who, when God is mentioned, their hearts quake, and when His signs are recited to them, it increases them in faith, and in their Lord they put their trust" (Qur'an 8, 2). This Qur'anic precedent enabled him to account for the fact that he unexpectedly broke into tears during his participation in ESQ. He said that this was a sign of "divine revelation [*wahyu*] from Allah. If we hear Allah's name [*asma Allah*] and we then tremble [*gemetar*], it means that our hearts have been touched [*hati tersentuh*]."

Other past participants in ESQ emphasized that spiritual training made them able to cry during Islamic ritual activity, often for the first time. To them this was an indication of the power of the program to develop the faith of nominal Muslims by turning them into pious practitioners. For example, often after I informed new acquaintances that I had participated in ESQ I was asked, "Did you cry?" or "Were you able to cry?" to ascertain how profound my participation had been. The fact that I had not wept during the training was met with a smirk and a knowing nod. The questioner would then respond that this was because my heart was "not yet opened."

This ability to move one to tears was frequently recounted when ESQ adherents explained how the program had become popular among elite members of the armed forces. During a retreat for high-level officials of the Indonesian military, a general named Syamsul was crying openly during a collective prayer session. Lieutenant General Syariefuddin, the head of SESKOAD (the army's officer candidate training school) noticed him shedding tears and afterward asked him how "he could be so devout [*khusyuk*] in his prayers." Syamsul affirmed that his experience at ESQ had made him able to cry during religious worship for the first time. Shortly thereafter Syariefuddin decided to enroll in the program himself and attended one of the four-day-long executive sessions in Jakarta. He was likewise moved to tears and attributed this experience to his newfound devotion to religious practice. He decided that it would also be beneficial for officers undergoing training at SESKOAD and brought ESQ to Bandung for officers in the Indonesian military training there.

Hydraulic Subjectification: The Message of the Medium

Water was a commonly repeated theme in lectures delivered by Ary Ginanjar or Rinaldi and a key material symbol of the subjective transformation that ESQ training was designed to achieve. Water was both a material medium circulated by the body and a metaphor through which a subjective transformation could be represented and understood. Experiences of a failure to change were metaphorically represented as dryness and as an inability to cry during religious practice. These metaphors were not strictly connected to ESQ but connected more broadly with how Indonesians explained the subjective transformation associated with enhanced religious practice. Suparman, a mechanic in the hot strip mill, invoked hydraulic metaphors to illustrate his own religious transformation that had occurred ten years prior to our conversation. He said that he had been inattentive to religious practice, would rarely attend his local mosque, and almost never prayed. He referred to this condition as "dryness overtaking the heart" (*kekeringan dalam hati*). He said that this dryness abated after he became more devout in his religious observance, which took place shortly after the birth of his first child.

These metaphors of dryness were common in explaining the effects of ESQ training. Sukromo, a senior manager in human resources, contrasted faith in development with efforts to develop faith. He said:

> Before the culture of the company was from outside [*budaya dalam perusahaan langsung dari luar*]. It was secular [*sekular*] because we adopted a notion of industry from Germany and the United States. This involved a separation of work from the rest of an employee's life activities. All the aspects of planning, operations, and control were done without the local culture, the

religious culture [*tanpa kultur lokal, budaya relijius*]. This resulted in dryness from the religious side [*sisi relijius kering*].

Here dryness metaphorically refers to the influence of the West, which is characterized by a strict separation of work and religious activity. This division, which he attributed to secularism, is depicted as something that was ultimately not commensurable with local culture and results in religious dryness. This dryness is redressed through the collective public circulation of tears that takes place during spiritual training. Tears serve as a material sign of a state that is otherwise only expressed metaphorically: having one's heart opened.

Represented as an effect of Western modernization, the remedy to religious dryness was the ritual weeping that ESQ enabled. Early on the first day of each training, Rinaldi alluded to the possibility that participants might be transformed through weeping. In metaphorically evocative terms he likened members of the audience to Umar bin Khattab, pronouncing "God willing at the end of these three days, we too will find the water inside of us." Shortly thereafter a custom-made animated video, played on the three large projection screens at the front of the hall, showed blocks of ice melt away to reveal a pulsating heart. Rinaldi alluded to the transformative potential of the circulation of tears, remarking that "hopefully we will be able to melt the ice and make water." He continued with numerous metaphorical references to water in various forms during a long communal prayer:

> Let these hearts bathe [*siram*], these hearts that are so hard, our hearts that are seldom bathed in Allah's verses. Our hearts have already become frozen [*beku*]. That is how hard our hearts are! Every piece of advice whatsoever we are given does not stick with us! Depicted here is their entombment in this ice [He gestured toward the animated image of the pulsating heart encased in dark ice projected onto the screens]. We see a deep freeze, how little light shines on it, hard like this ice, but with the permission of Allah, even this hard heart can be opened. Wherever there is a heart that is hard, there are actually the values of softness and wisdom that are symbolized [*dilambangkan*][4] by water, the water that gives life.

---

4. Given the reflexive methodology used in this study and described in the introduction it is germane to note that my focus on the symbolic importance of water is not something visible only

Like dryness, freezing is another metaphor related to water that is central to spiritual reform. References to freezing, ice, and bathing were also evoked in the concluding remarks to the second day of the training that are reproduced at the beginning of this chapter. Like ice melting to become water, so a hardened and closed heart could become soft and open. Rinaldi represented both tears and feelings of longing for repentance as "spilling over." Furthermore tears had the potential to extinguish the "fires of hell." This evocative phrase also shows how tears are invoked as capable of "washing away" one's past misdeeds.[5] Symbolically tears, or what are literally in Indonesian "water of the eyes" (*air mata*), represent melting ice. This ice is the symbolic material that shackles the emotional centers of those who are deficient in Islamic practice and, thus, whose hearts remain closed.

Circulating tears is a material means through which management of the heart could be achieved. Water was not only a symbol but an actual physical object that circulated on the bodies of subjects of spiritual reform. Enhancing Islamic practice, partially attained through ritual weeping, is depicted as the means to transform oneself. Further, crying was the embodied practice through which one demonstrated submission to a new regime of self-government. Spiritual reformers argued that by transforming oneself one could transform the company, and in transforming oneself and the company, one could transform the nation as a whole. Proponents of this project expected to achieve this economic transformation through a form of affective government that they termed management of the heart.

Management of the Heart

After one's heart had been opened through the circulation of tears one could manage one's heart and emerge from spiritual training as a new subject.

to the analyst but is something that those who participated in my research project also made explicit. This approach differs from leading approaches in symbolic anthropology in which it is unclear whether those under study are aware of the role of symbols (Geertz 1973b).

5. It is relevant here to note the material and symbolic importance of water in Indonesia. Historically water has been crucial to social relations and political organization in Southeast Asia (Geertz 1980, 69–86; Lansing 1991). Rinaldi alluded to the importance of water in what was until recently an agrarian society by emphasizing that water "gives life." Anthropologists have long argued that many features of social organization in inner Indonesia can be attributed to the elaborate irrigation systems that are an enduring feature of the landscape of Java and Bali (Geertz 1963a).

Management of the heart referred to achieving a form of self-government in which desire for personal gain was constrained and one's self-interests were harmonized with the broader collective interests of the company (and by extension the nation). The notion of managing the heart was not particular to ESQ but rather part of a larger formation in contemporary Indonesia in which the administration of affect was deployed to yield more effective government. Those who used this phrase to refer to practices associated with ESQ were in fact borrowing it from another of the moderate Islamic spiritual reform movements described in chapter 2, the hugely successful Islamic business Manajemen Qolbu Corporation. This prominent Islamic media and direct marketing company bears a name understood by Indonesians as Management of the Heart Corporation.

Although the term *management of the heart* did not originate with ESQ and was not used during the training, participants from Krakatau Steel would often invoke this idea in referring to the goals of the training. The two programs were understood as different means toward the same ends. While their audiences overlapped, Ary Ginanjar considered ESQ more narrowly as a human resources training, whereas Manajemen Qolbu sought to combine Islam and self-help principles to improve Indonesian national morality. The founder of Manajemen Qolbu, Aa Gym, cultivated a mass following through television, and he was a ubiquitous presence on numerous Indonesian stations in the early 2000s. In contrast, Ary Ginanjar was more limited with his television appearances, preferring to appeal to prospective followers through his training program. Indeed, for many the appeal of the executive ESQ training sessions was the fact that they offered participants an opportunity to encounter Ginanjar in the flesh.

Among ESQ participants, managing the heart was thought to enable one to become a more disciplined and responsible worker who would not engage in corruption because he or she was aware that all human action is subject to the gaze of Allah. Further, spiritual reformers argued that managing emotions facilitates better relations at work between employees of both equal and unequal rank. The heart was represented as the location from which material desires spring. By learning how to manage one's heart, the desire for material objects could be better controlled and the potential for employees to engage in corrupt activities could be reduced.

Indeed Djohan, the manager I discussed in chapter 3 who saw ESQ as a means of achieving what he termed "built-in control," illustrated the relationship between affect, management of the heart, and the emergence of what I have called a spiritual economy. Proponents of spiritual reform sought to inculcate an ethic of self-management to eliminate corruption and make the company more attractive to outside investment. As previously noted, he stated that ESQ enabled one to "manage your heart" and achieve "built-in control." His awareness of this mode of self-government emerged from the way in which he became enmeshed in the circulation of tears.

Toward the end of my fieldwork in Cilegon, Djohan spoke candidly with me about Islam, ESQ, and the problems Krakatau Steel had adjusting to new political and economic conditions in Indonesia. He had by this time warmed greatly to my presence and appeared comfortable with a foreign observer at the factory. In one conversation, he connected an experience that he had after completing the *hajj* for the first time in 2002 to a subsequent experience he had shortly thereafter when he participated in ESQ. He said, "After I did the *hajj*, I started to do *tahajud*[6] prayers.... This was the first time I cried during prayer. I had no idea why I cried. This happened again after ESQ....My heart saw that God sees us....We have to believe in two different worlds, this world and the afterlife. How do you see [the afterlife]? Not by the eyes, but by the heart." Djohan connects his immersion in the circulation of tears to achieving more effective self-management. In this instance, Djohan shows how crying is a physical sign of atonement that represents the personal transformation of a worshipping worker. Ritual weeping and an open heart enable development of built-in control. This produces a figure whose self-interest is no longer determined by a passion for individual gain but rather is harmonized with the interests of the collectivity.

I asked Djohan for an example of how he had changed following his new ability to manage his heart. He explained that, prior to his participation in ESQ, during business trips he would pocket any outstanding per diem allowance. However, after he had participated in the circulation of tears and learned how to better manage his heart, he realized that this was contrary to the central Islamic value of honesty. He declared, "It is not my money but the company's money....If everyone did it the company would

---

6. These are special prayers that are executed during the middle of the night. In the five-fold Islamic classification of human action *tahajud* prayers are not mandatory (*wajib*) but are encouraged (*sunnah*).

not exist anymore." Following his participation in ESQ he said that he was always certain to return the unused portion of his per diem allowance to the company. Given the precarious position of Krakatau Steel, which had to compete in an increasingly competitive global steel market, managers such as Djohan saw management of the heart as indispensable to corporate survival. Djohan's account of his transformation, in part achieved through the circulation of tears, represents this new regime of affect. In this sense it is reminiscent of the affective transformation from the passions to the interests that Hirschman described as facilitating the emergence of the modern economic order.

Later, in the same conversation, Djohan connected the affective dimension of built-in control to the new political realities that had reconfigured the problem of government in post–New Order Indonesia. He asked me rhetorically, "Why was Mr. Suharto so effective?" Without allowing me to respond he answered:

> Because at that time most people came from villages, so whatever Suharto said, everyone agreed with. One hundred percent agreed! And at that time the situation—political, economic—was very stable. "OK boss, I'll just support you"…but now it has changed. With ESQ, to control people it is not enough if it just comes externally, like the enforcement of regulations. It is more effective if the person has built-in control. Control to what? To do the right things! Control to have good behavior! If they can establish this control, discipline will emerge and if the people can be disciplined, the company will be ordered.

Djohan saw the Islam inculcated through ESQ training as a means of resolving the new problem of harmonizing government of the self and the collective in contemporary Indonesia. The New Order was characterized by external force, which was dependent on maintaining stability through the threat of physical violence. ESQ offered the possibility of internal control, a form of power that worked through the body, affecting it from the inside. This was designed to motivate people to act according to what corporate managers and spiritual reformers had decided matched both the individual interests of citizens and the population at large.

Not all who participated in ESQ, however, were able to achieve management of the heart. Toward the end of a training in May 2004 Sutiono, an engineer, expressed regret to me that he had not wept and thus remained outside the circulation of tears. He said that he had not been able to cry during the training, and he understood that this deficiency of affect indicated he had not achieved the personal transformation expected of participants in the program. I had come to know Sutiono well and we had often visited each other's houses after work hours. He was thoughtful, and I had come to respect his perspective on many issues regarding political and cultural aspects of life in contemporary Indonesia. He held an electrical engineering degree from one of Indonesia's elite universities and had worked at Krakatau Steel for fifteen years, rising to the position of midlevel technical expert at the company. His main project at the time was auditing the vast quantities of electricity that the company used in steel production, primarily in the electric arc furnace where steel pellets were melted to create the liquid steel that was cast into massive slabs. He was devising techniques to reduce the factory's demand for electrical power in this particularly energy intensive portion of the steelmaking process. This was a critical task, given impending reform of Indonesia's utilities, which included plans for the privatization of the state-owned electrical company PLN (Perusahaan Listrik Negara) and the likelihood that utility fees would increase. Krakatau Steel owned its own electricity generating facility that was separate from the national grid and considered more reliable because it was less prone to breakdowns and outages. Krakatau Steel managers hoped that utility deregulation would enable the company to sell surplus power in a new free market as a way of generating ancillary profits to help the company maintain viability given the increasingly competitive steel market and the pressure Krakatau Steel was facing from transnational competitors. Because their distribution was more reliable the service would be particularly valuable to the many private industries that were clustered in the sprawling industrial zone around Krakatau Steel.

Sutiono understood his inability to cry as a manifestation of the fact that his heart was "still closed, or just open slightly." He said that the goal of ESQ was to "learn the method of how to open your heart, if God wills it. If it is open I will have received divine guidance [*hidayat*] from Allah, but not all people can receive guidance.... I still have a lot of dirt inside me which I must have cleaned.... This dirt is the accumulation of sins that I have done in my life." He explained that these sins included not praying five times per day and sometimes having impure thoughts. The ability (or inability) to be affected and participate in what I have called the circulation of tears is the criteria by which one comes to know oneself as a successful (or unsuccessful) subject of spiritual reform. Circulating tears links hydraulic metaphors to embodied practices and is a potent signifier of personal change. Sutiono recognized his heart was not yet fully open, but he expressed optimism that, through learning to cry, he could eventually manage his heart and become part of the emerging spiritual economy.

Resolving Difference through Affect

Management of the heart also offered the potential to resolve long-standing conflicts between Krakatau Steel employees of different status and also to resolve cultural divisions. Overcoming distinctions based on education, status, employment position, and ethnicity was critical to the project of spiritual reform. ESQ invoked the Islamic tenet of the universal equality of all humans before Allah. Employees of Krakatau Steel often referred to the fifth pillar of Islam, the *hajj,* as evidence of human equality. Kadiono, an enthusiastic participant in ESQ, said that one of the strongest lessons he learned during the pilgrimage was that there is "no difference in race, wealth, tribes, and languages. We are all the same in front of Allah." By donning "simple clothes of white cotton" (the *ihram* clothes worn by *hajj* pilgrims) Kadiono asserted "we increase community through equality." This was a lesson that Ary Ginanjar sought to emphasize during the final exercise of ESQ training when participants simulated three of the main activities undertaken by pilgrims (see chapter 2).

Distinctions of status are a pervasive part of daily life in Indonesia (Bowen 2003; Siegel 1986; Wertheim 1977), but those advocating spiritual reform referred to them as an obstacle to the kind of egalitarian practices that characterized the market. Thus, the egalitarian ethos of Islam in which every believer is exactly the same in relation to Allah, was contrasted with what spiritual reformers referred to as "feudal" aspects of social relations in Indonesia. Participants were constantly reminded not to be "arrogant" (*sombong*), and humility was represented as an important Islamic value. Enactments of affect between strangers or coworkers who encountered each other as Muslims rather than as managers and operators, or as university graduates and those without college degrees, was designed to create a sense of equality among employees.

At Krakatau Steel an oft-cited problem was antagonism between employees of higher status and lower status. This problem had become acute enough that company managers feared it was threatening the productivity and efficiency of the company. Management of the heart was viewed as a means of overcoming these rifts. During Suharto's reign factory employees, like the rest of Indonesian citizens, were strictly classified according to an extremely rigid hierarchy. This system had survived in the post-Suharto period but was disliked by most employees and was under revision (see chapter 6). The three levels of employment classification were in turn divided into between twenty-five and thirty-two numbered ranks. Recent graduates starting at Krakatau Steel with the equivalent of a bachelor's degree in a technical field such as engineering started at the rank of A9 or A11 and moved up a carefully calibrated ladder as they gained experience. The A-level was for management-level employees, from foremen to general managers (*kepala umum*). The B-level was for operators (*pelaksana*) and the C-level was for clerical workers. The highest level was A25, while the lowest was C1 or B1. Each company employee was slotted into one out of over eighty possible positions in this vast grid. Although one could move up within one of the three classifications, from, say, a B12 to a B13, one could not move between the classifications. Thus, a B-level employee could not become an A-level employee. Proponents of ESQ sought to alleviate some of the antagonisms that this classification had created though advocating the Islamic principle of universal human equality before Allah.

One way in which they sought to overcome difference was through frequent bodily contact. The project of spiritual reform placed great emphasis on bodily contact between participants of the same gender (although cross-gender bodily contact was explicitly discouraged). At the end of particularly intense collective prayers for atonement, participants were urged to embrace one another in the still dimly lit room. Physical contact in public of this sort is unusual in Indonesia, and I found it somewhat awkward to adjust to as I had become used to maintaining a respectful distance, even from close Indonesian friends. Eventually, I became enmeshed in the circulation of affect that characterized ESQ training. Upon greeting me Ary Ginanjar's employees exercised the same informality with me that they did with each other. They would embrace me and then warmly brush each of my cheeks with their cheeks. Later, when I was allowed to observe ESQ trainings in Jakarta from backstage, I was surprised to see that the trainers on Ary Ginanjar's staff participated in the circulation of tears and mutual embraces with each other at precisely the same moment that the participants on the other side of the stage did.

This focus on physical contact was recognized by other participants as a specific intervention of ESQ but was not universally accepted. One afternoon in October 2003, close to the beginning of my fieldwork, I was chatting with a Krakatau Steel employee in the late afternoon. The sun had broken through for the first time in several days and a delightful breeze was blowing off of the Sunda Straits, keeping the air pleasantly cool. As Agum and I were chatting in an employee parking lot, a coworker of his Subekti, approached us. He said hello to Agum and then remarked that he had seen me at the ESQ training the previous week. Immediately after he mentioned ESQ Agum tried to give him a big hug, playfully evoking the emphasis on embracing during spiritual training, whereupon Subekti dodged away from him with a scowl and a raised fist, actions that appeared to be not entirely in jest. He quickly remarked, "That is the Islamic culture of the Middle East, that's not my Islam!" [*Itu budaya Islam Timur Tengah, bukan Islam saya*]. I asked him what he meant in making this cultural distinction, given Islam's claims to universality. He said that on television he had seen Muslims from Persian Gulf countries engage in bodily contact like embracing, but this was not a practice common among Indonesian Muslims. While some saw ESQ as introducing a more authentic form of Islam because of its reference to practices common in the Middle East, the fact that ESQ adopted foreign practices suggested to others that it was just one of multiple possible ways to practice Islam.

The goal of overcoming distinctions of status through mutual embraces and the circulation of tears was not completely successful. In a private conversation, Rinaldi lamented to me that he thought one of the reasons ESQ had not been as effective at Krakatau Steel as it was at other companies was that senior employees of the company (managers, general managers, and directors) usually attended the executive ESQ trainings in Jakarta, not the in-house training sessions offered at the Krakatau Steel training facility in Cilegon. He said that they avoided the onsite sessions because they were "ashamed that their subordinates might see them cry." He reiterated that part of the goal of ESQ was to make people realize that all humans were equal. He thought that some of the reason Indonesia had failed to progress was that there was a feudal mentality in which some were viewed as inherently inferior to others. In his eyes, the managers practiced their piety improperly and ignored Islam's injunction of universal human equality. He feared that employees were suspicious of supervisors who did not take part in the program with the same level of openness that managers at companies such as Pertamina and Garuda had. Demonstrating devotion through a collective act of asking for repentance from Allah with subordinates would have built a stronger corporate unit. He thought that only through a collective enactment of grief and mutual embracing between employees at different levels of the company hierarchy could divisions be overcome and reform of the company be successful.

"Emotional Development" for National Modernization

Governing through affect operated on individual and collective levels. Proponents of and participants in ESQ viewed spiritual reform as capable of resolving the moral crisis they understood to be at the root of a national crisis of faith in development. In Indonesia, national development is tantamount to modernization (Heryanto 1988). The two projects are virtually indistinguishable. Spiritual reformers sought to correct the crisis of national development through the inculcation of affects deemed conducive to business success. Management of the heart was a project that worked on the individual level, but through transforming individuals spiritual reformers contended that it held the possibility of reforming the nation as a whole.

One manifestation of conjoining affect to the project of national development involved emphasizing how the appropriate exercise of affect enabled business transactions. ESQ trainers emphasized that success in business is often dependent on successful interpersonal communication. Thus, the crisis of national development was connected to the ethical practices of individual citizens. As noted in chapter 3, part of the crisis of faith in development was attributed to prioritizing intellectual and technical knowledge over emotional connection and spiritual knowledge. Many thought that Krakatau Steel had for too long focused on technical intelligence to the exclusion of emotional and spiritual intelligence.

Affect was represented as a resource that could be cultivated to redress some of these failings. This lesson was illustrated in a story that was part of the regular ESQ training program at Krakatau Steel. It recounted a purported meeting between an executive director of PT Dirgantara Indonesia, the state-owned aerospace company, and the chief executive of Petronas, Malaysia's giant oil and gas conglomerate. Like Krakatau Steel, Pertamina, and Garuda, Dirgantara was a key corporate symbol of Indonesian national development. This company was a pet project of B. J. Habibie and a centerpiece in his "leap frog" development strategy (Amir 2004). Following the end of the Suharto years and Habibie's own brief stint as president, the loss of faith in development was illustrated by Dirgantara's spectacular collapse. The IMF targeted Dirgantara for major restructuring as it had failed to locate a market for its aircraft and thus never managed to break even. Ultimately the company was radically downscaled, its major product lines were shut down, and thousands of employees were laid off. Indonesia had little to show for the billions that the state had dedicated to the leap frog strategy, and Dirgantara's collapse was symbolic of this failure.

Rinaldi used Dirgantara as an example of Indonesia's crisis of developmentalism but attributed its mismanagement not to Habibie's overly ambitious schemes. Rather he suggested that Indonesia's economic problems were due to misunderstanding the relationship between affect and business transactions. In recounting a meeting between the executives of Dirgantara and Petronas, Rinaldi mentioned that the director of Dirgantara and his staff all had high IQs. In his words they were "very smart, smart enough that all their degrees would not fit on a single business card. They had to use the back of the card too!" However, while they were technically competent, their affect was wanting.

In Rinaldi's dramatic rendition of the story, this deficiency became evident as the company representatives prepared to negotiate a transaction in which Petronas planned to purchase aircraft from Dirgantara. The deal was to be finalized at the personal residence of the Petronas executive in Kuala Lumpur, but before beginning formal negotiations he gave the Indonesian delegation a tour of his estate. He relished the opportunity to show off his home, which included a proud presentation of his extensive antique collection. According to Rinaldi's account, when the Petronas executive asked his Indonesian colleague's opinion of his collection, the executive director of Dirgantara answered, "I have good news for you, since you like this kind of stuff. There are many things like these, sir, in

Indonesia. At the flea market on Surabaya Street! And even better sir, they are very, very cheap! I'll even send you a few things from the flea market, so that you can add to your collection, because there is a lot of stuff like this there." The Surabaya Street flea market is well known as the place to go in Jakarta to buy freshly produced "antiques" and other suspect goods at heavily discounted prices. On weekends, middle- and upper-middle class shoppers stop here to stock their homes with furniture and other household ornaments that appear to be antiques but are usually of recent vintage. The market has a reputation as a place to shop for those who value low prices more than high quality.

Rinaldi recounted the displeasure of the CEO of Petronas when his carefully composed collection of antiques was compared to shoddy flea market goods. The aircraft purchase was quickly cancelled, and Rinaldi remarked, in a mocking tone, that the surplus aircraft were ultimately sent to Thailand in exchange for a shipment of sticky rice (*ketan*).[7] He attributed this business failure to the inability of the Indonesian delegation to express appropriate affect, which in this case would have been "the ability to care for someone beside oneself." Rinaldi went on to explain that this was what is meant by "emotional intelligence...how to be empathetic, how to be sympathetic....How to do negotiations, how to speak, how to look intently with a sincere visage."

This story illuminates how spiritual reformers perceived the crisis of faith in development as a problem of personality, not a structural or technical deficiency. A potent symbol of modernization, the airplane, was the centerpiece of this story emphasizing the importance of emotions in negotiating business transactions. Indonesians with unmanaged hearts act crudely in comparison with their more cosmopolitan Malaysian counterparts. Rinaldi suggested that had the transaction been conducted in accord with the proper affective norms, the sale of the planes would have been successful.

Affect is a central feature of this story about the relative failure of Indonesia to develop economically in comparison to its close neighbor. The choice of Malaysia as a contrast to Indonesia is deeply resonant because Indonesians recognize a shared history between the two nations. In Malaysia

---

7. Indonesia did exchange several aircraft to Thailand for 110,000 tons of sticky rice (Erikson 2003).

modernity is a state project (Chin 1998; Ong 1990), pursued with single-minded, tunnel vision under former prime minister Mahathir Mohamad's Vision 2020 program. In Indonesia by contrast, modernization has been more haphazard. The Indonesian state has been much more willing to tolerate and even facilitate traditional institutions while pursuing development (Li 2007; Tsing 2005, 27–54). For example, informal arrangements and patron-client networks are critical in facilitating labor migration from Indonesia to other Asian countries, to which state bureaucracies are only peripherally involved (Rudnyckyj 2004). Rinaldi suggests that Indonesia's economic malaise is due to the ignorance of the affective enactments essential to negotiating global business deals.

Furthermore, the two state-owned companies epitomize the differing development fortunes of the two nations. Petronas, which built the tallest twin-tower skyscraper complex in the world, represented the triumphs of Malaysia's modernity project. Dirgantara, which had several widely publicized malfunctions with the airplanes it produced and ended up bartering some of them for sticky rice like a simple market trader, represents Indonesia's crisis of faith in development.

The contrast resonated with other conversations I had with Krakatau Steel employees in which the differences between Indonesia and Malaysia were occasionally broached. Whereas Malaysia had been successful in its developmentalist aspirations, Indonesia had fallen behind, culminating in the momentous crisis of 1998. Employees recalled nostalgically that Malaysia in the 1950s and 1960s had looked to Indonesia as a model of modernization, but by 2004 the direction of development envy had been reversed. One engineer lamented to me that "before Malaysian students used to come to Indonesia to study, but now Indonesian students go to Malaysia. No Malaysians want to come here anymore." A neighboring country once thought to be developmentally inferior to Indonesia had spectacularly surpassed it, precipitating a crisis of identity that spiritual reformers sought to redress through creating a spiritual economy and governing through affect.

Management of the heart and the crisis of faith development were closely linked. In a personal interview Ary Ginanjar exclaimed, "We have people with degrees from American universities, European universities. So many degrees! What for? What good is a degree if your heart is not right?" He suggested that while Indonesians have gained technical knowledge this knowledge was insufficient. Rather, what is required is the cultivation of affective norms—the ability to manage one's heart and achieve what Kusmanto referred to, in English, as "emotional development." Previous modernization efforts have pursued technical knowledge at the expense of self-knowledge and knowledge of others. Ary Ginanjar promotes emotional and spiritual introspection that is distinct from technical knowledge like engineering. By focusing only on technical knowledge important lessons about how to relate to others were lost. A paucity of affect, in this case sympathy and compassion, is viewed as responsible for the economic crisis that shook the national faith in development.

"All You Need Is Love": Affect and National Reconciliation

Governing through affect was represented not only as a solution to the crisis of economic development but also to the political crisis that called into question Indonesia as a nation. One of the most significant political conflicts that plagued the country until 2005 was the long-running clash between Acehnese separatists in northern Sumatra and the central government (Aspinall 2009). The Indonesian military had been in Aceh for several decades seeking to eliminate the Free Aceh Movement (Gerakan Aceh Merdeka or GAM), an armed resistance group that sought independence from the nation and greater local control over the territory's abundant fields of natural gas, one of Indonesia's largest and most lucrative natural resources.

As discussed in chapter 2, Ary Ginanjar conceived of ESQ as a national project of spiritual reform, and he frequently traveled around the archipelago to deliver trainings to employees of state-owned enterprises, military officials, private companies, and bureaucrats in the local and national governments. He conducted a number of programs in Aceh, where ESQ emphasized Islamic practice as a foundation for national unity. Avid participants in ESQ credited Ginanjar with facilitating the peace treaty between the rebels and the Indonesian government. Where some might have seen a coincidence in his visits to Aceh, others saw divine intervention.

In an email I received in March 2006 an ESQ participant wrote to me detailing how the circulation of tears that took place during an ESQ session in Aceh enabled peace in the province. I have minimally edited his message to maintain the texture of the original:

> Ary just gave the training to [the Indonesian military and separatist rebels] in Banda Aceh and what happened was a miracle.... Both side[s] burst into tears afterwards and realize[d] how fool[ish] they were all this time. Just like an old song from "the Beatles"...all you need is love...but this time it is love to "the almighty God." Everybody knew that part of people of Aceh had a big disappointment in the past and they had reason to desire their own state under the name of GAM. Of course there are some other countries who played a crucial part in the conflicts namely oil & gas companies. i'm really sorry to mention that some American businessman or companies are also involved in this matter, but the problem is still in Indonesian government and it started during ORBA[8] period.... So, what the people of Aceh need just a little touch of love from Pak[9] Ary, and they started to walk hand in hand again. Boy...ever since I followed the training I easily drop my tears if something touched my heart.

Several weeks later, in another email exchange he credited ESQ with actually precipitating the reconciliation of GAM and the Indonesian military:

> I had another session on training by Pak Ary last week end, the whole trainee were surprised on the second day of the training. By the [appearance] of GAM and the [Indonesian] Generals following the rest of the training. Every body was amazed and thankful of what happened, specially at the end of training the formal General of GAM Mr. Sofyan Daud (I believe his name was) gave a little speech about how stupid he was and GAM for what happened in the last forty years, but another surprise was the formal commanding officer [for the Indonesian military] in Aceh also gave him and every body warm regard and big hug to Sofyan Daud and promised as everybody as witnesses for true peace for the future in Aceh.... Great story isn't it?

By inviting members of the opposing sides in the Aceh conflict to ESQ training, Ary Ginanjar showed that his involvement in national reform

---

8. This is an abbreviation for Orde Baru, which is Indonesian for New Order.

9. The shortened form of *Bapak,* this is a term of respect that roughly translates as mister or father.

was not limited to making employees at state-owned companies more competitive internationally. The conflict in Aceh was something that called the nation into question, and by taking an active role in its reconciliation he addressed a pressing political problem. Past participants in ESQ credited the training with healing the rift. This was symbolically demonstrated by the embrace between the former Acehnese separatist leader Sofyan Daud and Indonesia's military commanding officer that occurred during the training. Thus, management of the heart and the frequent embraces that were a hallmark of ESQ training became a means of redressing the nation's political conflicts, in addition to its economic crisis.

Conclusion: Knowing through Feeling

Proponents of spiritual reform in contemporary Indonesia sought to refunction government through affect. Affect was a powerful means to modulate, manipulate, and reform the subjects of the emerging spiritual economy. Conceiving of the heart as an object of management and immersing program participants in the circulation of tears, spiritual reformers sought to elicit a set of personal transformations commensurate with this new economy. Affect was a central medium through which these transformations could be achieved. Proponents of spiritual reform engaged in a set of practices that resembled those analyzed by Hirschman, in which affect was deployed as an effective way of shaping the pattern of human actions.

In contrast to anthropological work on emotions, I approach affect as simultaneously internal and external to those enmeshed in a spiritual economy. It moved though them and both represented and enacted a new form of personhood. This dynamic, transitive quality of affect enables it to reflexively make both its subject and object. The immersion of subjects within affect was designed to have specific effects. Spiritual training would likely have had little effect on participants without this intensely affective component. Indeed the mobilization of affect was perhaps the main difference between ESQ and other training programs contracted by the company, such as the Seven Habits of Highly Effective People training.

This new form of governing entailed the mobilization of affect to forge a subject amenable to new norms. This form of government linked self-interest to collective interest through a powerful means of affecting action.

This was expressed by Djohan in his affirmation that through more effective management of his heart he became aware that the long-term survival of Krakatau Steel was more important than immediate personal gain. Further, the modulation of individual affect was linked to greater productivity and efficiency at iconic sites of national production, such as Krakatau Steel and PT Dirgantara. Drawing on the already existing cultural norm of *qolbun salim* (ritual weeping) and importing the norm of bodily contact from "Middle Eastern" Islam, spiritual reformers offered affect as a means of harmonizing self-interest with collective interest. Developing affect offered a means through which corporate employees could better participate in the transnational economy.

Management of the heart was the central preoccupation of spiritual reformers in contemporary Indonesia. Emotional quotient was not directed toward restricting emotional outbursts but of better *administering* them. This involved developing techniques intended to exercise constant control over one's emotional states. Employees were instructed in precisely when it was appropriate (and when it was not) to enact specific affects. These lessons were not only oral. Instead they were directed towards inculcating bodily practices (such as the circulation of tears) that both communicated and enacted affective transformation. Ultimately, affect was indispensable to spiritual reform because it offered a means to a personal transformation that was as much felt as known. As Ary Ginanjar noted, proponents of spiritual reform had decided that technical competence was insufficient for achieving global competitiveness. Yet spirituality itself was not something that could be known rationally; it could only be felt. The intense affects deployed at ESQ training sessions thus enabled participants to experience a spiritual transformation, something that was inaccessible through the forms of technical knowledge that dominated Suharto's New Order developmentalism.

Part III

EFFECTS

5

POST-*PANCASILA* CITIZENSHIP

In a darkened hall, amidst a cacophony of plaintive wails and heavy metal music, Arfan cried out for forgiveness from Allah. This seventeen-year veteran employee of Krakatau Steel was participating in the climax of ESQ training, the simulation of the *talqin* ritual that represented the transition from worldly life to the afterlife. He sat on a hard metal chair in the tight embrace of a coworker and called out in tears, "Allahuak-bar... subhanahu-wa-taala... astaghfirullah."[1] The chilling blast of the air conditioning created an odd frostiness in contrast to the sweltering tropical climate outside the room and from which participants protected themselves by overdressing in jackets and heavy wraps.

Suddenly, in the midst of calling out for repentance, Arfan fell to the floor in a set of fitful paroxysms. His body moved in violent spasms, but those around him were so deeply engrossed in this burial simulation that

---

1. These exaltations respectively translate as "God is great," "Praise be unto thee the almighty," and "May God forgive me."

they appeared unaware of his convulsions. Quickly a figure appeared beside him in the semidarkness and rapidly repeated turning on and off a flashlight focused at the ceiling directly above the spot where Arfan's body thrashed about. The pulsing beam attracted alumni of the program serving as ushers who quickly assembled around Arfan as he writhed on the floor. The crowd attempted to grab Arfan, but his legs kicked aggressively against their futile grasps while unintelligible words that some later identified as "Chinese" tumbled from his lips. Later he would tell me that he had no knowledge of the language, indicating a mysterious source for these nonsense enunciations.

Other participants appeared unaware of the escalating scene in their midst, as they shouted and wailed along with the simulation. Finally, the group seeking to contain Arfan swelled to eleven members, and they were collectively able to restrain his body and remove it from the room. With at least two people clutching each of his limbs, they carried his flailing mass into a smaller room adjacent to the hall. There he was given what his assistants called "pure water," Arabic prayers were whispered into his ears, and his wife, Sri, was summoned from home to assist with efforts at resuscitation.

From Authoritarian Pluralism to Democratic Exclusion

This chapter analyzes the implications of spiritual reform for the configuration of identity in Indonesia. I analyze some of the tensions that the explicitly Islamic program to develop faith precipitated after it was introduced in a diverse, plural workforce of a company that had been instrumental to the project of national development. I argue that an authoritarian pluralism is giving way to democratic exclusion in contemporary Indonesia as citizens are compelled to publicly proclaim pure identities, a transformation that yields post-*pancasila* citizenship. Pancasila is the founding doctrine of Indonesian nationalism and was initially formulated by the first president, Sukarno. It is a textual definition of both Indonesia as a nation-state and the principles of belonging in the imagined community. The five principles are: a belief in one God, a just and civilized humanitarianism, the unity of Indonesia as a territorial unit, democracy guided by wisdom through representative deliberation, and social justice for the whole of the Indonesian people (Darmodiharjo, Dekker, Pringgodigdo et al. 1970, 31). Post-pancasila citizenship captures how religious identity is substituted for nationalist identity in contemporary Indonesia. During the New Order pluralist nationalism was one of the choice technologies used by the state to foment unity and harmony. However, in the transition to democratic governance religion is an increasingly important criterion for inclusion in broader communities.

This chapter describes the tensions between the nationalist pluralism characteristic of the authoritarian state under Suharto and the modes of religious and racial exclusion that have emerged in conjunction with the country's democratization. While Ary Ginanjar and other proponents of the program argued that ESQ merely drew on an external manifestation of a universal underlying spirituality, non-Muslims disagreed. They saw ESQ as a sign of the Islamicization of the company. These micropolitics of religious and racial difference in contemporary Indonesia suggest that the pluralism that served as a key means of administering the national population during the authoritarian Suharto state is less possible in the aftermath of the New Order. It may appear counterintuitive that authoritarian rule is associated with pluralism and that democratization creates new modes of exclusion. However, as Douglas Holmes and Elizabeth Povinelli have shown in different contexts, democratic liberalism creates exclusion by positing a world of incommensurable social interests and identities (Holmes 2000; Povinelli 2002). Islamic spiritual reform suggests that the nationalist pluralism that was an important tenet of the authoritarian regime is eroding and religion is becoming an increasingly potent site of political conflict and existential dilemmas.

ESQ marks a transformation in how national belonging is being reconfigured in state-owned companies. At Krakatau Steel and other state-owned enterprises an older pluralist pancasila identity that embraced the five official religions recognized by the Indonesian state is giving way to increasing emphasis on Islam as a common denominator for belonging.[2] Whereas a religiously plural identity was a cornerstone of the nationalism

---

2. My argument draws on Michael Feener's description of the tensions between pancasila and Islam in postcolonial Indonesia (Feener 2007, 81–117).

promoted by both Sukarno and Suharto, Indonesian pluralism and its attendant criteria for citizenship are under revision. The unifying ideals of nationalism have ceded to new configurations of individual and collective identity that emerged in concert with democratic reform.

I refer to this new type of citizenship as *post-pancasila* because in spiritual training sessions employees are called on to publicly proclaim their membership in a community based explicitly in Islam rather than the nation. Below I describe how during the New Order Krakatau Steel employees had been obliged to affirm their membership in the imagined community through a nationalist training program that sought to apply the values of pancasila in everyday life and work. In contrast, after the end of the Suharto regime and the introduction of Islamic motivational training, managers did not say (as they might have during the halcyon days of faith in development) that one should work hard to build the Indonesian nation and further the project of nationalist development. Rather, they said that one should develop faith by being productive, disciplined, and individually accountable because those values are appropriate to Muslims. Not surprisingly non-Muslims expressed anxiety at this change, viewing it as an indication of the increasing Islamicization of the company. They also feared that it was a manifestation of the increasing political influence of Islam in the nation at large. This chapter documents some of the political tensions inherent in reconfiguring the project of faith in development to one of developing faith.

Due to the affirmative action–style hiring policies of the Suharto state, many state-owned enterprises in Indonesia historically employed Muslims in numbers greater than their proportion of the national population. Muslim Indonesians had been economically disadvantaged during the colonial period, and Dutch policies had favored those subjects identified as Chinese in the colonial economy (Rush 1990). The postcolonial state sought to redress this historical imbalance by giving priority to Muslim citizens for salaried positions in both the civil service and the expanding network of state-owned enterprises. While according to most estimates Muslims compose roughly 90 percent of the total population, the state officially recognizes six religions: Islam, Catholicism, Protestantism, Buddhism, Hinduism, and Confucianism. Today proclaiming adherence to one of these six faiths is an essential criterion for citizenship because one is required to list one's religious affiliation on the identity card (Kartu Tanda Penduduk or KTP) issued by the government and which every citizen is required to carry with them while they are in public.

During the Suharto years, the constitutive exclusion of the Indonesian nation was Chineseness. Chinese ancestry marked one as foreign, even though many of those marked as Chinese were descendents of migrants who had arrived in the archipelago five generations previously, if not before. In Indonesia religion is mapped on to designations of ethnicity because it is used to define those citizens considered indigenous and those presumed to be foreign. Liisa Malkki uses the term "sedentarist metaphysics" to refer to the conviction that a specific group of people has an inherent, essential tie to a particular geographical location (Malkki 1997, 61). Although Islam became established in the Malay Archipelago only in the twelfth and thirteenth centuries, today the religion is part of the sedentarist metaphysics that marks Chinese as foreign and makes Islam a central criterion of indigeneity. Indonesians use the word *pribumi* to refer to someone who is considered indigenous, a term which literally means "offspring of the soil." The major groups excluded in this sedentarist metaphysics are those of Chinese descent, who are commonly considered newcomers and therefore are not considered to have an essential connection to Indonesian soil. In sum, Islam and Chineseness are considered incommensurable in spite of abundant historical and contemporary evidence to the contrary (Sumanto 2003).

The project of spiritual reform resonates with the reconfiguration of citizenship in contemporary Indonesia because during the thirty-two-year Suharto regime, the state had explicitly discouraged discourse about "ethnicity, religion, race, and inter-group relations" (van Dijk 2001, 4) except for that which was directly promulgated by the government.[3] Operating under the official national motto of "unity in diversity" (*bhinneka tunggal eka*), the state promoted a harmonious vision of cultural diversity and religious pluralism, although, as Joe Errington has noted, in actual fact Javanese culture played a disproportionately influential role (Errington 1998). To be clear this was not liberal multiculturalism but a pluralism of a decidedly authoritarian stripe because national harmony was ensured through the threat of state violence.

---

3. These terms are translations of the Indonesian words *suku, agama, ras, dan antar-golongan,* which were grouped under the acronym SARA in the media and public discourse in Indonesia.

The erosion of pancasila multiculturalism is evident in other facets of Indonesian life as well. As a number of scholars have demonstrated, the political transition initiated in 1998 following the Asian financial crisis precipitated conflicts between religious and ethnic groups on an unprecedented scale in Indonesia (Peluso 2006; Sidel 2006; van Klinken 2007). However, the turn to Islam as a unifying force in a fragmenting nation did not spring fully formed out of the rubble of the New Order. As Robert Hefner has argued, the Suharto regime changed its governing strategy from viewing Islam as a threat to state power to openly courting Muslim causes in the 1990s (Hefner 2000). While the conditions of possibility for the emergence of religion as a criterion for inclusion in broader communities were evident during the later Suharto years, Indonesia's democratization has created the conditions for the emergence of new criteria of exclusion in which citizens are increasingly compelled to proclaim pure identities.

In examining the politics of religious difference in contemporary Indonesia this chapter shows how Islam has emerged as a critical criterion for inclusion in the post-pancasila nation. My argument about the centrality of religion to the politics of difference in Indonesia builds on James Siegel's work on the violence that accompanied the end of the New Order. He argues that mass killings of accused witches in Java following the end of the Suharto regime were the result of "a collapse of the structures that generate identities" (Siegel 2001, 52). In rural villages during the New Order, state surveillance had previously created rigid categories of belonging by promoting romanticized notions of village life. Episodes of mob violence exploded in its aftermath because the end of state surveillance produced suspicion of oneself as the state no longer served to confirm belonging in a larger collective (Siegel 2001, 67). Killing an other, marked as a witch, enabled the formation of an identity and thus was a means of assuaging existential anxieties. I build on Siegel's account by showing how the collapse of the structures that had generated identities during the New Order precipitated a similar search for identity among some employees of Krakatau Steel. However, the violence that this search precipitated was not directed toward an other but rather toward the self. Although participants were no longer safe in their affinity to the nation, they did not blame others for the loss of identity. Thus, the difference between the Javanese villagers studied by Siegel and the Indonesian factory employees with whom I worked is that the latter felt personally responsible for enunciating a pure Islamic identity.

Indoctri-Nation: Inculcating Pancasila Principles

The ESQ training program succeeded an earlier Suharto-era employee training program that was explicitly intended to forge subjects loyal to the nation-state. This now-defunct program was grounded in nationalist principles and, among other principles, strongly emphasized work as a moral duty for national citizens. Called Training for the Realization and Enactment of Pancasila (Penataran Pedoman Penghayatan dan Pengamalan Pancasila), this program was required of all state employees, including employees of state-owned enterprises, civil servants, teachers, and university faculty. Referred to by Indonesians as "P4 training," or more commonly simply "P4" (P *empat*), it sought to indoctrinate the principles of pancasila, the official state ideology. A comparison of this previous training program with ESQ training sheds light on how Islam has become an increasingly important criterion for belonging in Indonesia.

Pancasila was formulated at the founding of the nation to provide a frame of belonging that superseded the imagined community's distinct religious, linguistic, and cultural differences. Indonesia's founding president Sukarno proposed pancasila in 1945 specifically in "opposition to the demand that the independent Indonesian Republic be an Islamic state" (Morfit 1981, 844). This is evident in the first principle, a belief in one God. Hinduism and Buddhism were creatively reinterpreted as monotheistic religions to be recognized as comparable to what at the time were the other three official religions: Islam, Catholicism, and Protestantism (before 2000 Confucianism was not recognized by the state).[4] Muslim leaders were disappointed when the Jakarta Charter, an amendment to the five principles that would have enshrined a requirement that all Muslims in the country abide by Islamic *syariah* law, was dropped in late August 1945 (Feener 2007, 101–102; Ricklefs 1981, 213). This is one factor that led to Muslim rebellions such as the Darul Islam that threatened the viability of the nascent Indonesian state in the 1950s (Dengel 1995; Gunawan 2000).

In 1978 the authoritarian Suharto government developed the P4 pancasila training program as a technique to ensure the loyalty of citizens to

---

4. Catholicism and Protestantism are classified as distinct religions in Indonesia. Protestantism is referred to more generally as "Christian religion" (*agama Kristen*) whereas Catholicism is recognized separately (*agama Katolik*).

the nation-state. The training course, required of all civil servants including employees of state-owned enterprises such as Krakatau Steel, involved a training program of one week during which participants were systematically instructed in principles of pancasila. Emphasis was placed on how the authoritarian New Order government reflected pancasila values and on the duties of citizens to the nation (McGregor 2001, 47). During the 1980s the population required to participate in the pancasila education program was broadened to include religious leaders and students at all levels (Weatherbee 1985). Philip Kitley has described how a children's television program on the state-owned channel TVRI was one means the state used to extend the P4 program to Indonesian children (Kitley 1999, 130–131). By the 1990s pancasila "became the prescribed set of guiding principles for the press, the law, the economy, industrial relations and morality" (McGregor 2001, 48).

The P4 training sought to inculcate nationalist pancasila principles among citizens of the nation. It was devised in the late 1970s and early 1980s by senior government officials including the Minister for Economics, Finance, and Industrial Affairs, the Minister for State Security and the Minister for Administrative Reform. The P4 training lasted from 8 A.M. until 6 P.M., and participants were required to complete homework assignments and a final test on the last day of training. Grades were awarded to participants based on their performance and were recorded in their employment files. These were later factored into personnel decisions for promotions and salary adjustments (Morfit 1981). The P4 program was consistent with the regime's strategy of presenting nationalism as an alternative to both political Islam, of which some variants advocated the implementation of *syariah* law, and communism, which advocated the redistribution of material wealth. It was closely associated with the repressive New Order state and, after Suharto's fall in 1998, the training program was terminated.

Prior to 1998 all employees of Krakatau Steel were required to participate in P4 training. Sutiono, the engineer described in chapter 4 who found himself unable to open his heart, related how seriously the company took P4 training. He said, "Even wives were required to attend.... It took place in strategic years (*tahun strategis*) like before elections.... There would be case studies, lectures, question-and-answer sessions. The teachers were usually professors or lecturers from universities...but after *reformasi* it was stopped." The program lasted for one week and government employees were expected to attend the program at least once every five years. Universities served as sites for the development of techniques for "indoctrinating the pancasila" (*santiaji pancasila*). Thus, the state teacher's training college (Institut Keguruan Ilmu Pendidikan) in Malang had a "pancasila laboratory" (*laboratorium pancasila*) where Indonesian academics formulated techniques for indoctrinating the five principles to produce loyal subjects of the Indonesian state (Darmodiharjo, Dekker, Pringgodigdo et al. 1970). By the time of my fieldwork P4 training was no longer required for public employees, so my knowledge of P4 comes from books published by organizations such as the P4 laboratory in Malang, the recollections of participants, and the writings of earlier scholars who have analyzed P4 (McGregor 2001; Morfit 1981; Weatherbee 1985).

Both proponents of and participants in Islamic spiritual training contrasted ESQ with the P4 pancasila training program that preceded it. Most had concluded that P4 was a failure. Sutiono told me that he thought "the theory" of the P4 program was "good, but the problem was that it was never properly implemented." The program was derided by employees and spiritual trainers at Krakatau Steel. In the second morning session of an ESQ training session in May 2004, Rinaldi compared ESQ to P4:

> Why did P4 fail? Was the project [*proyeknya*] successful? The procurement [*pengadaan*] of the book was successful! If you make a program the *manggala* [chief] will benefit [*berhasil*], isn't that right ladies and gentlemen? … The program was implemented across Indonesia, but was the goal achieved or not? No! Why? Because it went against divine characteristics [*berlawanan dengan sifat ilahiayah*]! What did they hope to build [*tegakkan*]? The characteristics of Allah! Do you agree or not? They hoped to build these characteristics of Allah: honesty, justice, love, and affection. But they forgot to ask for permission [*ijin*] from he who possessed those characteristics!

Rinaldi suggested that the P4 program failed because it was not sufficiently Muslim. This was reflected in the fact that he used the term *manggala,* a Sanskrit term given to officials licensed to give the P4 training. He claimed that although P4 sought to inculcate proper moral values, it did so in a manner inconsistent with Islam, which was represented in the ESQ training as the ultimate source of those values. Thus, while ESQ training drew on Indonesia's Muslim present and recent past, P4 was premised on the country's more distant Hindu and Buddhist history. The use of the

Sanskrit term *manggala* identified the program with Hinduism and Buddhism rather than Islam. Although Rinaldi noted that officials sought to implement the program on a national scale "everywhere in Indonesia," he suggested that the failure of the P4 program was at least in part due to the fact that it invoked the wrong religious and historical tradition.[5]

Further, Rinaldi alluded to the fact that P4, like many programs associated with Suharto's discredited New Order, was corrupt (Pemberton 1999; Schrauwers 2003). In contrast, ESQ was specifically intended to redress the problem of chronic corruption at state-owned enterprises. Rinaldi's allusions were conveyed through the words *proyek* (project) and *pengadaan* (procurement). Among factory employees, the procurement of equipment for the company from outside suppliers was widely known to provide opportunities for corruption by senior and midlevel managers who held the authority to sign off on purchase orders (see chapter 3). The term *proyek* is often used in Indonesia to refer to illicit and quasi-licit business dealings, such as government contracts obtained through political connections rather than through open bidding. Although P4 was developed by the state, Rinaldi suggested that the program was a moneymaking scheme rather than an earnest attempt to bring about moral reform in the nation as a whole. This suggestion was conveyed through his claim that the program achieved the goal of procuring books but fell short of fostering national development by implementing the virtues (honesty, justice, love, and affection) that ESQ asserted were conducive to business success.

Although it is difficult to directly compare the defunct P4 program with ESQ, the latter was more popular among Krakatau Steel employees. In general they disparaged P4 as a propaganda tool for a corrupt state but had more positive things to say about ESQ. This was in part due to its association with Islam. ESQ was dedicated to enhancing individual Islamic piety, as opposed to nakedly serving the aims of a state that by 2003 was viewed as crooked and morally bereft. Although employees were aware that some sought to use it as a means to increase corporate productivity and efficiency, employees themselves saw it as an opportunity to enhance their personal religious practice and knowledge. Further, employees unenthusiastically

---

5. Roughly 2 percent of the population of contemporary Indonesia is Hindu, but this population lives overwhelmingly on the island of Bali. At Krakatau Steel the percentage of employees identified as Hindu was less than 1 percent.

recalled the dry delivery of the P4 program, which consisted of monotonous lectures and emphasized rote memorization. In contrast, ESQ was conveyed through sophisticated technology that merged elaborate audiovisual presentations with collective calisthenics and impassioned group prayers.

Another indication that ESQ held broader appeal than P4 is evident in the fact that P4 was dependent on direct state support, whereas ESQ's success was based in the market. P4 was designed and implemented as a state project of forging the national loyalty of civil servants and other state employees. It was devised by the state and would not have existed but for the fact that the New Order state invested heavily in its development and dissemination. In contrast, ESQ was created by an independent businessman and although various government institutions contracted the training, it was not an explicit state project. Furthermore, as noted in chapter 2, ESQ managers saw the greatest potential for expansion through offering the training to members of the general public rather than relying on the limited pool of state-owned enterprises and government institutions. Future growth would be dependent on attracting people who paid out of their own pockets to participate. Thus, ESQ was disseminated primarily through the market rather than by the state and operated as a private, for-profit company rather than in a state-supported university. ESQ's orientation toward the market was reflected in the construction of a skyscraper and convention center based in part on donations of past participants, further testament to its independence from state financial guarantees.

In the years following Suharto's downfall many of the same groups of employees that formerly participated in the P4 pancasila training program were enrolled in ESQ spiritual training sessions. Bureaucrats, employees of state-owned enterprises, and other public employees such as teachers in the national educational system at all levels were previously required to participate in P4 training. After the end of the New Order some of these constituencies were compelled or recommended to participate in ESQ training. However, whereas the nationalist program developed by the authoritarian state sought to create solidarity in spite of Indonesia's pluralism, ESQ confronts its participants—Muslims, non-Muslims, and those who identify as of plural heritage—with an explicitly Islamic message to guide individual ethical comportment. The fact that the program was grounded in Islam precipitated a number of tensions of identification, both for individual employees of plural heritage and for members of other religious groups.

Fixing Identity: The Politics of Possession

To understand why ESQ training spurred the dramatic episode of spirit possession that I described at the outset of this chapter, it is helpful to understand something about the historical construction of Chinese and Muslim identities in Indonesia. People with ancestors who came to the Malay Archipelago from what is today mainland China were first defined as foreign during the colonial period. Prior to Dutch rule, historians have concluded that conceptions of identity in the archipelago were fluid as seagoing traders from other parts of Asia and beyond established households in diverse coastal cities as they waited for the trade winds to shift (Reid 1988; Wolters 1999). Only with the onset of colonial rule and the formation of what James Furnivall called "plural societies" (Furnivall 1948) were fixed racial and religious categories created, in part as a means of furthering colonial rule (Roff 1985; Stoler 2002). "Chinese" as a distinct category emerged only at that time. Their ambiguous position in the colonial order of things was reflected in the fact that colonial civil law codes classified Chinese together with "natives," but in commercial matters they were subject to laws governing the conduct of Europeans. There were also strict codes regarding personal appearance that required Chinese men to wear their hair in a long braid and clothes in what was considered Chinese style (Schulte Nordholt 1997). This made those marked as Chinese easily identifiable to the colonial state.

After the formation of the Indonesian nation in 1945, the colonial construction of "Chinese" as a distinct racial and ethnic category persisted, a distinction that was further fixed and amplified by Suharto's authoritarian government (Mackie 1976; Suryadinata 2007). Although state multiculturalism framed public discourse about ethnicity, religion, and race through the national motto of "unity in diversity," those identified as Chinese were ambiguously positioned in the ethnic map of postcolonial Indonesia, and the category remained particularly complicated (Lee 2003). While those marked as Chinese were given wide latitude to participate in the economy, to the extent that some of those so marked became among the wealthiest tycoons in Indonesia (Robison 1986), Suharto constrained their political influence so that they would be beholden to him for their security. Furthermore, New Order cultural policies put strict limits on the public practice of activities marked as Chinese. All but one Chinese-language newspaper was closed, Chinese-language schools were contracted and all were closed by 1974, and Chinese script was banned from public places such as storefronts (Schwarz 1994). The downfall of Suharto was simultaneously accompanied by widespread violence directed at those identified as Chinese and somewhat later followed by the lifting of restrictions on Chinese cultural practices (Purdey 2006).[6] After the end of the New Order Confucianism, which was not recognized as an official religion by the Suharto regime, was given status equal to Islam, Catholicism, Protestantism, Buddhism, and Hinduism in the pantheon of religions that received official sanction (Friend 2003, 468).

The complex tensions between Islam, Chineseness, and national citizenship were graphically demonstrated in Arfan's episode of spirit possession described at the beginning of this chapter. His experience is particular to his personal biography and was not representative of the experiences of every Indonesian of plural heritage that encountered spiritual training. The significance of Arfan's experience lies in the fact that it was well known and often invoked in conversations that I had with other employees of Krakatau Steel. They cited it as evidence of the power of the program to resolve potential conflicts of identification among those of plural heritage such as Arfan who recognized both Chinese and Muslim ancestors.

Episodes of spirit possession analogous to those that Arfan experienced were not unprecedented during ESQ training. During ESQ training sessions at Krakatau Steel there would usually be a handful of participants who were similarly afflicted. An interesting facet of these events was the different explanations and conflicting interpretations that were provided to account for them. Lower-level employees, such as operators and foremen,

---

6. It should be noted that in Indonesia *orang Cina* (Chinese people) contains within it subcategories of *peranakan* and *totok*, which mark differing degrees of "nativeness" based on when the group in question arrived from "China" (Aguilar 2001). Totok are recent immigrants to the archipelago, whereas peranakan denotes descendents of Chinese immigrants who mixed in with inhabitants of the Malay archipelago during the early modern and colonial periods. In practice many Indonesians fail to make this distinction. I thank Christopher Vasantkumar for helping me to clarify this point.

for the most part attributed them to "spirit possession" (*kesurupan*). However, Rinaldi, other proponents of ESQ, and senior-level employees who proclaimed themselves to be better educated invoked medical explanations for these events and referred to them as "shock," "trance," or most innocently "resting." Gusniarto, the engineer quoted in chapter 2, told me that these events occurred when people realized their sins, "they feel regret and then realize the consequences of their activities. They realize that one should be responsible for one's activities. Before they were ignorant [of this fact]...so it leads to an emotional shock." The episodes were regular enough that the Krakatau Steel organizers ensured that a nurse from the company hospital was on site during ESQ training. In a pristine white uniform she circulated throughout the hall dragging a small, battered tank on wheels behind her so that she could instantly administer oxygen to those who had collapsed.

Some months after Arfan's dramatic episode of spirit possession I met him and his wife, Sri, at their home in a middle-class neighborhood in the provincial capital of Serang where a number of Krakatau Steel employees lived. Although this section of the city was about twenty kilometers away from the main factory compound, the company used a fleet of buses to transport workers who lived in Serang to the industrial zone adjacent to Cilegon. Arfan was an avid reader and a pile of *Kompas* newspapers, Indonesia's leading daily, sat beside him in his small living room as we chatted. He alluded to the complex politics of religion in contemporary Indonesia by joking that *Kompas* was an abbreviation for *komando pastor* (priest's command), which was a reference to the fact that the newspaper is owned by a prominent Catholic family. In so doing, he made an oblique reference to how he was complexly positioned in the ethnic and religious frames through which Indonesian citizenship is constituted, because he is a member of the imagined community constituted through a Catholic-held newspaper (Anderson 1991). He mentioned that he found *Republika,* the newspaper discussed in chapter 1 and directed toward an Islamic audience, "too Muslim-focused."

Arfan explained to me the long history behind the violent episode of spirit possession that I had witnessed some months prior. He was born in Jakarta and, like many Indonesians who hail from the plural societies along Java's north coast, claimed a mixed heritage. He referred to himself as Betawi, an appellation considered appropriate to people native to

Jakarta. Betawi people are regarded as ethnically heterogeneous and can often trace ancestors to the Arabian peninsula, India, China, and other parts of the Indonesian archipelago, such as Java, Sunda, Sulawesi, Sumatra, and Ambon (Budiati 2000). Arfan told me that although his maternal grandfather was Chinese, his other ancestors were not. He had gone to Muhammadiyah[7] Islamic schools through junior high, but he said that although he had received an Islamic education as a child he had not been a particularly devout observer as an adult.

Arfan's invocation of a Chinese grandparent was further significant, as to be Chinese in Indonesia is by implication to be non-Muslim. The sedentarist metaphysics at work in Indonesia frequently defines Islam as a criterion for indigeneity, in contrast to Chineseness, which is still frequently considered an attribute external to the archipelago. One operator at Krakatau Steel illustrated this when he identified himself as Chinese but maintained that Chinese is not an ethnic category in Indonesia because there is no Chinese territory (Peluso and Harwell 2001). He expressed his understanding that "an ethnicity is like Javanese, Balinese, Batak, Sundanese, and Ambonese. An ethnicity [*suku*] must have its own territory [*wilayah*]. Chinese is just a lineage of descent [*keturunan*]. We are newcomers [*pendatang*] here." This demonstrates how "Chinese" was represented as a category of belonging external to the nation. Postcolonial politicians emphasized ethnic diversity as constitutive of the nation but many notably excluded those labeled Chinese. Although some families identified as Chinese can trace ancestors that first came to the archipelago more than five generations ago (and thus long before the nation itself even existed) a common perception is that they are still somehow newcomers (Aguilar 2001). Furthermore, during the colonial period restrictions were placed on the ability of those marked Chinese to own agricultural land, and today many Indonesians who identify as Chinese live in urban areas. Following the isomorphism of blood, soil, language, and culture that often comes to constitute modern conceptions of belonging (Moore, Kosek and Pandian 2003), territory is understood as a critical attribute in constituting identity

---

7. Muhammadiyah is a "modernist" Islamic organization that was founded as a response to both the increasing activity of Christian missionaries in the early-twentieth-century Dutch East Indies and reforming traditional Islamic practices in Indonesia. The organization administers schools, hospitals, and orphanages throughout Indonesia (Noer 1973).

in contemporary Indonesia. Thus, Chinese are often excluded from membership because they are not connected to a discrete territory, unlike those who are unambiguously considered citizens.

The startling reaction that Arfan demonstrated during spiritual training was connected to events that had punctuated his life for over twenty years. After graduating from high school in the early 1980s Arfan left Jakarta for Borneo. There he worked as a manual laborer for the French oil and gas conglomerate Total, which at that time was developing oil and gas fields off the coast of East Kalimantan. He was living in informal worker's dormitories adjacent to the home of a more prosperous local trading family. Arfan continued, "One Sunday evening, it was right around *maghrib*. I heard the maid for the family next door start screaming. I wanted to help out, so I went to see what I could do. As I held her, it was like there was a movement, or something mysterious [*ghaib*], and suddenly it entered inside of me. I didn't know what it was … suddenly I didn't feel well, I felt something heavy here [gesturing toward his shoulders]." As it turned out the maid had accompanied her employers to a beach that was adjacent to what was locally regarded as a Chinese cemetery. Arfan concluded that a magical being had entered the maid's body while she was near the cemetery and then later inhabited his body as he tried to calm her from the outbreak.

For the next twenty years this spirit periodically occupied his body and would occasionally manifest itself. Arfan said that the spirit was particularly active around the time of Chinese New Year. This is noteworthy as public celebration of this holiday was prohibited in Indonesia during the Suharto regime. Only during the presidential administration of Abdurrahman Wahid in 2000 were Chinese New Year's celebrations again permitted publicly. Arfan's inclusion of this detail suggests that the spirit was distressed by restrictions on cultural practices marked "Chinese" during the New Order.

Arfan returned to Jakarta from Kalimantan in 1985, and his parents were increasingly concerned about the unprecedented but recurring episodes of spirit possession that seized him. Seeking to alleviate the outbreaks they brought him to some of the most renowned shamans (*dukun*) in Jakarta and West Java, but all were incapable of expelling the spirit from Arfan's body. After a number of vain attempts Arfan said that he was told by several of the shamans he visited that he had to take individual responsibility for the exorcism. They told him that only he had the ability to expel the spirit that occupied his body and no one could do it for him.

At about that time he had started to work at Krakatau Steel as a dispatcher in the newly established cold rolling mill. His employment at the mill is significant because the mill's existence illustrates the complex political economy of Indonesian citizenship and its constitutive exclusions. The cold rolling mill was a paradigmatic example of collaboration between the Suharto regime and those Indonesians of Chinese descent who were central players in the country's spectacular economic growth during the New Order (Robison and Hadiz 2004). These tycoons held scant political power and thus were ambiguously positioned in the nation because they were dependent on the patronage of the Suharto regime. Although that patronage enabled them to become some of the leading players in Indonesian commerce, it also made them beholden to Suharto. The cold rolling mill was constructed in the 1980s out of this convenient alliance. Falling oil prices and a sudden dip in economic growth in 1982 slowed down a decade of massive state-directed investment in Krakatau Steel. Pertamina, the state-owned oil company, had been generating huge profits due to historically high global oil prices throughout the 1970s. The boom in oil prices had subsidized the expansion of facilities, production, and employment at Krakatau Steel. However, despite these massive outlays the grand vision of a fully-integrated steel mill had yet to be realized.

In light of Pertamina's struggles, government technocrats called on the longtime Suharto crony Liem Sioe Liong to complete the modernist vision of development planners for whom an integrated steel mill was a central feature of faith in development.[8] A migrant from the southern Chinese province of Fujian who arrived virtually penniless in the Dutch East Indies, Liem became the wealthiest businessman in Indonesia in large part due to his connections with Suharto that dated back to the 1950s. In partial exchange for investing $875 million in a cold rolling steel mill located within the Krakatau Steel industrial zone, Liem received an exclusive monopoly on the domestic sale of cold rolled coil. This enabled him to profit

---

8. The strength of Liem's connection to Suharto cannot be understated. Liem was born in Fujian, China, in 1916 and arrived destitute in central Java on the eve of World War II. By the 1950s he had become a supplier to the Diponegoro division in Semarang. The division's chief financial officer was Suharto, who at the time was a young lieutenant colonel (Robison 1986, 297).

from a huge markup on this critical industrial product, selling it for \$550 per ton at a time when the international price was about \$380 per ton (Robison and Hadiz 2004, 97). In spite of such advantageous market conditions the operation managed to rack up huge debts, resulting in a bailout in which the Indonesian government agreed to purchase Liem's 40 percent investment in the project and assume his outstanding debt. The entire labor force of the cold rolling mill was absorbed as employees of Krakatau Steel in 1991, although employees proudly affirmed that the mill was more like a private business compared to the other company mills. Thus, Arfan's initial job at Krakatau Steel was facilitated by Liem's investment capital, and later he became dependent on the Suharto state for his employment. In this sense, Arfan's career at Krakatau Steel was the product of an alliance between Chinese capital and indigenous (*pribumi*) political power, in a way that parallels his family tree, which contains both Chinese and *pribumi* ancestors.

Like other employees, Arfan and Sri attributed characteristics they associated with Chinese culture to the spirit that inhabited his body. They said that the spirit would emerge in the guise of a Mongol emperor (*kaiser Mongol*).[9] In addition to Chinese New Year, the spirit would make its presence felt when Arfan became angry or irritated. Sri mimed the behavior of Arfan's body when it experienced inhabitation. When the spirit came, she showed me how he would fall to the ground and then begin to grind his teeth while he slowly rose into a kneeling position. Sri told me that when he was possessed his hands shook "like a tiger's" and he threw aside his beaten, coke-bottle glasses with discernibly taped rims. From a kneeling position, he would bow forward in a manner she described as characteristic of "someone praying at a Chinese temple." This involved a repeated set of prostrations from a kneeling position. She imitated his movements and showed me how, when possessed, he stood up and began to stroke an imaginary handlebar mustache with floppy ends, fluttered an invisible pigtail (*kuncir*), and reached for an imperceptible samurai sword on his back. All these traits are associated with Chineseness, as it is commonly represented in dubbed programs from Taiwan and mainland China that are a regular feature of Indonesian network television. Although they had no

---

9. In explaining Arfan's spirit possession episodes, Arfan and Sri conflated Mongolian and Chinese identities. From their perspective these were the same.

knowledge of the language, several Krakatau Steel employees mentioned that when Arfan was in a state of possession he was able to speak what they understood to be Chinese. Arfan likewise explained that he had no knowledge of the language outside of the times that his body was inhabited by the spirit.

The descriptions that Arfan and Sri gave of his episodes of spirit possession reflected a common Indonesian perception that Islam and Chineseness are opposed. Sri was told by one of the shamans Arfan's family had visited that she should try to bring him out of his states of possession by reading him Qur'anic verses. She found this partially effective, but occasionally she would whisper holy passages in his ear while he was possessed and Arfan would reply, "I will get my revenge on you" (*gue dendam sama lu*). The pronouns that she attributed to Arfan while he was possessed were not the common Indonesian language forms *aku* and *kamu* but *gue* and *lu,* which are associated with the southern Chinese dialects and have influenced the Betawi speech that is identified with those native to Jakarta.

In another instance of his affinity for his self-professed Chinese heritage, Arfan told me that he felt "refreshed" whenever he visited the Klenteng Avalokiteswara, a Buddhist temple frequented by local Chinese families and an important landmark in the nearby historic city of Banten Lama. After he visited the temple he said felt "better there" than he did at the mosque. Immediately after he expressed the contentment he derived from visiting the temple, Sri commented, "Strange isn't it? Before he didn't pray [*sholat*] at all." She said that he would pray only at home, never at the mosque. She would pester him about his lack of devotion and he would dismissively reply that praying at home "was enough to quiet the creator" (*menghening pencipta*). Sri then told me that after he attended ESQ he became "much more diligent at praying and *zikir*.[10] Now, if he is home during Friday prayers he always goes to the mosque."

Arfan said that he had postponed attending ESQ three times despite having been repeatedly invited because he was scared that it would rouse the spirit that had intermittently possessed him for over two decades. He said that he finally chose to participate because he thought that it might offer a way to divest himself of these recurring episodes. For the first two

---

10. *Zikir* is ritualized chanting associated with Islamic devotion in Indonesia.

days of the training he experienced no sign of inhabitation. The spirit became active only on the third day when the group was performing the climactic *talqin* simulation. According to members of the Krakatau Steel ESQ committee, other participants in the training also had the most extreme reactions to spiritual training during this simulation, when participants simulated the transition to the afterlife.

It was precisely at the point of enacting this liminal state that Arfan's long existential crisis precipitated the events I described at the beginning of the chapter. Sri told me he ran amok (*mengamuk*) as he was calling out for forgiveness from God. She and Arfan understood that the Islamic ritual had incited the Chinese spirit. Arfan said that at that time he wanted to be healed, but the spirit became angry when Arfan exclaimed Arabic phrases such as *Allahuakbar, Subhanahu-wa-taala,* and *Astaghfirullah.* He then fell under the control (*dikendalikan*) of the spirit and it caused him to collapse. After his collapse, he awoke, stood up, and began to go into the series of convulsions that Sri referred to as amok. After he was removed from the room she was summoned from their home to restore him to full consciousness (*sadar penuh*). She took pride in the fact that she was the only one who could bring him out of his altered state and did so by whispering the throne verse (*ayat kursi*), a Qur'anic passage, into his ear.[11]

Arfan's experience demonstrates the effectiveness of ESQ training, although not precisely in accordance with the expectations of proponents of the program. Arfan said that after he attended ESQ, he was better able to control the episodes of spirit possession that had previously seized him unsuspectingly. He also attested that he was more diligent about praying at the mosque, reading the Qur'an regularly, participating in Qur'anic study groups in his neighborhood (*pengajian*), and fasting during Ramadan. In the year since he participated in ESQ the spirit did not seize him unexpectedly any longer. Toward the end of our conversation, he asked me if I wanted him to call the spirit. Sri ardently pleaded that I decline the offer, explaining that it was difficult to settle his body once the spirit

---

11. Many Indonesian Muslims consider the throne verse (Qur'an 2, 255) to be one of the most powerful in the Qur'an. I was told that, in terms of the spiritual merit one attained, memorizing this single verse in Arabic is considered equivalent to memorizing one quarter of the Qur'an. Ong also documents use of Qur'anic verses to resuscitate those afflicted by spirit possession (Ong 1987, 206).

was incited. She said that after ESQ he was occasionally inhabited but, in addition to greater devotion to pious practices, he was also more able to control the episodes in which he experienced possession. The resolution achieved through his attendance at spiritual training was not so much the exorcism of the spirit that haunted him but his enhanced ability to *manage* his states of inhabitation. In contrast, his colleagues from work did not draw this distinction but proclaimed that he had been exorcised of the haunting. Arfan had been partially reformed, although not precisely according to the terms laid out by proponents of spiritual reform, who were more concerned with constituting spirituality as an object of management and inculcating an ethic of work as worship.

Arfan's experience illuminates certain tensions between the spiritual economy and the historical legacy of how religion and ethnicity have been constituted in Indonesia. The existential power and emotional force of preparing for one's own death through a simulation of one's burial cannot be underestimated, especially in the context of post–New Order Indonesia. As previously noted, James Siegel has described how villagers in rural parts of the country killed those they identified as witches to assuage their own existential anxieties following Suharto's downfall (Siegel 2001). The evaporation of the state that had for so long conferred being and belonging left them to define themselves against the only available other. In the semi-urban setting where my research was conducted, a similar crisis of identity was evident as factory workers literally called their own identities into question, asking each other, "Who are you?" In the countryside where no answer to this question was forthcoming, villagers physically killed those who were marked as others to convince themselves that they were not witches. In contrast, in the factory, a structure (to use Siegel's term) was provided that was intended to generate a new, explicitly Muslim identity in place of the old nationalist identity premised on unity in diversity. As Siegel observes, being and belonging were life and death matters. However, the resolution to this existential crisis entailed not the killing of an other but rather the simulation of the beginning of one's afterlife.

The central difference between Siegel's research on rural Java and my account of the racial and religious politics of spiritual reform at a critical site of nationalist development has to do with the object of violence. In the former, the protagonists kill others to find themselves. In the latter, the object of violence is not an other but the self, because the protagonists performed their own afterlife. Thus, the subjects of spiritual reform made themselves into the objects of a prior, obscured violence. It is not known when or how they will die, just that death is inevitable. In staging a confrontation with the angels of death in the afterlife, they submit to an ethics of personal responsibility in which they are accountable for living as devout Muslims. It is precisely at the moment when confronted with the question "Who are you?" that Arfan experienced his intense episode of spirit possession. Proclaiming a religious identity that did not completely conform to his understanding of his plural heritage precipitated an existential crisis as the spirit prevented him from fully affirming faith in Islam. In the spiritual economy participants are called on to take responsibility for their practice *as Muslims*. This stands in marked contrast to Siegel's account in which people see the responsibility for their own existential crises in the actions of another.

Further, Arfan's intense episode of spirit possession while performing the experience of the afterlife illustrates the relationship between the afterlife of development and national identity. The introduction of programs to develop faith at key sites of state-directed development in the country challenged the uneasy truce between Islam and Chineseness that characterized the later years of the Suharto regime. Never assigned a territory in the ethnic map that made up Indonesia (Pemberton 1994b; Roff 1985), the Chinese were treated as internal others and tolerated by the regime for their investment capital until they no longer served Suharto's strategic agenda, at which point they were vulnerable to mass violence (Kusno 2003). Although Arfan could claim Muslim identity because he was brought up in the religion and went to Islamic schools, he also recognized a Chinese grandparent. During the Suharto regime, such a subject position could be tenuously occupied, as Chinese were ambiguously positioned at the peripheries of the pancasila. However, after the regime fell, this unstable assemblage was ruptured and Chineseness and Islam became incommensurable. Explicitly Muslim spiritual training precipitated a conflict between these two components of his identity. Plural identities were carefully managed during Indonesia's period of authoritarian pluralism as the state sought to minimize religious and ethnic differences and emphasize unity in diversity to facilitate faith in development above all. However, as the state's identity-building project was being challenged in the wake of the Suharto regime, pluralist identifications became more fraught.

Individuals of plural identity such as Arfan were no longer publicly called on to proclaim their allegiance to the nation but rather to Islam. Instead of being able to live somewhat tenuously as both Muslim and Chinese, the afterlife of development compelled him to publicly proclaim a position as a member of the *ummah*.

Exclusion and the Politics of Conversion

Arfan's dramatic experience during ESQ is a manifestation of a broader politics of religious difference in contemporary Indonesia. To better understand the contours of these politics, it is useful to move from considering the plural identity of a specific individual to the pluralism of Krakatau Steel's workforce as a whole. Although they were a clear minority, many non-Muslim employees at the company expressed anxiety about the increasing prominence of Islam at the company in the aftermath of the political changes associated with *reformasi*. These tensions were illustrated by the reactions of Christian employees to the ESQ training program and the increased role of Islam in the everyday life of the factory. Calls for company employees to proclaim religious faith created anxiety not only for individuals of hybrid identity but also for non-Muslims at the factory. This was an effect not only of, on the one hand, the religious pluralism inherent in the pancasila but, on the other hand, the fact that many ESQ participants claimed that the program had successfully brought non-Muslims to Islam.

Nelson, a Christian supervisor in one of the mills, attested to the change that had taken place in religious politics at Krakatau Steel. He maintained there was an increasing tendency to publicly proclaim religious identity among factory employees: "In the past five years...there is pressure from the environment [*tekanan dari lingkungan*] to become more religious, because the community here does not accept Christianity." He self-identified as a Batak and was originally from North Sumatra but had started working at Krakatau Steel in the late 1970s. Our halting conversation was held in his sweltering and cramped plywood-paneled office deep inside the bowels of a plant where massive steel slabs and billets emerged from thundering machines. I sensed that he felt, as someone who had worked his way up to a supervisory position at the company, he should be confident in speaking openly and at times our conversation was fluent. However, at other points he appeared tense and reticent to share his thoughts on the politics of religion both at the factory and in the overwhelmingly Muslim province of Banten at large.

Nelson felt that the company was fostering Islam to the exclusion of other religions practiced by factory employees. He told me that although his work colleagues were more tolerant of other religions than indigenous inhabitants of Banten, he was disturbed that since *reformasi* there had been an increase in the public practice of Islam at the company. He was especially concerned that company management supported Islam to a greater degree than Christianity. This was particularly evident in the fact that the company had recently completed construction of "mosques in every mill but no places for Christians to worship." Furthermore, Nelson said that while Muslim celebrations are observed, the "attention to Christian holidays is limited." With a pained expression he lamented a lack of equal representation: "I don't want to make problems, but I too must be recognized" (*Saya jangan membikin yang berat, tapi juga harus diakui*). Although he had taken no part in the spiritual reform programs, he viewed ESQ as an indication that Islam had become more prominent in factory life. He said, "Muslims are taught to manage their emotions through ESQ. I was offered the opportunity to attend, but I didn't want to go. Maybe they would try to convert me!"

Christian employees reported that there was little discussion of conversion to Islam during the Suharto years, but increasing compulsion to do so in the years following the end of the New Order. Nelson's suspicion of possible ulterior motives echoed the concerns of other Christian employees regarding ESQ, who reported pressure to convert to Islam either during or shortly after their participation in the program. One employee, Marius, related that members of the company labor union, SKKS,[12] encouraged him to convert. He said that this occurred immediately after he had attended an ESQ training session in Jakarta. "They tried to approach me after I had just attended ESQ because they thought that I would be influenced, but I held on to my religion." He continued, "The SKKS thinks that their religion is the true one. That is why they support ESQ!"

---

12. An abbreviation for Serikat Karyawan Krakatau Steel (Krakatau Steel Employee Union).

Marius said that several union officials had confronted him in a hotel room immediately after he had attended an early off-site training before the program had been brought to the factory. They expected that ESQ would have inspired him to reconsider his religious affiliation. Marius explained, "They asked me to convert [*masuk*] to Islam." Moreover, he claimed that he was offered material incentives to do so: "They told me that my family would be taken care of and given good positions at the factory." He said that he deflected the pressure by appealing to an argument that echoed the first tenet of the pancasila: "When they asked me to convert, I told them that I would if they could answer just one question." He told those confronting him that "the Allah that I pray to is the Allah of Adam, the Allah of Moses, the Allah of Abraham. Is the Allah to whom Muslims pray not included in that Allah? If the answer is yes, I will become a Muslim! But if not, it means that the religions are the same! That there is only one God." Thus, Marius rebuffed the entreaties to conversion through an appeal to the Judeo-Christian roots of Islam (Bulliet 2006). He was able to invoke the first principle of pancasila, the "belief in the one and only God" (*ketuhanan yang maha esa*),[13] by virtue of the fact that in many parts of Indonesia, Christians sometimes refer to God as Allah rather than the generic *tuhan,* which is also occasionally used.[14] Marius invoked the linguistic ambiguity of this distinction in spoken Indonesian, to convey the idea that he already believed in the one and only God.[15] Thus, deploying a logical appeal to the prophets of monotheism shared by Islam, Christianity, and Judaism, he was able to rebut entreaties for his conversion.

The notion that ESQ had the ability to convert non-Muslims resonated beyond Marius' confrontation with members of the union. Many participants attributed to the program an almost mystical prowess in bringing non-Muslims into the faith. In the wake of the dissolution of the authoritarian

---

13. The use of the term *maha esa* (greatest one) was designed to encompass diverse religious groups: Christians, Hindus, and Buddhists as well as Muslims. Hindus and Buddhists were included under the rubric of monotheism only by virtue of skillful hermeneutic exegesis.

14. For example, during my tenure living in parts of the archipelago as diverse as Manado, Yogyakarta, Jakarta, and Cilegon, I heard Christians refer to God as Allah. In addition, televised Christian preachers on the Sunday religious shows would use the word Allah to refer to God.

15. Aware of this linguistic ambiguity, some Indonesian speakers would sometimes differentiate the two concepts in pronunciation. Thus, they would articulate the Christian Allah in a much flatter intonation, which sounded more like "A-llah." In contrast, in referring to the God of Islam, the intonation was enunciated in the back of the throat and sounded like "U-llah."

New Order state tension between religious communities in Indonesia increased. While a few highly visible cases escalated into violent clashes (Sidel 2006), in most of the archipelago the tension simmers below the surface. When I lived in the predominately Christian region of Manado, North Sulawesi, in 2001, anecdotes about discrimination against Christians circulated widely. Edy, the eldest son in the Christian family with which I was living, invoked the Indonesian state's Suharto-era family planning program, which operated under the motto "Two children is enough" (*Dua anak cukup*) as evidence of a Muslim conspiracy. The program had been lauded by international development institutions, including the World Bank, as one of the most successful in the world and was credited with enabling Indonesia to achieve self-sufficiency in food production. However, Edy said that the program covertly discriminated against Christians, because "Muslims are permitted up to four wives. That means that a single man could have eight children, while a Christian is restricted to one wife and only two children!" He was convinced this was a state strategy to turn Indonesia into a Muslim country by devising measures to suppress the size of the Christian population, while fostering the growth of the nation's Muslim population.

These suspicions were reciprocal as Muslim employees of Krakatau Steel occasionally expressed distrust of Indonesian Christians. One common indication of this suspicion occurred in conversations I had with employees about Irena Handono. She is a former Catholic nun from central Java who converted to Islam and regularly gives lectures in which she describes a looming Christian menace in Indonesia, manifested in efforts by Catholics to convert Muslims and in which she claimed to have formerly participated.[16] Videorecordings of her lectures were popular among some employees. They were produced by Irena's NGO, the Irena Center, and featured her personal account of engaging in efforts to convert Indonesian Muslims. Irena's advocacy and the videos she produced demonstrated the

---

16. Irena Handono founded the Irena Center, which is "an organization active in Islamic proselytization, with activities in the fields of Comparative Religion and in guiding the Islamic *ummah,* especially recent converts [*mualaf*]." This description and more information about the organization can be found on the group's website, www.irenahandono.or.id (accessed August 2, 2009).

complicated legacy of pancasila religious pluralism. When I went to visit Umar (a leader of a group of activist workers discussed in the next chapter) at his home for the first time, before we sat down to talk in his living room he ushered me into an adjacent room with a television and VCD player where he played the first ten minutes or so of one of Irena's videos. The video consisted of a long lecture in which Irena provided an account of her life as a nun, her conversion to Islam, and plans by Christians to convert Indonesian Muslims. After several minutes Umar commented on Irena's claims about Christian conversion efforts in Indonesia. He articulated the widespread impression that Christian charitable projects such as bringing aid to disaster victims and providing food to the poor were in fact tactics intended to encourage conversion. He expressed a common sentiment that such practices had been quite successful: "Forty Muslim scholars [*ulama*] from Padang have become Christian.... They were bribed with money to change religions." He then said that Muslim groups were organizing in response to this threat and invoked the efforts of the emerging Prosperity and Justice Party (Partai Keadilan Sejahtera or PKS) to deliver aid to disaster victims and food and medicine to the poor.

From Authoritarian Pluralism to Market Multiculturalism

Although Krakatau Steel employees interpreted ESQ as a vehicle to strengthen Islamic identity and to purify those of plural faith, those directly affiliated with the program were more equivocal in their articulation of the goals of the program. Although the program was based in explicitly Islamic principles, as discussed in chapter 3 Ary Ginanjar and his employees contended that Islam was but one manifestation of a universal spirituality that God had imparted to all humans. Thus, Ary Ginanjar and his protégés sought to simultaneously negotiate the complex politics of religious affiliation and Indonesia's historical legacy of pancasila pluralism. In general, the ESQ trainers represented spiritual reform in much less aggressive terms than it was interpreted by some of those who participated in it. Although all the trainers were devout Muslims, they never expressed the conviction that the training was designed to persuade non-Muslims to convert to Islam.

Indeed, the religious specificity of ESQ training posed a problem for the universal claims of spiritual reform. On the one hand, Ary Ginanjar explicitly stated that the training was "based on the 6 pillars of the faith and the 5 pillars of Islam." This proclamation was the subtitle to his first and most popular book. However, Ginanjar also was convinced that the principles he identified linking spirituality to corporate success were universal and that the training would enable participants, irrespective of their religious faith, to adjust their actions to the ethical imperatives of globalization. His transnational ambitions were evident in his Vision 2050, which was an addendum to Developing a Golden Indonesia 2020. After disseminating ESQ throughout Indonesia, Ginanjar expected to compete globally with other modes of management knowledge such as the Seven Habits of Highly Effective People. Thus, he planned to disseminate the training program around the world by the middle of the twenty-first century.

Ginanjar's argument for the universality of the training was that it was premised on spirituality, which was taken to be a characteristic intrinsic to all human beings. Thus, in a theological claim that somewhat surprisingly no one exposed to spiritual training had yet identified as problematic, he represented Islam as an external manifestation of an underlying, universal spirituality. In a sense Ginanjar's claims about universality of spirituality echoed the historical legacy of pancasila, which creatively interpreted Hinduism and Buddhism as monotheistic religions to make the nation possible. However, his resolution to the problem of difference did not stop at national borders. The spiritual economy that emerged out of this assemblage was contiguous with all human beings. Pancasila, in contrast, notably excluded practices such as Confucianism, Judaism, and animism that were evident in the Indonesian archipelago.

Ginanjar's claims regarding the universality of spirituality illustrate market multiculturalism because it extends the limits of the spiritual economy beyond the borders of Indonesia and the Muslim world to all humans. Indeed, one of the initial PowerPoint slides of the ESQ training program was titled the "Peaceful Greeting" (Salam Perdamaian) and read, "If the pillars of faith and the pillars of Islam are referred to in this training it does not indicate that the training is exclusive to a specific school or religion, but rather a wish to deliver the truth. If the Qur'an is invoked in this training it is not for a specific group, but for all of humanity. The Qur'an is not for

Islam and the world is not for Islam, but the Qur'an and Islam are for the world. Islam yearns for genuine peace and joy, for oneself and for others."[17] In addition, during collective prayers, non-Muslim participants were encouraged to "pray in accordance with their own religions." There was an explicit recognition that the religious practices used in the training were not universal, even if the spirituality that they were purported to represent was considered universal. Furthermore, during the *talqin* simulation that precipitated Arfan's crisis of identification, non-Muslim participants were paired with other participants with whom they shared a common religious identity and told to pray in accord with their own religious traditions.

By market multiculturalism I refer to the fact that constituting a universal spirituality intrinsic to human beings was an important commercial strategy. Spirituality is configured as a universally valid form for the expression and explanation of pious practice. Making the program exclusive to Muslims would have limited the potential audience for the training, both nationally and globally. Thus, to achieve Ginanjar's goals, spirituality was an advantageous concept because it offered the possibility of universal appeal. In contrast to spirituality, religion is tied to a specific discursive tradition (Asad 1993). Finally, within Indonesia the economic clout of Christians outsized their numerical proportion among the national population. Businesses owned or managed by Christians were an important potential market segment for ESQ training, were Ary Ginanjar to achieve his grand vision.

Ultimately, whereas some enthusiastic participants at Krakatau Steel saw ESQ as a means of enhancing the Islamic practice of employees, ESQ trainers strategically invoked a more generic spiritual development as the goal of the training. The trainers were certainly less aggressive in their promotion of the Islamic face of ESQ training in favor of its spiritual visage. Some employees of Krakatau Steel saw identity in absolute terms, calling on those of hybrid identities to adopt Islam and intimidating non-Muslims. However, those directly affiliated with the ESQ Leadership Center advocated market multiculturalism in the wake of the demise of specific programs intended to inculcate pancasila ethics. In this latter formation spirituality was an absolutely critical concept and object, as it

---

17. A version of this statement can also be found in the first book Ary Ginanjar wrote about ESQ (Ginanjar 2001, xxii).

offered the promise of resolving the differences between particular religious traditions.

Conclusion: Democratization and the Pressure to Proclaim

This chapter demonstrates how the formation of a spiritual economy posed a challenge to Indonesia's legacy of pancasila pluralism that underlay its nationalist developmentalism. Whereas pluralism was a technology of rule used by the New Order state, it was contested in the latter years of Suharto's reign as Islam increasingly became a common denominator for the nation's population. This involved a shift in the exclusions constitutive of the nation. During the New Order Chineseness existed in an uneasy, tenuous position vis-à-vis the nation in which Indonesians of Chinese descent were never included in the national map of ethnicized provinces that constituted the polity (Thongchai 1994). However, they were instrumental to the nation because the capital held by those marked Chinese was indispensible to national modernization, particularly as the state could no longer rely on oil profits to fully fund its development ambitions. The violence against the Chinese during the 1998 economic and political crisis called this contingent truce into question. In the post-Suharto period, while official state limits on expressions of Chinese cultural practice were eliminated, other technologies of belonging produced new configurations of citizenship. Mechanisms such as spiritual training introduced new criteria for belonging. Amid the plural workforce of Krakatau Steel, the explicitly Islamic program of spiritual training suggested the Islamicization of the company to non-Muslim employees.

This conjuncture demonstrates the emergence of post-pancasila citizenship. During the Suharto era Krakatau Steel employees were represented as the purveyors of progress and development. Hard work and employee productivity were represented as virtues conducive to nationalist modernization. After the project of national development underwritten by an authoritarian state ended, spiritual reform entailed recasting productivity not as service to the nation but as religious duty. This was evident in a new configuration of citizenship in which, at a critical site dedicated to the project of national development, managers abandoned Suharto-era programs intended to cultivate the loyalty of workers through a nationalist propaganda program. In place of the state-directed P4 pancasila training program, Krakatau Steel substituted a program premised on the principle that enhanced Islamic practice was conducive to business success. The increasingly high stakes politics of religious difference in Indonesia placed an increasing burden on citizens of plural heritage to publicly proclaim their religious identities.

The events described in this chapter demonstrate how Indonesia's democratization posed a challenge to the country's nationalist pluralism. As a centerpiece of national development, Krakatau Steel once was a site for overcoming heterogeneity, as employees from across Indonesia found employment there. However, after the crisis of national identity in the wake of the collapse of the Suharto regime, Islamic spiritual reform was substituted for pancasila training as a technology for the production of citizen-workers. While these events were met with anxiety by non-Muslim employees of the plural workforce, they triggered more profound crises of identification among those of plural identity. Thus, employees such as Arfan were no longer publicly called on to proclaim their allegiance to the nation but rather to enunciate the truth of their being as Muslims (Foucault 2001). However, doing so elicited an unavoidable conflict with the portion of his heritage that he identified as Chinese. Calls to proclaim a pure identity resonate in other domains of Indonesian life as well.

Arfan's experience of inhabitation sheds light on the new practices of inclusion characteristic of democratization in Indonesia. Although during the New Order his Islamic identity and his Chinese identity were to some extent incommensurable, they were not forced into sharp relief against one another in the space of the factory. It was only after the introduction of spiritual reform and its insistence that he proclaim the truth of his being by answering the question "Who are you?" that Arfan's Chinese heritage and Muslim heritage were forced into explicit conflict, eliciting his dramatic haunting. The earlier P4 nationalist training program did not compel such existential reckoning because the answer was already assumed: one was an Indonesian. This was the identity that the authoritarian state conferred on its subjects. Thus, belonging was not posed as a question. By virtue of participation in the P4 program, one was a member of the political community. One's belonging was never in doubt and the training was more of an elaboration on what it meant to be a citizen of the nation. However, democratization compelled one to choose one's membership, on one's own and for oneself. Thus, the recurring refrain of spiritual training required participants to consistently proclaim the truth of their being.

This pressure to proclaim was perhaps more disconcerting to Christian employees of Krakatau Steel. During the New Order their monotheistic compliance with the first principle of pancasila, a belief in one God, had cast no doubt on their full membership in the nation. The introduction of explicitly Islamic spiritual reform into a site for the material production of the nation called into question the religious pluralism that was a founding principle of the nation. Furthermore, some expressed the fear that spiritual training had emboldened some managers to pressure other employees to convert to Islam. Whereas the authoritarian state had guaranteed religious pluralism under the banner of pancasila, democratization enables new exclusions from the political community because one is compelled to choose.

Finally, the tension between Islam and the nationalism evident in Arfan's episodes of spirit possession and the anxieties of non-Muslim employees of Krakatau Steel offer insight into how globalization entails the reformulation of individual identity (Comaroff and Comaroff 2009; Park 1999). The introduction of Islamic spiritual training at Krakatau Steel illustrates the connection between the erosion of an economy defined in national terms and the corrosion of nationalist identity. These simultaneous dissolutions are not abstract but evident in the constitution of new practices designed to address the challenge posed by globalization and the afterlife of development. Krakatau Steel was faced with the elimination of a protected national steel market in which it enjoyed a privileged position due to tariffs on imported steel and reliable infusions of state investment. Concordant with this vision of development was the state's promotion of a nationalist identity among state employees through the notion of unity in diversity. By 2005 both of these technologies for delimiting a national subject were rusting away. On the one hand, the protected national steel market was undone by policies associated with open borders, the end of state support, and investment capital sourced in the market. On the other hand, a program intended to promote unity in diversity and forge national solidarity out of a resolutely plural society conceded to a market-based program that suggests membership in a global *ummah* as a central axis of belonging.

6

Spiritual Politics and
Calculative Reason

I met with Umar during Ramadan in 2004 at his compact house located in the same housing development as Arfan's on the outskirts of Serang. After pestering him for several months he had finally agreed to recount the history of an employee activist group that he had led at Krakatau Steel. We had just begun our conversation when I made what Umar considered a significant gaffe by referring to him and his colleagues as workers (*buruh*). He responded gruffly, "We're not workers, we're from a state-owned company! Employees [*karyawan*] are different from workers! Workers are like those over in Cikande.... As for us at Krakatau Steel, we're not workers but employees!"[1] His response illustrated the legacy of the Suharto

---

1. Cikande refers to an export processing zone about fifteen kilometers east of Serang. Among other companies it is home to PT Nikomas Gemilang, a giant shoe company that serves as a contractor to Nike and Adidas, among others. Ill treatment of workers at this factory had led to several highly publicized labor demonstrations (for example, see www.oxfam.org.au/campaigns/nike/reports/julianto.html).

regime's efforts to discourage left-wing political activism based in notions of labor solidarity and class consciousness. The distinction that Umar assumed was self-evident was not entirely clear to me, which led to the following exchange:

> DR: I see. So you are employees. What's the difference?
>
> UMAR: Employees have permanent positions [*berkeja tetap*]. . . . They usually have a salary, maybe benefits [*kesejahteraan*]. . .
>
> DR: Oh, I see. So they are better off compared to normal workers?
>
> UMAR: The connotation of workers is . . . The head of the workers is Mochtar Pakpahan,[2] right? As for workers the connotation is employees who can be let go [*karywan yang kerja lepas*].
>
> DR: What do you mean "let go" [*lepas*]?
>
> UMAR: Not stable, they can be laid off whenever [*di-PHK kapanpun*], their wages are small, their benefits are not so good.[3] They always make demands and demonstrate in front of the parliament when they are laid off. That's the difference.
>
> DR: OK, so "employee" means that you can't be laid off at any time. That's the definition of an employee?
>
> UMAR: Well, we can be laid off, but there is a long process. . . . It takes a long time to lay us off . . . It is not as easy as with workers. That's a worker. If you say, "You're a worker, you're an employee" there has to be a distinction. If a person works in Cikande, in a shoe factory, or a clothes factory, those are all workers! But employees work at Krakatau Steel, at PLTU Suralaya, at Chandra Asri.[4] Those are all employees!

Umar's indignation at being called a worker sheds light on a recurrent question regarding labor politics after the Suharto regime. For the most part, scholars of Indonesia have been puzzled as to why organized labor

---

2. Mochtar Pakpahan was the longtime leader of the Indonesian Workers for Prosperity Union (Serikat Buruh Sejahtera Indonesia or SBSI) and a vocal advocate for worker's rights under the Suharto regime. In 2001 he founded the Social Democratic Labor Party (Partai Buruh Sosial Demokrat or PBSD). In the April 2004 Indonesian parliamentary elections the PBSD finished 24th out of 24 total parties with a total of 0.56 percent of the vote.

3. PHK is an abbreviation for *putus hubungan kerja,* which literally translates as "to sever the work connection."

4. PLTU Suralaya refers to the massive state-owned electricity plant in Suralaya. It is about fifteen kilometers north of Cilegon. Chandra Asri is a privately owned petrochemical factory located about ten kilometers southeast of Cilegon.

did not play a larger role in the political transformations associated with *reformasi* and their aftermath. This is in spite of the fact that between two and six million Indonesian wage laborers lost their jobs in the wake of the economic crisis (van Dijk 2001, 94). In the years leading up to Suharto's downfall some had predicted that workers would play a leading role in the nascent prodemocracy movement (Hadiz 1997). However, as Jeffrey Winters has noted, "labor had failed to step into the new political space...Not only did no major parties try to mobilize workers qua workers, the word '*buruh*' (worker) was scarcely ever mentioned by any political elites during the election campaigns" (Winters 2000, 148–149). The failure of an active working-class political movement to emerge after the end of the authoritarian state has puzzled scholars. Nicolaas Warouw argues that the failure of mass working-class political mobilization after the end of the New Order is due to the fact that workers were content because of their increased access to material goods. Thus, consumption foreclosed the emergence of class consciousness (Warouw 2005).

In contrast to these approaches, I contend that workers have seized certain political possibilities but that these possibilities have not taken the form of political action articulated in terms of common class interests. Rather, given the extensive political repression that characterized the New Order, workers have been more cautious and tactical. In this chapter, I show that some workers at Krakatau Steel took advantage of the new political space available to them, but they did so in a manner not of their own choosing. Indeed, the political action in which they engaged was shaped by both the history of New Order suppression of organized labor and the emerging spiritual economy. Ultimately, by their own account, they were moderately successful in achieving the changes they sought but also sensitive to the limitations on their political action. A goal of this chapter is to show that the analysis of developing faith cannot simply end with the observation that it is a management tool for disciplining corporate employees. While labor discipline was definitely one component of spiritual reform, it also produced effects that did not align with such designs. Thus, the chapter analyzes some of the unintended consequences of ESQ training at Krakatau Steel.

Following discussion of an employee activist group precipitated in part by ESQ, I describe the remuneration project, another technical intervention that Krakatau Steel managers deployed to address discontent and poor motivation at the company. I compare efforts to develop faith with the remuneration project and show that they were both neoliberal, in the sense that they both entailed the extension of economic rationality into domains from which it was previously constrained. However, whereas the spiritual economy involved enhancing religious practice to meet the imperatives of economic calculation, the remuneration project relied on purely market principles and calculative reason to motivate and discipline corporate employees.

Spiritual Politics

In February 2003 employees in the hot strip mill initiated an unprecedented movement to bring about structural changes in the hierarchy of mill management. The movement is notable because it operated outside the Krakatau Steel Employee Union (Serikat Karyawan Krakatau Steel or SKKS). Furthermore, the movement became a primary target of spiritual reform. Its members were immediately dispatched to ESQ training in spite of the fact that they were mostly lower-level operators and the early trainings at the factory were directed toward managerial staff. This movement started on February 27, 2003, when employees of the hot strip mill wrote a letter to managers threatening to shut down the factory if their demands for better working conditions were not met.

Of the six most prominent plants at Krakatau Steel, employees of the hot strip mill claimed their mill was the most vital because most of the company's revenues were generated by sales of its products. Furthermore, they took pride in the fact that the mill had the most costly and advanced high-technology equipment of any of the other mills. The high profile of the mill was a legacy of the position it held during the New Order. The construction of the hot strip mill was a landmark achievement in Indonesia's aspirations to modernity and it had served as a material symbol of the country's industrialization because it produces a commodity with widespread industrial applications. Close to the mill's most frequently used entrance was a huge bronze plaque that displayed Suharto's engraved signature and proudly commemorated the president's role in formally opening the mill in 1983. An adjacent monument, blackened with soot, prominently displayed the first hot rolled coil ever produced in Indonesia.

Because the mill generated the greatest revenue, had the most sophisticated machines, and held an important symbolic position, employees of the mill contended that salaries and conditions at the mill should mirror its importance.

The political struggle that took place at the hot strip mill was in part precipitated by historical hiring practices that had led to obstacles for employees at lower levels of the company hierarchy to attain promotions. This was due to the fact that employees from roughly the same age cohort were usually hired at around the same time. Thus, there was very little natural attrition due to retirement. Even lower-level managerial positions did not open very frequently. The movement in the hot strip mill took obstacles to promotion as their primary grievance for redress. The movement was headed by a group of longtime employees of the hot strip mill who called themselves both the team of five (*tim lima*) and, after they added a sixth member, the team of aspirers (*tim aspirasi*).[5]

The movement was significant because it operated independently from Krakatau Steel's new labor union, which was formed in 1999. From 1966 to 1998, the ability of workers at state-owned enterprises to organize was highly constrained by the Suharto regime. The official organization for employees of the company was Korpri (Korps Pegawai Republik Indonesia, the Republic of Indonesia Civil Service Corps), the civil servants' representative organization.[6] Korpri was less intended to represent state employees and more designed to support the political goals of the authoritarian state. Every member of Korpri was required to register as a member of Golkar, which was the dominant political party during the New Order. At Krakatau Steel, the structure of Korpri mirrored that of the corporate hierarchy. Thus, the chairman was a director, the second in command was a general manager, the third in command was a manager, and so forth.

---

5. Groups operating under the label of a team (*tim*) had resonance in Indonesian history. For example, under Suharto, in the so-called Sixth Development Cabinet (Kabinet Pembangunan VI), a team of six was particularly influential in setting national development policies. This group consisted of Minister of Research and Technology B. J. Habibie, Minister of Information Harmoko, Minister of Transportation Haryanto, Minister of Housing Akbar Tanjung, Minister of National Development Ginandjar Kartasasmita, and Armed Forces Commander Feisal Tanjung. These politicians maintained their influence in Indonesia in the years following Suharto's downfall.

6. Korpri was established on November 29, 1971, as the representative organization for all Indonesian government employees. Employees of state-owned enterprises were required to be part of this organization and could not establish independent unions.

Following Suharto's resignation and the events collectively referred to as *reformasi,* Krakatau Steel employees dismantled Korpri and formed a new representative organization, SKKS. While some employees appreciated the new union, the team of five was dismissive of the SKKS. They objected to the fact that, as in the Korpri hierarchy, there was no distinction between labor and management in the union's organization. This meant that all employees of Krakatau Steel were members of the union, from the level of operator to general manager. Thus, everyone who held a formal employment position at the company was a member and the only excluded employees were the five directors and the CEO. Furthermore, as in Korpri the powerful executive committee of the union was made up of employees who held managerial positions rather than lower-level operators.

Krakatau Steel employees were of mixed opinions about the efficacy of the new union. A number of employees thought that employment conditions had improved markedly after the new labor union was founded. One operator said, "There have been several successes. Wages have gone up and the welfare of the employees is better. The new buses have air conditioning so that we arrive at work fresh.... The SKKS represents the aspirations of the workers, not the management as Korpri used to do." However, a number of lower-level workers were suspicious of the new union. Some alleged that nothing had changed in spite of the formation of the independent body.

Muliadi, a critic of ESQ was also not impressed by the SKKS, claiming that it was "just a tool of management." I asked if this meant they were the same as Korpri, to which he replied that whereas Korpri had been 100 percent supportive of management, SKKS was "about 80 percent pro-management." He continued, "They are supposed to rein in the employees [*mengendalikan karyawan*]." Another operator in the hot strip mill, Heddy, concurred that "SKKS is about the same as Korpri." He said that under Korpri "the aspirations [*aspirasi*] of the employees were frozen. Korpri was predisposed toward the government. When Korpri would ask for a raise in salaries, the company would show the budget to Korpri, and they would reduce their demands." I asked him if SKKS was the same. Like Muliadi, he consented that some things had changed, but "in general" the situation remained the same. Heddy was not a member of the team of five but, like many employees of the hot strip mill, supported their activities. He explained that the actions of the team of five were necessary because

SKKS did not fully represent the interests of workers, particularly lower-level employees. He explained that the "team of five is different from the SKKS. The SKKS only supports the company [*mendukung perusahaan*], but the team of five's proposals are sometimes contrary to the policies of the company."

One member of the team of five, Hadi, explained that the group chose not to advocate through SKKS because SKKS dealt only with salary and benefit demands, not with the employment structure and work hierarchy at the company. He said that SKKS was largely ineffective about changing things that really mattered to employees and that they "only have control over things like vacation pay, money for food, and wages, but structural problems are outside their purview.... They can't achieve things like promotions [*naik pangkat*] for employees." He was also suspicious of SKKS because many of the leaders of SKKS were managerial staff, and he felt that they would not adequately represent the interests of lower-level employees. He added that although the team of five operated outside the purview of the union, this did not mean that they were radical:

> We are not anarchists [*anarkis*], we didn't demonstrate but used our brains [*kami tidak demo tapi pakai otak*]. ... We spoke to our colleagues in the canteen on our own time, we asked for a change in our position [*minta perubahan jabatan*]. ... When we met with our superiors, we asked that they address our needs. The essence [of our demands] was that we had achieved our production targets, but there were no promotions and there was no career ladder [*jenjang karir tidak ada*]. Our careers were blocked, but in other mills we saw that our colleagues were advancing.

Hadi framed the actions and demands of the team of five to make them nonconfrontational. The team of five was aware that the demise of the New Order had enabled a new space in which they could engage in political activities that would have been impossible beforehand. Umar also claimed that the training did not diminish their efforts: "We were considered provocateurs [*provokator*]. Maybe if it had happened during the New Order we would have been fired, but since it is the *reformasi* era it is more difficult, right?"

Managers responded to the demands of the team of five by attempting to incorporate them in the new spiritual economy. After the initial demands were expressed the team was dispatched to ESQ training. The program was still relatively new, as the first group of Krakatau Steel employees had only completed the program at one of the early trainings in August 2002. In April 2003, less than two months after the team of five had sent a letter of their demands to management, they were "invited" to attend the fourth cohort (*angkatan*) of ESQ at Krakatau Steel. Managers may have expected that subjecting them to spiritual reform would mitigate the increasingly vocal demands of the group.

Both Hadi and Umar claimed their participation in ESQ achieved effects directly contrary to those expected by managers because it made them more resolute. Umar said, "We were considered obstinate [*bandel*]. We were considered provocateurs, so we were sent to ESQ so our hearts would be purified." Hadi concurred that enlisting the team in spiritual training was a strategic effort to discipline the members. Using similar metaphors to those I discussed in chapter 4, he said this intervention was an effort to "soften" workers who were previously considered "hard." He said:

> We were enrolled in ESQ so that we would become soft, so that we wouldn't be hard any more [*tidak keras lagi*], but it only served to enhance our courage. ESQ teaches the truth, and when we learned the truth, we were more resolute [*jadi kita lebih tegas*]. We didn't become soft but remained hard! Our friends were oppressed [*tertindas*] and we got even more conviction [*lebih semangat*] from ESQ because we saw the truth....Maybe it was intended to extinguish the blaze [*meredam kejolakan*], but we learned from ESQ that we have a conscience [*punya hati nurani*] and what is wrong must be acknowledged as wrong!

Both Hadi and Umar asserted that they became even more steadfast in their cause because of the emphases on individual initiative and being proactive that were stressed in the training program. Thus, ESQ produced effects that did not always conform to the desires of managers to instill greater employee discipline. Hadi invoked central themes of ESQ training: that participants must learn to trust themselves, become more proactive, and take responsibility for their worldly and otherworldly fates. Hadi and Umar also became enthusiastic proponents of ESQ to the extent that Umar took to reenacting portions of the training with other colleagues at his home, as described in chapter 2.

After they completed spiritual training, managers sought to further neutralize their political activism through ongoing exposure to ESQ. The team of five was "invited" to be members of the ESQ committee. This meant that during each three-day training session they would serve as the liaisons between Ary Ginanjar's staff and the Krakatau Steel employees who were participating in the training. They assisted by shepherding participants back into the room after breaks and passing out props during interactive portions of the training. They were also responsible for monitoring participants, encouraging full involvement in the training activities, and ensuring that access to the training space was restricted exclusively to registered participants. Entrance to the hall was strictly controlled so that only officially registered participants and alumni were able to enter the room. Due to the widespread popularity of the program and the interest that it had incited among company employees, some who were not officially registered frequently sought to attend the trainings.

Hadi and Umar claimed that participation in spiritual training only enhanced their activism, which illustrates how an aspect of their struggle resonated with ESQ in an unanticipated fashion. Umar asserted that the members of the team of five all had "supernatural powers" (*kelebihan*). For example, prior to any meeting during which they had to present their demands to management one member would "sterilize" the meeting space to ensure that, according to Umar, it was free of any "evil spirits" (*jin*). Another manifestation of these powers was the ability to resuscitate those, such as Arfan, who suffered the extreme physical reactions during the ESQ training that were variously described as shock, trance, or spirit possession. Afflicted participants would fall to the floor, slump in their chairs, or wander aimlessly about the room until they were attended to by a member of the ESQ committee.

Umar asserted that the group's spiritual prowess was conducive to their political action. He told me that originally the team of five was much larger, but a number of members withdrew. He asserted that those who left "did not have spirituality... They were spies. Secret information was passed on to the directors." In contrast, those that came to constitute the team of five had a "spiritual ring through the ESQ training.... You must be honest, religious, and have good intentions to pass through the spiritual ring and become part of the team of five." Umar thus asserted that those who had betrayed the movement were deficient in their spirituality. He explained that the team often prayed together prior to meetings in which they planned advocacy activities.

Proactive Power

The team of five framed its political struggle in management idioms similar to those which ESQ sought to fuse with Islamic practice. Their central demands were distilled in another document they wrote collectively in November 2003 and titled somewhat awkwardly "The Secret to Raising the Production of the HSM to Enable Competitiveness in the Free Market Era 2004 Through Raising Work Motivation and Management as a Point of Departure for Making the HSM New, Faithful, Pure and a Prima Donna."[7] The document is significant because it provides insight into the contours of Indonesian labor activism in state-owned enterprises in the immediate post-Suharto period. Initially the members of the group were hesitant to share the document with me, citing its sensitivity, but ultimately I persuaded them to provide me with a copy.

Rhetorically the tone of the document was not confrontational. By accepting the free market as a given, the team of aspirers represented their struggle as in concert with the concerns of managers, who were increasingly worried about the ability of the company to survive given that the Indonesian steel market was being opened to foreign competition and that government subsidies were no longer forthcoming. For example, the goals stated in the proposal were to raise production and competitiveness. Furthermore, the document adopted the language of what Nigel Thrift has called "soft capitalism" (Thrift 1999). The team of five dexterously incorporated management knowledge into their demands for reform. Thus, productivity and competitiveness were directly linked to "motivation and management." Finally, the team linked "faith" and "purity" to the business goals of enhanced productivity and competitiveness, further reflecting the efforts of proponents of developing faith to introduce religious practice into workplace operations.

The proposal was framed as a set of suggestions to improve the performance of the hot strip mill and consisted of two chapters (*bab*). The first

---

7. "Kiat untuk Meningkatkan Produksi Hot Strip Mill Menuju Persaingan Era Pasar Bebas Tahun 2004 Dengan Melalui Peningkatan, Motivalsi Kerja dan Management sebagai Titik Tolak Menuju HSM Baru Beriman, Bersih dan Primadona."

chapter outlined a series of problems at the mill that led to declining productivity and the second chapter contained a list of eleven proposed solutions to these problems. The cover of the proposal is dated November 27, 2003, two days after the end of Ramadan that year. The document opens with a long sentence that positions the team of aspirers as "contributing suggestions" to the "Top Management." It states, "With the blessed mercy of God [*Tuhan*] the one and only and with his favor, at long last we make this proposal as a contribution and suggestion [*sumbang saran*] to the Top Management as a sign of our care [*kepedulian*] toward the development [*perkembangan*] of the hot rolling process, that for several years now has suffered a decrease in production because of numerous problems." It then lists a number of problems that the plant experienced, including divisiveness between employees, mechanical failure, the purchase of unnecessary equipment, the purchase of substandard spare parts, too much freedom for employees, a decline in employee motivation, and finally a lack of new promotions in spite of the fact that in the past ten years many new machines had been added.

These grievances can be divided into three broad categories for which the team of five sought intervention: interpersonal relations within the workplace, corruption, and the structural conditions of work within the factory. Interpersonal relations had become strained as factions had developed in the plant when individuals competed over access to positions and the right to sign off on purchase orders. Illustrating these turf battles Umar compared the hot strip mill to the Indonesian Army's elite Special Forces (Kopassus) because it was lucrative for midlevel managers to obtain postings there. Just as a leadership position in Kopassus provided ample opportunities for personal enrichment, he suggested that the hot strip mill likewise afforded the most opportunities to get rich [*cari kaya*] through illicit deals and collusion. He said that the mill, due to its large budget and expensive machinery, provided a greater opportunity for corruption than any other plant at Krakatau Steel. Because the team had expressed a commitment to fighting corruption in the mill, it had cultivated "sympathizers from the highest to the lowest level.... They have data [about corruption] but they don't know where to go with it." Umar said that these employees would often share data with the team of five anonymously because they were fearful of reprisals from senior managers.

The foremost demand of the team of five was to create new managerial positions at the hot strip mill. Historically, the addition of new machinery, such as a sizing press, had always entailed the creation of new supervisory jobs. Although the mill had recently added new machines, there had been no corresponding increase in the number of positions as foremen and supervisors. Umar explained that they wanted the company to expand the "number of superintendents from one to three" or the number of "supervisors from two to five" in places where new machinery had been added. He was somewhat bitter because although he had completed a university degree by going to night school and had expected that his credentials might at some point enable him to move up in the company hierarchy, this had not come to pass. He said, "I am at the lowest level, operator. Even though I am a university graduate my education was never recognized." As his voice rose and his open palm pressed down repeatedly on this thigh, he exclaimed intensely, "We [operators] have always been repressed, repressed, repressed [*ditekan*]." Employees had come to expect that the addition of new machines would mean an expansion of the plant hierarchy, but due to changes in the economic environment managers had ended this policy.

Furthermore, Umar said that members of the team had not benefited from networks based on either ethnicity or university alumni affiliations, which were a frequent avenue for employees to garner promotions. He gave a hypothetical example of how an ethnic network might serve such a purpose: "Say that a superintendent is from a certain part of Java. Then he chooses those below him, supervisors and foreman, who are also from that region. Below them there are many *kroco*.[8] [Those from Java] are more likely to get a promotion to supervisor then any of the other foremen." Umar explained that to advance in the company hierarchy one had to take a test, but the results of the tests were never made public. Thus, it was unclear if promotions were actually based on test results or whether they were attained through personal connections.

The team of five proposed ten specific solutions to the problems outlined at the beginning of the document. These included:

1. A change in the management of the hot strip mill "as soon as possible" from the level of manager through superintendent and supervisor, including a list of the specific positions that the group wanted changed.

---

8. A *kroco* is literally a small snail, but it was also used as a pejorative term for operators at the bottom of the company hierarchy. Umar belittled himself as a *kroco* several times during our conversations.

2. A change in the organizational structure of the hot strip mill and the creation of new management positions to enable greater opportunities for promotions.

3. The active solicitation of suggestions for improvements to the mill from employees so that they would be more willing to share recommendations with management.

4. The systematic implementation of the safety program. They specifically requested a return to an older schedule in which heavy equipment was changed during shift two (the day shift) instead of during shift one (the night shift), which would be less dangerous for employees.[9]

5. The installation of new television monitors to enable employees to observe parts of the plant, diagnose problems, and prevent the destruction of machinery, such as the flooding of the laminar cooling pump that had recently been destroyed because it was difficult to monitor.

6. The use of spare parts "of true quality with official Japanese or German licenses." The team asserted that the use of better parts would reduce breakdowns and corresponding decreases in mill productivity. Furthermore, they requested that the purchase of spare parts be strictly audited so that "certain dishonest people" [*oknum-oknum*] could not continue to cause the factory to lose money through illicit deals.

7. Changing the procurement process for spare parts so that office staff in the hot strip mill order such parts rather than employees of the logistics division. This call for the devolution of procurement power was a bold reference to alleged widespread corruption in the logistics division.

8. A prohibition on non-Krakatau Steel employees, specifically suppliers, visiting the factory floor.

9. The better integration of midlevel technical experts into plant operations to facilitate communication in the production process.

10. The cessation of operations in the hot strip mill between noon and 12:30 P.M. every Friday to enable employees to participate in Friday prayers.

The proposal concluded with an invocation that combined religious idioms with the managerial imperative toward proactive action. It read, "If our suggestions have a weakness, it is only because we endeavor to save the HSM from destruction and deliver it to an era of success. But if

---

9. There were three time blocks for shift workers at Krakatau Steel. Shift one (night) was from 10 P.M. to 6 A.M., shift two (day) began at 6 A.M. and ended at 2 P.M., and shift three (swing) was from 2 P.M. to 10 P.M.

these suggestions are true then they are part of a divine truth that clutches our souls and holds the heavens and earth. Amen." The closing sentence quoted from the Qur'an, "be not as those who forgot Allah, and so He caused them to forget their souls" (Qur'an 59, 19). By ending the document first with a demand for enhanced ability to participate in religious activities during the workday and then closing with a quote from the Qur'an, the team of five represented their struggle in terms that resonated with the emerging spiritual economy. Given that the company had recently begun to promote the enhanced Islamic practice of employees through spiritual training, such language was politically astute.

The tactics of the team of five illustrates a key dynamic of labor activism in the *reformasi* period because it shows how political mobilization took a subtle form that did not entail open resistance. They explicitly invoked Islamic practice as justification for their political action. Eight months before they had collated their demands in the proposal, they were assigned to spiritual training. Umar explained, "Certainly there was a plan to ESQ-ize [*meng-ESQ-kan*] the team of five. The management also did it with other colleagues who were tough [*rekan yang keras*]." However, their experience in the training did not soften their resolve. Rather the team drew on the language used and practices advocated in ESQ to advance their cause. For example, ESQ emphasizes principles of universal human equality that are central to Islam yet have not been characteristic of Muslim practice in hierarchical Java (Peacock 1978, 101–112). The very fact that people who in other circumstances had identified themselves to me as snails (*kroco*) would deign to make suggestions to senior-level managers in such a hierarchical institution shows how they had enacted the principle of universal equality that was a central tenet of ESQ.

ESQ created a new frame for political action that drew on the idioms deployed in the training but did not necessarily conform to the desires of corporate managers. The team of five couched their grievances in the idioms of the spiritual economy. One predominant theme of spiritual reform was that employees should be proactive, a notion that represented a radical change of practice in state-owned companies. Historically, decision making was considered the purview of those who held senior positions and commands were unidirectional from supervisors to their subordinates, yet ESQ promoted a democratization of knowledge because lower-level employees were encouraged to make decisions without necessarily first receiving direction from those above them.

Proactive behavior was promoted in several interactive sessions during ESQ training that stressed employees should not wait for orders if they saw a problem but rather should rely on their own judgment to remedy it. For example, the virtues of being proactive and personally accountable were graphically illustrated on the last day of ESQ training. This occurred before the final exercises when an assistant trainer led the participants in a collective rendition of a popular Indonesian schoolchildren's song. At this point, late in the day, all the participants were a bit giddy and seemed to relish the opportunity to sing a lighthearted tune. About midway through the song loud popping noises appeared to emanate from behind the three screens. The popping persisted for several minutes but no one paid much attention. Several trainees looked around with bemused and quizzical expressions. Suddenly three participants stood up and ran behind the screens at the far end of the hall. A woman returned carrying two balloons and two men came out holding Rinaldi's arms. He wore a mischievous grin, and it became apparent that he had been popping balloons backstage. He grabbed a microphone and chastised the rest of the audience for idly singing a "kiddies' tune" while allowing the disruptions to proceed unabated. He lampooned them in chiding tones, "Just a moment ago there was a disturbance with the balloons. A few of us, three people who exercised initiative, saved the nation [*bangsa*] while the others sat around dazed and confused [*terbengong-bengong*]!"

The lesson was that employees must take it upon themselves to solve problems they encounter in the workplace and not wait for others to do it for them or tell them what to do. Rinaldi said that by becoming proactive the "servants of Allah" demonstrated they were "ready for the free market" (*sudah menunggu pasar bebas*). Being a proactive, responsible worker was a central aspect of the emerging spiritual economy and was represented as indispensible to Krakatau Steel's survival amid increasing transnational competition. Examples such as the incident with the balloons were designed to encourage employees to shift from a sense of entitlement to the largesse of the state based on their credentials to the realization that only through proactive behavior and individual initiative could state-owned companies survive given the end of state support and apparently inevitable transnational competition.

The actions and resolve of the team of five demonstrate how management interventions do not necessarily achieve their intended effects. In contrast to the expectations of managers, the team of five took the incitement to being proactive as a frame through which they could further their own interests by representing their struggle in terms similar to those deployed in ESQ. The title and content of the proposal written by the team of five shows how they had adapted the frame of management knowledge to suit their own ends. Umar couched the struggle of the team of five in terms of a desire to save Krakatau Steel. He claimed, "Our goal was actually to save [*menyelamatkan*] the hot strip mill. In fact now production is expanding because of the struggle of the team of five [*bangkit karena perjuangan tim lima*]. Before *reformasi* we produced between three thousand and forty-five hundred tons per day, but after the movement [*setelah gerakan*] we did six to seven thousand tons per day. Workplace motivation was higher after our struggle!"

The success of the team of five was marked in December 2003 when Suwono replaced Ibnu as manager of the hot strip mill. Umar told me emphatically that Suwono's selection was "arranged by Allah" [*diatur oleh Allah*]. As evidence he explained:

> On his first day working here in December 2003, [Suwono] met with the managerial staff of the HSM at 10 A.M. At that meeting, he pounded his gavel [*ketok palu*] and said that he planned to stop activities during Friday prayers. Afterwards, at 11 A.M., he met with the team of five for the first time. We showed him our proposal. He read through it and when he came to solution number ten, he stopped and said, "Just an hour ago I told the managerial staff at the HSM that we would stop rolling during Friday prayers." He just pounded his gavel and determined that Muslims should observe Friday prayers [*menentukan orang Islam harus sholat Jumat*]....This means that the proposal is a sign from Allah [*berarti proposal ini merupakan petunjuk dari Allah*]....We all cried [*menangis semua*] and hugged one another. We could no longer speak, we could only cry, because after fifteen years our struggle had finally been successful.[10]

Solution ten was the team of five's request that the mill should stop rolling on Fridays at noon to enable Muslim employees to attend weekly prayers. Umar commented that Ibnu, the former manager of the hot strip mill "was not brave enough to stop activities for Friday prayers."

---

10. See chapter 4 for an explanation of the role that the circulation of tears played in constituting the spiritual economy.

In seeking to advance their interests the team of five tactically adopted a nonconfrontational approach that converged with management desires to make the company operate more efficiently. The solutions they proposed to resolve strife within the hot strip mill were unprecedented in as much as they included a call for the replacement of a cadre of mill managers. The demand that the organizational structure of the mill be changed to enable more operators to be promoted to managerial positions was similarly bold. However, the team deployed language intended to garner the favor of senior company managers in making these appeals. They framed their proposal as a means to overcome factions within the mill. Furthermore, the issues they sought to address were the large-scale problems that senior managers dealt with on a daily basis: competition, free markets, work motivation, and corporate productivity. They avoided terms such as *justice, equality,* and *class* that might have appeared threatening to the company leaders who would ultimately decide the fate of their unprecedented proposal.

Managing Motivation: From Spiritual Economies to Regimes of Calculation

As a type of rationality that entails organizing conduct according to norms of economic efficiency, the power of neoliberalism lies in its ease of combination. Thus, it can be readily integrated as an element in diverse assemblages. The creation of a spiritual economy asserted a precedent for efficiency, transparency, and rationality in Islamic practice and doctrine. Such a message appealed to managers at Krakatau Steel and other state-owned firms and private companies in Indonesia. At a later moment, although the popularity of the training program was growing sharply across the country, an increasingly influential cohort of managers at Krakatau Steel became disenchanted with the program. They had concluded that the training did not elicit the kind of cultural change that it purported to achieve. Furthermore, the team of five had drawn on the discursive practices of ESQ to advance interests that did not comply directly with the wishes of managers to instill greater corporate discipline.

At roughly the same time that some company managers were losing confidence in developing faith, a new technology—the remuneration project—

was generated to manage the conduct of corporate employees. Rather than representing economic rationality as a religious imperative this new technology sought to elicit workers motivated by calculation and fiscal self-interest. The economic calculation of the remuneration project did not necessarily wholly replace the religious rationality of the spiritual economy. Rather, like intersecting circles in a Venn diagram, they overlapped one another. These two configurations entailed different techniques to optimize human conduct according to rational calculation. The difference lay in their component parts and the means through which they were implemented.

Toward the end of my research at Krakatau Steel I interviewed several members of the rising cadre of managers who had begun to express skepticism that ESQ was achieving the transformations that would improve the human resources of the company. This disenchantment emerged gradually during the period I carried out fieldwork at the factory. Some managers who were enthusiastic proponents of the program at the beginning of my tenure at Krakatau Steel had become disillusioned with it by the end. Jajang, a senior manager in the human resources directorate, expressed this growing dissatisfaction. When I spoke with him in August 2004 Krakatau Steel had recently completed its fourteenth ESQ training session at the factory, indicating that almost three thousand employees had been subjected to ESQ.

Jajang said that he was initially attracted to ESQ because he was impressed by the possibility that spirituality could enhance the motivation of company employees. He said the most attractive aspect of ESQ was that "it reminds us not to sin, because we will have to account for it later." Jajang expected that the individual changes brought about through spiritual reform would precipitate changes on the scale of the company as a whole. He found the message that spirituality was strongly connected to individual motivation and action persuasive. He also found compelling the contention that faith in development had emphasized IQ to the exclusion of emotional and spiritual intelligence. He said, "Spirituality was not affected in our previous training programs.... The spiritual is important because it can make people do what is right...[because] it comes from the heart." According to him the biggest problem ESQ was intended to address was the problem of personal responsibility. He said that the program was expected to make employees "understand that what they do now, they must be responsible for [in the future]. . . . ESQ states that individual spirituality can be set alight so that [employees] understand that work is not just for earning money, but is also a good deed [*beramal*] . . . that work is a form of worship [*bekerja adalah ibadah*]. That work is nothing less than the individual search for Allah." However, Jajang was dismayed at the implementation of ESQ because he felt that employees by and large did not make the association between individual spirituality and their job performance. Thus, while individual religious practice was enhanced, at Krakatau Steel this had not had the effect on work motivation that Ary Ginanjar claimed it would.

Jajang's criticism of the program captured an emerging consensus among managers at the factory that the company needed techniques of employee motivation and management that were based in explicitly economic rationality rather than spiritual experience. Jajang asserted that while ESQ was a good program in general, there was no "consistency" in its "absorption." He said that although the theories on which it was based were sound, it was not "implemented well" at Krakatau Steel. In terms of "constructing a person individually, it was good, but when they return to the work environment, the environment is not conducive to the change." He explained that there was no "culture of reward and punishment" at the factory, and the ESQ principle that hard work was a worldly means of accumulating otherworldly merit had not been effective.

Jajang explained that poor workplace conduct was the effect of long-standing hiring policies at state-owned enterprises in Indonesia, specifically the notions of *padat karya* and *hajat hidup orang banyak* that were discussed in chapter 3. He invoked the Booz, Allen and Hamilton management consulting report released in 1995 that had identified a surplus of about 1,500 workers among the 5,865 full-time employees of Krakatau Steel. Jajang alleged the surplus in workers was a product of the earlier strategy of the Suharto-era state that used state-owned enterprises to create salaried, middle-class employment with the justification that the social mission of the enterprises was as important as the business mission. He said that the transformation to more "professional" management oriented to "competition" meant that the company could no longer rely on its "monopoly" position. He explained that until the early 1990s Krakatau Steel held a monopoly not only on the production but also on the marketing of steel domestically. This meant that the company was the only licensed vendor for all steel imported into Indonesia. This retailing monopoly was intended to protect the company from transnational competition under principles of import substitution industrialization. However, according to Jajang and other managers, the monopoly had been bad for the company in the long run because it had contributed to a situation in which it did not operate as a "pure business."

Jajang said the motivation of employees declined as the expansion of the company slowed. For two decades the company had steadily added new production facilities. As long as the company was building new plants, there was a corresponding expansion in the company's organization, creating new managerial level positions for workers who felt they had earned promotions. However, Jajang said that it had been "ten years since there has been any expansion in the company's capacity." Thus, "the competence of employees has gone up," but "motivation is down" because there was little possibility for promotions.

According to Jajang there were three main sources for the declining motivation of company employees. The first was that many employees had reached a glass ceiling in which employees could not move up in the company hierarchy. A point system, devised in 1973, determined salaries and organized the company's employment structure. Many employees had attained the maximum points (*poin mentok*) and thus were ineligible for raises. If a foreman had worked for twenty years as a foreman, he could not obtain any further salary increases. A second issue was that Krakatau Steel salaries were less than those at other companies, both state-owned firms and private concerns. Finally, the company had begun a practice of paying an increasing portion of employee salaries as bonuses rather than as base pay. Thus, pensions at Krakatau Steel were relatively small compared to those offered by other similarly sized companies because they were based on a percentage of an employee's base salary. Salaries no longer constituted the bulk of employees' total pay because a larger percentage of pay was based on bonuses (*tunjangan*).

Calculating Labor Value

Alongside ESQ, Krakatau Steel managers deployed other techniques to enhance employee motivation and alleviate the problems that Jajang elaborated. In late 2003 they contracted the Hay Group, a management consulting firm, to conduct an external review of salaries and benefits and their relationship to employee motivation at the company. This resulted in what was referred to as the remuneration project (*proyek remunerasi*). The goal of the project was to enhance motivation by rationalizing the company hierarchy and salary structure by concretely and clearly linking compensation to employee performance through apparently objective mathematical formulas. The old system of assigning economic value to labor was deemed ineffective because it disproportionately rewarded credentials, particularly in the form of educational degrees, rather than labor value. The remuneration project was designed to objectively calculate the contribution of individual labor relative to the company's core business, producing steel.

As described in chapter 4, under the old point system there were three separate levels of employment classification, which were each in turn divided into between twenty-five and thirty-two numbered ranks. The A-level was for management level employees, from foremen to general managers. The B-level was for operators (*pelaksana*), and the C-level was for lower-status clerical workers who did not possess advanced degrees. One problem with this system was that operators who worked in production resented the fact that people who did much less physically demanding work in air-conditioned offices were often positioned higher in the point system than those who did the more intense labor inside the factories.

A further problem with the point system was that it facilitated the notion of distinct and separate categories of employees at precisely the moment that the company was advocating collective unity in the face of increasing transnational competition and the global integration of the steel market. A common refrain of management was that in the face of these threats employees should unite to prevent the collapse of the company. The need to unify to ensure the survival of the company was often invoked in official corporate communications. This message was repeated in corporate communications. For example, the cover page of the December 2003 company magazine had a huge headline quoting the chairman of the company's board of trustees and read "God Willing Krakatau Steel Will Continue to Survive" (Insyallah Krakatau Steel Tetap Eksis). The tenuous condition of the company in an increasingly global steel market was often reiterated. This message was also expressed later that month when the CEO,

Daenulhay, delivered his annual address to an assembly of employees, who were seated in the grandstand of the stadium built for Pelita KS, the company-sponsored soccer team. He stood on a podium meagerly sheltered from a steady drizzle and invoked the specter of the extraordinary growth of Chinese steel production as an incentive for employees to pull together and exercise more diligence at work. He ominously declared, "They will soon be able to produce almost three hundred million tons per year and we only produce two and a half.... We must be cautious of global oversupply." In dire tones he continued, "I want to remind you of the possibility of the death of the company" (*mati perusahaan*), before adopting a motivational approach and exhorting "in spite of these challenges, we can prevent it" through "hard work and cooperation."

These admonitions rang somewhat hollow given the history of inequity between employees of different rank. Efforts had been underway since the end of the Suharto regime to eliminate distinctions between ranks. Suwono, who before his appointment as the lead manager of the hot strip mill had been the leader of the SKKS, told me that one of his first initiatives after he was made the organization's founding chief was to insist that all the identification badges be of the same color. Before the year 2000 badges for management employees were of a different color than those for nonmanagers. This had made status differences instantly apparent between workers.

In spite of these repeated appeals for common cause among factory employees, the three separate tracks at Krakatau Steel created the impression of categorically different employees. The main problem was that it was difficult, if not impossible, for most employees to move between tracks. Thus, B- and C-level employees could never reach the managerial positions restricted to A-level employees. The goal of the remuneration project was to enhance employee motivation by forging a single track. In so doing the consultants sought to create the appearance that even the lowest-level company employee could ascend to the upper echelons of the company hierarchy. A major innovation of the remuneration project was to replace the three-tiered hierarchy of the point system with a single-tiered grade system.

In addition to reforming status distinctions, the remuneration project also sought to more accurately calculate salaries and raises with respect to the company's core business. A recurring grievance among plant workers was that they were paid less than office workers even though their labor was more critical to the survival and profitability of the company. Further, employees from different plants sought to claim that their plant was the most critical to the financial health of the company. One senior manager provided me with the PowerPoint slides from the final presentation that the Hay Group consultants made to Krakatau Steel managers in March 2004. The presentation consisted of fifty-three slides divided into four sections: "the evaluation and classification of positions," "the system and structure of remuneration," "the incentive system," and "recommendations for future steps." According to the slides, the objectives of the remuneration project were threefold. First was to "develop and implement a remuneration system that is just and competitive to create a better work climate." The second objective was to "develop a remuneration system that can be applied for long-term but nevertheless is flexible enough to face business changes and the needs of the company." The third objective was to "have a human resources system and policy that more closely corresponds with systems that are used by other leading companies."

In technical language the report carefully defined the central terms it used to describe efforts to revise the system of employee compensation. "'Just' refers to [*adil berarti*] the correspondence between status and function at the factory. 'Competitive' [*kompetitif*] means a system that works according to market practices [*praktek pasar*] and can successfully recruit, maintain and motivate employees [*memotivasi karyawan*] to perform work effectively and efficiently. A 'good work climate' refers to human resources systems that are of sound basis so that employees can optimize [*mengoptimalikan*] their contribution and energy to support the achievement of company goals and targets." Thus, the remuneration project sought to reorganize workplace conduct according to neoliberal principles by extending market rationality into a domain that had previously been organized to norms that were not strictly economic. Previously employees had been compensated according to the prestige of their credentials, but the remuneration project sought to tie compensation directly to one's function in the factory. Whereas under the old regime recruitment and promotion had been based on personal connections, the remuneration project was designed to ground them in competition and merit under the presumption that so doing would more effectively motivate employees. Moreover, by making the knowledge of this system public, the remuneration project was designed to create a system in which employees, *of their own accord,* would optimize their own labor in accordance with the goals of the company.

The introduction of market rationality to influence the will of company employees was apparent in the reclassification of job rankings according to a set of abstract norms. Jajang asserted that the new classification system was based on three "objective" criteria: "know-how, problem-solving, and accountability." Know-how referred to the technical knowledge a given job required, its management breadth in terms of the number and diversity of subordinates, and the "human relations skills" critical to performing the job. Problem-solving was defined as the skills needed to address the everyday challenges for which a particular employment position was responsible. This included the number of challenges that an employee faced during an average workday. Accountability was defined as how much "freedom to act" was characteristic of a specific employment position; specifically it measured the number of independent decisions that a given position required. It also attempted to measure the "area of impact" one's decisions affected and the "nature of impact" of those decisions. This evaluation of job rankings enabled the production of a quantitative index by which all employment positions could be objectively ranked. The result was a single hierarchy into which every company employee could be assigned.

The second intervention the Hay Group made was to the system and structure of remuneration, which proposed two significant changes. First, salaries at Krakatau Steel would be benchmarked to other leading Indonesian companies. Second, an employee's total remuneration would consist more of base salary than bonuses and other benefits. In the 1990s and 2000s the company increased employee compensation by giving out large bonuses rather than increasing salaries because managers were concerned about the increasing pension burden that the company faced. By handing out substantial cash bonuses the company alleviated employee demands for increased compensation in the present without committing themselves to huge future payouts, due to the fact that pensions were indexed to base salary (but not bonus income). Employees were conscious of this strategy because stories circulated about colleagues who had retired only to find their pension incomes did not meet their living expenses. This became a particularly acute problem after the 1997–1998 financial crisis when the value of the rupiah dropped precipitously, triggering steep price increases for basic commodities. According to the Hay Group, base salaries at Krakatau Steel in 2004 composed only 31 to 43 percent of an employee's average total compensation whereas at other leading Indonesian companies base salaries amounted to 64 percent of the total.

The remuneration project also introduced a new incentive system, which was designed to increase work motivation through the implementation of an objective and transparent system for the payment of incentive bonuses. The system was to be formula-based so that the "calculation of incentives paid to employees would be based on a formula agreed to [by the SKKS and company management]." The Hay Group devised the following formula to calculate the sum total of incentive payments:

(Conversion Costs + Composite Spending + Yield and Purchasing Efficiency + Margin Trading + Plant Availability + Interest Expense) × (Claims + Collection Period + On Time Delivery) / 3

Once the total incentive funds available were known, managers and employees could use another set of equations, the distribution formulas, to calculate the bonuses to which they were entitled. In order to derive this figure four successive equations were devised:

1. progressive value = total incentive funds/(grade factor × work unit factor)
2. total incentive funds = 20% × efficiency value
3. maximum total funds for distribution = maximum of 30% of total funds
4. incentive per employee = progressive value × grade factor × work unit factor × key management performance factor

Grade factor, work unit factor, and key management performance factor were all variables the Hay Group created to facilitate the calculation of the incentives that each worker was due.

The variables to be used in calculating these bonuses would be mutually agreed on and made widely available to company employees. The report stated, "Targets from each parameter used in the incentive program should be agreed upon and communicated to every employee and unit in the organization." The impetus for reforming incentive payments was that doing so would "avoid delays in deciding and paying incentive to employees, reduce subjectivity [*mengurangi subyektifitas*], be easy to socialize [*sosialisasi lebih mudah*],[11] be transparent [*transparan*], enable employees to calculate the incentives they were to receive themselves, and be more effective in increasing the motivation of employees."

These revisions to the incentive system marked a profound transformation in corporate practice at Krakatau Steel because it represented a shift from restrictions on the circulation of knowledge to a new regime in which the broad circulation of knowledge among employees was viewed as the best means to enlist employees in their own government and to enhance their work motivation. During the Suharto years, secrecy was a paramount value in management practice at Krakatau Steel. Like the results of the entrance test that Umar referred to above, the process for determining incentive payments had never been disclosed publicly. The formulas and criteria for the distribution of incentive bonuses were unknown to all but a select few senior employees. This corresponded with one of the guiding principles of the New Order state, as secrecy had been a central strategy of political control in Indonesia during Suharto's rule (Butt 2005; Schrauwers 2003; Siegel 1998). However, advocating that certain kinds of previously concealed knowledge be made available to all employees was a radical change for governing employees of state-owned enterprises. The remuneration project entailed making knowledge about incentive payments public under the assumption that the employees would then apply this knowledge to their own practices and modify their comportment accordingly.

Neoliberalism is at work here in that rather than being told the value of their bonuses, employees would be enlisted in their own government by being empowered with the tools necessary to calculate incentive payments themselves. Bonuses would be based primarily on how much steel a given mill was producing, the time it took to reach production targets, and the operating costs of such production. Employees would be informed of the exact formula that captured these variables and thus could calculate themselves exactly how much extra income they would generate in so doing. This relatively mundane change had far-reaching implications because it reframed the relationship between knowledge and power. The new regime sought to make knowledge public under the rubric of transparency. Transparency was expected to engender increased productivity, which was

---

11. Meaning that employees could understand the system easily and would be receptive to its adaptation.

mutually beneficial for both the company and individual employees. The company would accrue increased profits and the workers would receive more income. The introduction of market logic was premised on making knowledge about the distribution of workplace resources transparent. By making production data and the formulas on which incentives were calculated widely available, managers expected employees to perform a task that was previously the exclusive domain of a few experts: calculating the incentive payments to which employees were entitled. In addition to disclosing the formulas for calculating these incentives, production and sales data would also be broadly disseminated. Thus, a whole set of statistics, such as composite sales (*penjualan komposit*), mill efficiency, and the percentage of on-time deliveries, would be made available to employees so that they could rationalize and optimize their own productive capacity.

One of the final slides in the report illustrated the Hay Group's competence concept (*konsep mengenai kompetensi*). The slide showed a photograph of an iceberg with the massive submerged portion labeled "behavioral competence" while the smaller portion of the iceberg above water was labeled "technical competence." In the image, technical competence corresponds to "skills" and "knowledge," while behavioral competence corresponded with "social role," "self-image," "characteristics," and "motivations." Although the graphic was secular in its content, it further illustrated how the afterlife of modernization entailed posing development as an ethical rather than a technical problem. The implication was that "soft" competencies are less visible in an industrial organization like Krakatau Steel but more important because they constituted a larger portion of the competencies necessary for a successful organization (Huczynski 2006; Jackson 2001).

The remuneration project was designed to address discontent among employees in the production facilities. The response was mixed, but as expected the project was most appreciated by employees who worked in various aspects of the company's core steelmaking business. Employees in those roles were pleased with the revision of corporate compensation policies because they felt it more accurately reflected their contributions to the company's bottom line. However, employees that worked in office jobs, such as the company's education and training or public relations departments, were by and large unhappy with the program. This latter group had been largely located in the lower-tiers of the A-level under the old point system. Operators who worked in the plant were all on the B-level.

The remuneration project eliminated the lettered tracks and substituted a single fifteen-grade hierarchy for what had previously been three lettered tracks. As a result, many office workers suddenly found themselves equal in status to factory operators who, although less well educated (at least formally), nonetheless were classified as performing labor that was perceived as more instrumental to producing steel, the core business of the company.

Many hot strip mill employees saw the implementation of the remuneration project as a victory for the team of five. One operator in the mill, Heddy, said he thought that remuneration would equalize wages between those that worked in offices and those that worked in production. He said, "According to remuneration, the biggest raises would be in the factory. The office only prepares things for production. The factory employees sweat and use their own power." Heddy spoke about the team of five with admiration and attributed their success in effecting remuneration to their previous participation in ESQ: "After ESQ the team of five understood their duties and rights. It emboldened them to seek justice."

Support for the remuneration project was premised on the contention that it was a universally valid standard. Suwono, the newly appointed manager of the hot strip mill, said that the introduction of the grade system had incited a lot of protest among supervisors and superintendents at Krakatau Steel because they did not feel that the new system recognized their positions and abilities adequately. He said that although some changes would be made, the old point system had served the company for nearly thirty years and needed to be reformed to reflect new approaches to human resources management. In his eyes, the grade system was a universal standard that Krakatau Steel had to adopt to enable it to compete. He said, "All the world-class companies use the grade system. That is why we have to use it too."

Conclusion: Two Manifestations of Neoliberalism

The spiritual economy evident in the project of spiritual reform and the secular remuneration project overlap in some respects but also contain key differences. Both entailed contracting outside consultants that recommended prescriptions based in management knowledge and were designed to enable the company to better compete in an increasingly global steel market. However, the objects that were created in achieving this goal differed. Spiritual economies refer to the assemblage of religious practice and management knowledge to inculcate work ethics conducive to corporate competitiveness. The remuneration project was grounded in entirely secular reason in that it recommended the introduction of transparency, the democratization of corporate hierarchy, and mechanisms that purported to objectively calculate the value of employee labor.

Both projects saw boosting employee morale and motivation as critical to achieving the goal of greater competitiveness. In the spiritual economy labor was transformed into religious worship. Thus, hard work, self-discipline, and efficiency were reconfigured as moral values that enabled otherworldly salvation. Spiritual economies entailed inspiring confidence in something that is ultimately unknowable: one's fate after death. In contrast, the secular neoliberalism of the remuneration project was based entirely on transparent, worldly reason. Employees were provided with the criteria by which their labor would be valued and the calculation of such value would be composed according to objective, rational criteria. Labor had absolutely no significance other than its ability to produce earthly value.

To raise employee motivation, both projects presumed a self-interested subject who would be motivated by incentives, but the spiritual economy was based on fear of the unknown and self-interest in salvation, whereas the remuneration project was premised on the assumption that economic rationality was a universally valid means of human motivation. Spiritual economies refer to the creation of subjects who are motivated by self-interest in their otherworldly salvation. The primary incentive was the prospect of such salvation. This subject was expected to act in a way that was also conducive to the interests of the corporation because according to this scheme hard work benefited the company as much as the individual. In contrast, the remuneration project presumed a subject who was above all interested in advancing his or her individual economic interests. Thus, an employee's economic self-interest would encourage him or her to act in ways that are simultaneously in the interest of the corporation. The incentive used to excite worldly self-interest is a system that transparently represents the relationship between worldly labor and personal profit.

Further, both systems sought to instill individual accountability, but the means through which subjects were made accountable differed. The spiritual economy described the introduction of market rationality into religious practice. Compliant with the norms of so-called audit cultures (Strathern 2000) participants in spiritual reform were instructed that their otherworldly fate would be determined by their record of actions in the present. Thus, each good deed and sin were recorded by angels, and only a surplus of merits would enable someone to be admitted to heaven. Similarly, the secular remuneration project was designed to make employees personally accountable but based on entirely worldly calculations. The value of their labor was not evaluated by supernatural beings beyond sense experience but by employees themselves through mathematical equations. Thus, employees would be enlisted in the project of calculating their own incentive bonuses through publicly disclosed statistics on corporate performance and the dissemination of the formulas used to compute bonuses.

At Krakatau Steel, both the spiritual economy and secular neoliberalism shared a similar scale because both were envisioned as universally valid. However, the basis on which they made these claims to universality differed. Proponents of spiritual reform assumed that it was universal, because it is based on Islam which was depicted as an outward manifestation of a universal spirituality. Further, Ary Ginanjar envisioned the scope of ESQ training on a global scale. His Vision 2050 entails disseminating ESQ around the planet, just as other management knowledge brands, such as the Seven Habits of Highly Effective People, are found worldwide. Similarly, the remuneration project was grounded in what was represented as a universal principle: all human beings are motivated by rational self-interest. Thus, work motivation could be enhanced through objectively representing the value of labor so that every employee would seek to maximize his or her financial benefit. The grade system was designed to enhance motivation by creating the appearance that even the lowliest operator could ultimately become a CEO. Assigning corporate employees to a position in a single hierarchical table was thought to be a universally valid way of structuring organizations, as is evident in Suwono's claim that Krakatau Steel had to adopt this system because it is utilized by all "world-class companies."

Finally, the mode through which each of these reforms was introduced was similar in that neither relied on the coercive force of state violence. The authoritarian New Order had relied on violence to ensure social and labor control. In contrast both spiritual reform and the remuneration project enlisted workers in their own self-government through the exercise of their own reason. Spiritual reform was designed to elicit the ethics of worshipping work through an elaborately choreographed multimedia presentation. This presentation was designed to elicit the affective responses deemed conducive to cultivating spiritual discipline. In contrast, the secular remuneration project entailed a sparer presentation without enthusiastic displays of affect. PowerPoint was used, but there were no inspirational videos on Islamic history and doctrine, no group cheers, no collective pleas for atonement from Allah, no paeans of praise for the prophet, and no communal prayers. It involved the introduction of a new bureaucratic system with wholly transparent rules to enlist the governed in the project of their own government.

Thus, spiritual reform was just one tool at the disposal of corporate managers to address the challenges that the company faced as an effect of broader-scale political and economic changes. When spiritual reform reached the limit of its effectiveness—demonstrated when the team of five reinterpreted ESQ to advance their own interests—managers turned to other interventions to ameliorate employee discontent. Each of the schemes that I have described, the ESQ training program in earlier chapters and the team of five and the remuneration project in this one, entails a specific intervention designed to resolve real world problems. The passing of the Suharto regime had opened up a new space in which unprecedented forms of action were suddenly possible. This included the unique assemblage of Islamic practice and management knowledge represented in the spiritual economy. It also included the ability for lower-level company employees to make demands for better working conditions. Finally, the end of massive New Order support for industrialization precipitated the introduction of a new hierarchical arrangement that was premised on instilling motivation through incentives and transparency rather than coercion and secrecy.

The contrast between the two technologies that were deployed to enable Krakatau Steel to compete in an increasingly global marketplace bring into relief some of the salient differences between what I call a spiritual economy and the secular neoliberalism represented in the remuneration project. Both are neoliberal in the sense that they share many formal similarities. Both seek to enhance workplace motivation, accountability, self-interest, and employee discipline. They also make common assumptions about human nature and the universality of their attendant modes of practice. Yet in terms of content there are key differences. One seeks to bring otherworldly calculations into worldly action and the other is based on purely worldly concerns. What is at stake here are two distinct types of rationality; the first seeks to combine otherworldly and worldly concerns and the second is premised on making decisions based on variables that are fully known and knowable.

These two systems demonstrate the flexibility of neoliberal governance. The introduction of economic rationality into domains that were previously not subject to calculation took different forms. Yet, both were premised on common values of accountability, self-interest, and personal responsibility. The goal in both cases is to elicit a type of power that links self-government with collective government by aligning self-interest with collective interest.

Conclusion

Life Not Calculated?

This book has examined the assemblage of religious resurgence, economic globalization, and fading nationalist developmentalism in Indonesia. I have shown how the spiritual economy that emerged from this assemblage is composed of a unique combination of religious ethics and principles for business success. In so doing, I treat globalization not as an era, nor as a culture or system, but rather as a set of practices. While some have shown that globalization entails the configuration of new spaces (Appadurai 1996; Gupta and Ferguson 1997b), my account has focused on the rationalization of practices. Thus, I have charted an anthropology of globalization attentive to the reconfiguration of everyday life created by the extension of economic rationality into domains from which it was previously limited. A spiritual economy entails the development of worldly asceticism, the practice characteristic of this extension. It is precisely this asceticism that is deemed conducive to corporate survival in the face of the end of state support and an increasingly integrated transnational economy.

In contrast to approaches that examine the globalization of religion and globalization as religion, I have analyzed religion as globalization in that I have demonstrated how religious values are made compatible with the integration of financial markets, production systems, and labor markets across national borders. In addressing this articulation, I shed light on the question with which Max Weber concluded *The Protestant Ethic*. Weber suggested that the ultimate reach of the ethic of worldly asceticism at the heart of the spirit of capitalism was unknown, writing "no one knows who will live in this cage in the future, or whether at the end of this tremendous development entirely new prophets will arise, or there will be a great rebirth of old ideas and ideals, or, if neither, mechanized petrification, embellished with a sort of convulsive self-importance" (Weber 1990, 182). Ary Ginanjar could be interpreted as a new prophet. ESQ might be seen as a kind of mechanized petrification. However, what I found most striking about spiritual reform was that it sought to configure an ethic of worldly asceticism grounded in Islam. This sober, austere, rationalized way of life entailed reconfiguring labor as a religious calling and the methodical cultivation of Islamic virtues. At Krakatau Steel and beyond, the spiritual economy I describe entailed the construction of an iron cage, in which calculative reason was conjoined to a particular interpretation of Islamic practice.

Examining the effects of globalization, anthropologists have focused on the end of state social guarantees, the dissolution of the borders of the nation, and growing class inequality. This book reveals a less discussed dimension of globalization: the fact that it demands more individual labor, in terms of greater individual responsibility and accountability and ultimately more time invested in labor. Perhaps because work holds a privileged place in our morality, critiques of globalization and neoliberalism that have emerged in anthropology and its allied disciplines in recent years have been less attentive to this imperative. However, this was precisely what was at stake for employees of Krakatau Steel as they faced increasing transnational competition and the end of a development regime in which the viability of the company was guaranteed through state investment and protection. Spiritual economies capture the technical approaches through which managers at the company sought to instill the ethical maxim that "work is worship."

I have also demonstrated that the assemblage of religious practice and economic globalization does not necessarily elicit either false consciousness or resistance. For methodological, ethical, and empirical reasons, I have avoided these explanations. The methodological approach I adopted in this book precludes false consciousness as an explanation of religious resurgence because the latter presumes that the analyst has greater insight into the predicament of those under analysis than the analyzed themselves have. In addition, false consciousness fails to explain spiritual reform movements such as ESQ on other grounds. As described in chapter 2, spiritual intervention was primarily directed at, and more successful among, managerial staff than it was among the lower-level company employees, such as operators. Thus, spiritual reform was as much an intervention that managers targeted at each other and themselves as it was something directed at those over whom they exercised administrative authority. To managers who had long benefited from the Suharto regime, now discredited as corrupt, the new spiritual economy offered a means to publicly renounce their complicity with the authoritarian state and atone for the benefits they had accrued by virtue of their association with it.

Furthermore, spiritual economies elucidate a dimension of the articulation of religion and capitalism that has perhaps been under recognized in contemporary social scientific work. Rather than seeing religion as a reservoir of resistance against, or realm of refuge from, globalization, I have shown how novel interpretations of religious practice make Islam conducive to increasing transnational competition, free markets, greater political freedom, and the end of state guarantees. Such an articulation does not represent a retreat into magic, mystery, or the occult but rather the cultivation of ascetic practices according to which work is reconfigured as a form of worship.

Does It Work?: Regimes of Calculation

This book has analyzed a particular sociotechnical scheme for managing and optimizing human conduct by designing a new laboring subject congruent with the afterlife of development. I have shown how reformers in Indonesia produced a spiritual economy by designing a mode of Islamic practice that is conducive to corporate competiveness and productivity. They argued that the principles for success found in human resources, life-coaching, and self-help primers were latent in the prescriptions for a devout Muslim life contained in the Qur'an and the *hadiths*. By intensifying the Islamic practice of employees, ESQ trainers expected to ensure the viability of Krakatau Steel and other state-owned firms given the end of state support for industrial modernization, the looming specter of privatization, an economy no longer defined in national terms, and the formation of new and potentially more confrontational labor unions. Given the substantial investment in this project, corporate managers, spiritual reformers, company employees, and outside observers were left with an obvious question: Does it work? Such a question is deceptive in its apparent simplicity and presents a variety of methodological, ethical, and ultimately political challenges.

First, a definitive claim about the efficacy of spiritual reform presents a methodological challenge. Simply put, what techniques exist to resolve this question? That is to say, what evidence would prove or disprove the effectiveness of spiritual reform? Given that the object of spiritual reform is to reconfigure human conduct, what are the criteria by which one could evaluate such reconfiguration? Measuring changes in human conduct is not the same kind of intellectual enterprise as counting the number of electrons around an atom or determining the rate at which a rainforest is shrinking (Latour 1999). Although there is some evidence to suggest that it was effective, such evidence is more anecdotal than statistical, more para-ethnographic than positivist.

The method of para-ethnography developed by Holmes and Marcus argues that anthropologists should attend to how those under study addressed this question, and indeed, it was a question that was not merely academic. Proponents of ESQ also often wondered whether the techniques deployed actually achieved the ambitious goals expected and there was an economic imperative for proving their success. Perhaps predictably, Ary Ginanjar had some calculative metrics for evaluating the success of spiritual reform, which he readily shared with his audience and other observers. When I asked him whether ESQ was achieving its goals, he told me that after Krakatau Steel started using ESQ its Good Corporate Governance ranking rose to "fourth best in the country among state-owned companies, its highest ever."[1] Managers concurred that the steel company's

---

1. The Good Corporate Governance program is described in chapter 2. It was designed to increase the transparency of corporate information. As noted in chapter 6, secrecy was a hallmark of

performance in this index had improved around the same time as spiritual reform was introduced, although they did not attribute it wholly to the introduction of ESQ training.

ESQ trainers cited other examples of the efficacy of their methods. In the morning of the first day of the training, a chart was projected that showed a remarkable increase in production following the implementation of ESQ at a sprawling Pertamina fuel production facility near Cirebon, West Java. The slide illustrated that oil production at the facility rose from fourteen thousand barrels to twenty-two thousand per day. A subsequent slide reproduced an article from the Pertamina employee newsletter that attributed the rise in production to the fact that company employees had recently participated in ESQ. Participants in the training remembered this story and retold it to me afterwards in justifying the efficacy of spiritual reform in improving economic productivity.

However, even ardent proponents of spiritual reform were not wholly convinced by this kind of evidence. Haidar, the young ESQ trainer who had previously delivered Seven Habits training programs at Krakatau Steel and elsewhere, expressed an interest in enrolling in a graduate program in the social sciences in the United States. He told me that he wanted to complete a dissertation because he wanted to prove that the principles on which ESQ was based on were true. He said that such research was needed because "we need valid methods to prove that spirituality can increase effectiveness. Then we can be more effective marketing the idea to institutions and businesses.... [But] we need systematic research to prove this." I encouraged him to pursue graduate study but cautioned that most methodological approaches in use in reputable scholarly institutions in North America discouraged academic studies in which researchers knew the answers to the questions they posed before investigating them empirically. Several proponents of ESQ intimated that they thought I would be in a position to verify the efficacy of their program. However, when these suggestions were broached, I explained that I understood the role of anthropology as the documentation of practices, the analysis of their disciplinary relevance, and the diagnosis of their implications for human life rather than their mechanistic evaluation.

---

government practice during the Suharto era. The move toward promoting transparency is complicit with the introduction of initiatives such as the remuneration program.

In typically visionary fashion, Ary Ginanjar realized that the uncertainty over the efficacy of ESQ provided a business opportunity as well as a chance to more deeply inculcate the values he advocated. In response, in April 2008 he launched the Mission Statement and Character Building (MCB) training as the second step of ESQ training. Oriented toward alumni who had completed the first-stage training, MCB focused on practical methods to more solidly implement the principles developed in the initial training in daily work life. He also initiated the ESQ Parenting program to extend the values advocated in ESQ into the family life of past participants.

The facts presented in chapter 2 indicate that many Indonesians were convinced that the program achieved its objectives. By 2007 the number of people enrolling in the program was growing by two hundred thousand annually. ESQ had attracted the support of some of Indonesia's most powerful political, business, religious, and military figures. Past participants in ESQ continued to support it by attending alumni meetings, recommending it to their friends and relatives, buying books and other media that ESQ produced, signing up for the second-stage program, and perhaps most materially by investing in shares to support the construction of a twenty-five story skyscraper and convention center in south Jakarta. There was no shortage of anecdotal accounts, some of which I have reproduced, of people who had experienced what they understood to be instances of profound spiritual transformation as a result of the training.

Conversely, there is also evidence that indicates that ESQ did not achieve its intended effects in every case and at times led to consequences that were unintended. Some saw the program as management propaganda intended to deceive employees. Others said that it tainted Islam by associating the religion with commerce. Others expressed concern that the explicitly Islamic content of the training threatened the pluralist, pancasila value of unity in diversity on which Indonesia had been founded. Furthermore, certain events exceeded the imperative toward rationalization. The episodes of spirit possession precipitated during ESQ were far removed from the effects that the authors of ESQ intended, as was the team of five movement that drew on practices advocated in ESQ to advance their own political goals. Schemes for social engineering do not always achieve their designed effects with perfect precision. They are put into motion in the world and their outcomes are effects of the vagaries and contingencies of social life.

Evaluating the effectiveness of ESQ is further problematic because a central presupposition of this book is that scientific reason creates social formations as much as it transparently represents them. Thus, in chapter 2 I showed how Ary Ginanjar used mathematical formulas, statistical studies, and accounts from leading scientific institutions that purported to show a positive correlation between spirituality and business success to create the truth of ESQ. I do not adopt this position to suggest that science is untrue but rather to show that it is not transcendental. Because human beings are both the subjects and objects of scientific knowledge, scientific representations are social facts (Rabinow 1986). Thus, they make the world as much as they represent the world.

Ultimately, the greatest obstacle to addressing the question, "does it work?" is an ethical one, because the question is a product of the very reason that this study takes as a central object of analysis. I hope that this book inspires reflection on the increasingly widespread presumption that economic rationality and calculative reason are universally valid means for organizing and living human life. My goal has been to show that, given the inheritance of modernist social science in which religion and the economy were consigned to distinct spheres (Asad 1993), anthropologists have been inattentive to the extent these two domains could be made compatible. Thus, spiritual economies show how economic and religious rationalities can be combined and market logic can be introduced into domains that were previously considered external to the market.

The key ethical issue then is that the question, "does spiritual reform work?" is a product of the very economic rationality that is the central object of analysis in this study. The question presumes that objective calculation, rational manipulation, and social improvement are necessary or desirable outcomes of scholarly inquiry. It is a question born of a threefold impetus in our modernity toward social engineering, the calculated improvement of human life, and the rationalization of human conduct. My objective is not to answer the question but rather to encourage reflection on why it is posed and ultimately, perhaps, to inspire ways of living not structured by such calculus. Thus, if this book is a critique, it is a critique of the reason that demands that we live our lives according to the principles of rational calculation inherent in such a question.[2]

Faith in Numbers

Developing faith through calculative intervention is occurring not only in Indonesia, Asia, or what in more halcyon times was called the developing world. The financial crisis of 2008 has made this fact readily apparent. In the wake of the near cataclysmic meltdown in global financial markets, political leaders and technocrats alike responded by seeking to restore faith and confidence in the economy. In a March 2009 address to the U.S. Congress, British prime minister Gordon Brown intoned that America's "faith in the future has been, is, and always will be an inspiration to the whole world." He concluded his address by enjoining the Congress in terms resonant with the historical echo of faith in development, "Let us restore prosperity and protect this planet and, with faith in the future, let us together build tomorrow today" (Brown 2009). In addition to his quasi-ecclesiastic appeals to "hope" during his election campaign, U.S. president Barack Obama likewise saw the economic cataclysm as a crisis of faith. Following a G-20 summit in April 2009, he said, "I have no doubt, though, that the steps that have been taken are critical to preventing us [from] sliding into a depression.... I think that they will have a concrete effect in our ability ... to create jobs, save jobs that exist, grow the economy, loosen up credit, restore trust and confidence in the financial markets" (Obama 2009a). These entreaties were not solely the provenance of the avatar of hope. In response to Democratic initiatives, Republican members in the U.S. House of Representatives introduced the Free Market Protection Act (HR 7223) to, in the words of one member, "provide Wall Street a mechanism to use private capital to restore faith in financial markets" (Bartlett 2008).

Such efforts characterized not only new world optimism. In October 2008, after the leaders of the four largest European economies (Germany,

---

2. As such this book contributes to a broader anthropological conversation that has sought to reduce the chasms that often separate theory and practice, object and analysis, and ethics and knowledge (Holmes and Marcus 2005; Maurer 2005; Miyazaki 2004; Ong and Collier 2005; Rabinow and Dan-Cohen 2005; Riles 2004; Strathern 1988).

France, the United Kingdom, and Italy) met to devise regulations for a co-ordinated response to the crisis, Jean-Claude Trichet, the baronial president of the European Central Bank, stated, "We are doing our best to maintain and restore confidence. There can be no doubt that confidence is the most vital factor in the current circumstances. I am convinced that the decisions we make here will help restore confidence once more" (Chancellor's Press Office 2008). In addition to politicians, no shortage of pundits appeared in numerous media outlets definitively declaring that, in the wake of the financial catastrophe, political leaders had to restore faith in financial mar-kets (Appelbaum and Cho 2009; *Economist* 2009; Lehigh 2008). These en-treaties to develop the faith of borrowers, producers, and consumers were not calls to pious practice or religious devotion but rather to implement a specific set of technical interventions to elicit such action.

In response, a variety of mechanisms have been developed to achieve precisely this goal. Governments and other institutions such as the IMF and World Bank (Dattels and Kodres 2008) sought to apply concrete measures that would elicit this elusive aspect of human conduct that was variously referred to as faith, confidence, or trust. They included lowering interest rates, insuring the solvency of banks and other lenders, limiting execu-tive pay, and devising new government regulatory institutions such as the Consumer Financial Protection Agency (Obama 2009b). Interest rates in particular are perhaps the most effective means that modern states have at their disposal to manage the conduct of their subjects, at the scale of both the individual and the population at large. These interventions illustrate how faith is not an object outside the realm of calculation or opposed to economic action but rather something at the very heart of the practice of the market—an object developed through decidedly rational interventions (Miyazaki 2007).

Regimes of calculation, audit cultures, and spiritual economies have be-come constitutive features of modern life. It might be tempting to dismiss the efforts to develop faith represented in ESQ as a cult. Yet, it is perhaps less so if one were to take a step back and reflect on the fact that if it is a cult, it may be one from which we are not entirely insulated, if we are not already enmeshed within its icy grasp. An earlier generation of social scien-tists debated whether economic calculation and rational choice were essen-tial attributes of human beings (Popkin 1979; Sahlins 1972; Scott 1976). In recognition of the historicity of the object known as the human (Foucault

1970), contemporary anthropology has changed its focus to the norms and knowledge through which the human is created rather than a search for its essential nature. Nonetheless, these earlier debates enable us to move past analyses that debate the inherent rationality of humans and to investigate the processes through which human beings are rationalized. Thus, this book documents the techniques, practices, norms, and knowledge that are configured to make economic calculation the organizing principle for human life. In so doing, I have sought to encourage reflection on why and how this is occurring and how we might think and live otherwise.

References

Abeng, Tanri. 2001. *Indonesia, Inc.: Privatising State-Owned Enterprises.* Singapore: Times Academic Press.

Abu-Lughod, Lila. 2005. *Dramas of Nationhood: The Politics of Television in Egypt.* Chicago: University of Chicago Press.

Abu-Lughod, Lila, and Catherine Lutz. 1990. Introduction: Emotion, Discourse, and the Politics of Everyday Life. In *Language and the Politics of Emotion,* ed. Catherine Lutz and Lila Abu-Lughod, 1–23. Cambridge: Cambridge University Press.

Aguilar, Filomeno V. 2001. Citizenship, Inheritance, and the Indigenizing of "Orang Chinese" in Indonesia. *Positions: East Asia Cultures Critique* 9 (3): 501–533.

Akbar, Faidil. 2003. Krakatau Steel Terancam Bangkrut [Krakatau Steel is threatened with bankruptcy]. *Tempo Interaktif.* August 18.

Amin, Riawan. 2004. *The Celestial Management.* Jakarta: Senayan Abadi.

Amir, Sulfikar. 2004. The Regime and the Airplane: High Technology and Nationalism in Indonesia. *Bulletin of Science, Technology and Society* 24 (2): 107–114.

———. 2007a. Nationalist Rhetoric and Technological Development: The Indonesian Aircraft Industry in the New Order Regime. *Technology in Society* 27 (3): 283–293.

———. 2007b. Symbolic Power in a Technocratic Regime: The Reign of B. J. Habibie in New Order Indonesia. *Sojourn* 22 (1): 83–106.

———. 2008. The Engineers Versus the Economists: Disunity of Technocracy in Indonesian Development. *Bulletin of Science, Technology, and Society* 28 (4): 316–323.

Anderson, Benedict. 1991. *Imagined Communities: Reflections on the Origin and Spread of Nationalism*. London: Verso.

———. 1998. Nationalism, Identity, and the Logic of Seriality. In *The Spectre of Comparisons: Nationalism, Southeast Asia, and the World*, 29–45. London: Verso.

———. 1999. Indonesian Nationalism Today and in the Future. *New Left Review* 235:3–17.

Anderson, Benedict, Ruth McVey, and Frederick Bunnell. 1971. *A Preliminary Analysis of the October 1, 1965 Coup in Indonesia*. Ithaca: Modern Indonesia Project, Cornell University.

Appadurai, Arjun. 1996. *Modernity at Large: Cultural Dimensions of Globalization*. Minneapolis: University of Minnesota Press.

Appelbaum, Binyamin, and David Cho. 2009. Geithner to Propose Vast Expansion of U.S. Oversight of Financial System. *Washington Post*. Accessed August 7, 2009, from http://www.washingtonpost.com/wp-dyn/content/article/2009/03/25/AR2009 032502311.html.

Apter, Andrew. 2005. *The Pan-African Nation: Oil and the Spectacle of Culture in Nigeria*. Chicago: University of Chicago Press.

Aragon, Lorraine V. 2000. *Fields of the Lord: Animism, Christian Minorities, and State Development in Indonesia*. Honolulu: University of Hawai'i Press.

Aragon, Lorraine V., and James Leach. 2008. Arts and Owners: Intellectual Property Law and the Politics of Scale in Indonesian Arts. *American Ethnologist* 35 (4): 607–631.

Arberry, Arthur J. 1955. *The Koran Interpreted*. New York: Macmillan.

Arndt, Heinz W. 1975. P. T. Krakatau Steel. *Bulletin of Indonesian Economic Studies* 11 (2): 120–126.

Asad, Talal. 1993. *Genealogies of Religion: Discipline and Reasons of Power in Christianity and Islam*. Baltimore: Johns Hopkins University Press.

———. 1994. Ethnographic Representation, Statistics, and Modern Power. *Social Research* 61 (1): 55–88.

———. 2007. Explaining the Global Religious Revival: The Egyptian Case. In *Religion and Society: An Agenda for the 21st Century,* ed. Gerrie Ter Haar. Leiden: Brill.

Aspinall, Edward. 2009. *Islam and Nation: Separatist Rebellion in Aceh, Indonesia*. Stanford: Stanford University Press.

Barber, Benjamin R. 1996. *Jihad vs. McWorld*. New York: Ballantine Books.

Barker, Joshua. 1999. Surveillance and Territoriality in Bandung. In *Figures of Criminality in Indonesia, the Philippines, and Colonial Vietnam,* ed. Vicente Rafael, 95–127. Ithaca: Southeast Asia Program, Cornell University.

———. 2005. Engineers and Political Dreams: Indonesia in the Satellite Age. *Current Anthropology* 46 (5): 703–727.

Barry, Andrew, Thomas Osborne, and Nikolas S. Rose. 1996. *Foucault and Political Reason: Liberalism, Neo-Liberalism and Rationalities of Government*. Chicago: University of Chicago Press.

Bartlett, Roscoe. 2008. Rushing to Bail Out Wall Street Won't Protect Main Street. U.S. House of Representatives website. Accessed August 7, 2009, from http://www.house.gov/hensarling/rsc/doc/ca_092908_bartlettrescue.pdf.

Beck, Ulrich. 1992. *Risk Society: Towards a New Modernity.* London: Sage Publications.

Beck, Ulrich, Anthony Giddens, and Scott Lash. 1994. *Reflexive Modernization: Politics, Tradition, and Aesthetics in the Modern Social Order.* Stanford: Stanford University Press.

Boellstorff, Tom. 2005. *The Gay Archipelago: Sexuality and Nation in Indonesia.* Princeton: Princeton University Press.

Boellstorff, Tom, and Johan Lindquist. 2004. Bodies of Emotion: Rethinking Culture and Emotion through Southeast Asia. *Ethnos* 69 (4): 437–444.

Bornstein, Erica. 2005. *The Spirit of Development: Protestant NGOs, Morality, and Economics in Zimbabwe.* Stanford: Stanford University Press.

Bourdieu, Pierre. 1990. *The Logic of Practice.* Stanford: Stanford University Press.

Bowen, John R. 1984. Death and the History of Islam in Highland Aceh. *Indonesia* 38:21–38.

———. 2003. *Islam, Law, and Equality in Indonesia: An Anthropology of Public Reasoning.* Cambridge: Cambridge University Press.

———. 2007. *Why the French Don't Like Headscarves: Islam, the State, and Public Space.* Princeton: Princeton University Press.

Boyer, Dominic. 2001. Foucault in the Bush. The Social Life of Post-Structuralist Theory in East Berlin's Prenzlauer Berg. *Ethnos* 66 (2): 207–236.

Brenner, Suzanne April. 1996. Reconstructing Self and Society: Javanese Muslim Women and "the Veil." *American Ethnologist* 23 (4): 673–697.

———. 1998. *The Domestication of Desire: Women, Wealth, and Modernity in Java.* Princeton: Princeton University Press.

Bronson, Bennet. 1977. Exchange at the Upstream and Downstream Ends: Notes toward a Functional Model of the Coastal State in Southeast Asia. In *Economic Exchange and Social Interaction in Southeast Asia,* ed. Karl Hutterer, 39–52. Ann Arbor: Southeast Asia Studies Program.

Brown, Gordon. 2009. Speech to Congress. *Daily Telegraph.* Accessed August 7, 2009, from http://www.telegraph.co.uk/news/newstopics/politics/gordon-brown/4938252/Gordon-Browns-speech-to-Congress-the-full-text.html.

Budiati, Tinia. 2000. *The Preservation of Betawi Culture and Agriculture in the Condet Area.* Leiden: KITLV Press.

Bulletin Krakatau Steel. 1977. Cocktail Party Menyambut Tahun Baru 1977 [Cocktail party welcomes New Year's 1977]. 25:6–7.

Bulliet, Richard W. 2006. *The Case for Islamo-Christian Civilization.* New York: Columbia University Press.

Bunnell, Tim. 2004. *Malaysia, Modernity, and the Multimedia Super Corridor: A Critical Geography of Intelligent Landscapes.* London: RoutledgeCurzon.

Butt, Leslie. 2005. "Lipstick Girls" And "Fallen Women": AIDS and Conspiratorial Thinking in Papua, Indonesia. *Cultural Anthropology* 20 (3): 412–441.

Callon, Michel. 1998. *The Laws of the Markets.* Malden, MA: Blackwell.

Castells, Manuel. 1997. *The Power of Identity.* Malden, MA: Blackwell.

Chancellor's Press Office. 2008. Confidence Must Be Restored in Financial Markets. The Chancellor of the Federal Republic of Germany. Accessed August 7, 2009, from http://www.bundeskanzlerin.de/nn_704284/Content/EN/Artikel/2008/10/2008–10–04-g4-paris-finanzmarkt_en.html.

Chin, Christine. 1998. *In Service and Servitude: Foreign Female Domestic Workers and the Malaysian "Modernity" Project.* New York: Columbia University Press.

Collier, Stephen, and Aihwa Ong. 2005. Global Assemblages, Anthropological Problems. In *Global Assemblages: Technology, Politics, and Ethics as Anthropological Problems,* ed. Aihwa Ong and Stephen Collier, 3–21. Malden, MA: Blackwell.

Collins, Elizabeth. 2007. *Indonesia Betrayed: How Development Fails.* Honolulu: University of Hawai'i Press.

Comaroff, Jean, and John L. Comaroff. 1999. Occult Economies and the Violence of Abstraction: Notes from the South African Postcolony. *American Ethnologist* 26 (2): 279–303.

———. 2000. Millennial Capitalism: First Thoughts on a Second Coming. *Public Culture* 12 (2): 291–343.

Comaroff, John L., and Jean Comaroff. 2009. *Ethnicity, Inc.* Chicago: University of Chicago Press.

Connor, Steve. 1997. "God Spot" Is Found in Brain. *Los Angeles Times.* October 29.

Cribb, R. B. 1991. *Gangsters and Revolutionaries: The Jakarta People's Militia and the Indonesian Revolution, 1945–1949.* Honolulu: University of Hawai'i Press.

Csordas, Thomas. 2007. Introduction: Modalities of Transnational Transcendence. *Anthropological Theory* 7 (3): 259–272.

———. 2009a. Modalities of Transnational Transcendence. In *Transnational Transcendence: Essays in Religion and Globalization,* ed. Thomas Csordas, 1–29. Berkeley: University of California Press.

———. 2009b. *Transnational Transcendence: Essays in Religion and Globalization.* Berkeley: University of California Press.

Darmodiharjo, Darji, Nyoman Dekker, A. G. Pringgodigdo, M. Mardojo, Kutjoro Purbopranoto, and J. W. Sulandra. 1970. *Santiaji Pancasila* [Indoctrinating Pancasila]. Surabaya: Usaha Nasional.

Dattels, Peter, and Laura Kodres. 2008. IMF Warns about Failure to Act Decisively on Turmoil. *IMF Survey Magazine.* Accessed August 7, 2009, from http://www.imf.org/external/pubs/ft/survey/so/2008/new100708A.htm.

de Certeau, Michel. 1984. *The Practice of Everyday Life.* Berkeley: University of California Press.

Deeb, Lara. 2006. *An Enchanted Modern: Gender and Public Piety in Shi'i Lebanon.* Princeton: Princeton University Press.

Delaney, Carol. 1998. *Abraham on Trial: The Social Legacy of Biblical Myth.* Princeton: Princeton University Press.

Dengel, Holk H. 1995. *Darul Islam Dan Kartosuwirjo: Langkah Perwujudan Angan-Angan Yang Gagal* [Darul Islam and Kartosuwirjo: Pursuing a failed illusion]. Jakarta: Pustaka Sinar Harapan.

Dhofier, Zamakhsyari. 1999. *The Pesantren Tradition: A Study of the Role of the Kyai in the Maintenance of the Traditional Ideology of Islam in Java.* Tempe: Arizona State University Southeast Asian Studies Monograph Series.

Djajadiningrat, Hoesein. 1913. *Critische Beshouwing van de Sadjarah Banten: Bijdrage ter Kenshetsing van de Javaansche Geschiedschrijving.* Haarlem: Joh. Enschede en Zonen.

Dreyfus, Hubert L., and Paul Rabinow. 1983. *Michel Foucault: Beyond Structuralism and Hermeneutics.* Chicago: University of Chicago Press.

Dumit, Joseph. 2004. *Picturing Personhood: Brain Scans and Biomedical Identity.* Princeton: Princeton University Press.

Economist. 2009. Looting Stars. Accessed August 7, 2009, from http://www.economist.com/businessfinance/displaystory.cfm?story_id=13035696.

Eickelman, Dale F., and Jon W. Anderson. 2003. *New Media in the Muslim World: The Emerging Public Sphere.* Bloomington: Indiana University Press.

Elyachar, Julia. 2005. *Markets of Dispossession: NGOs, Economic Development, and the State in Cairo.* Durham: Duke University Press.

Engels, F. 1968. Letter to Franz Mehring of July 14, 1893. In *Marx and Engels Correspondence.* Moscow: International Publishers.

Erikson, Soren. 2003. Indonesia's Aircraft Industry: Technology and Management Impediments. *International Journal of Technology Transfer and Commercialisation* 2 (2): 207–226.

Errington, Joseph. 1998. *Shifting Languages: Interaction and Identity in Javanese Indonesia.* Cambridge: Cambridge University Press.

Escobar, Arturo. 1995. *Encountering Development: The Making and Unmaking of the Third World.* Princeton: Princeton University Press.

Evans-Pritchard, E. E. 1969. *The Nuer.* Oxford: Oxford University Press.

Feener, Michael. 2007. *Muslim Legal Thought in Modern Indonesia.* Cambridge: Cambridge University Press.

Ferguson, James. 1999. *Expectations of Modernity: Myths and Meanings of Urban Life on the Zambian Copperbelt.* Berkeley: University of California Press.

———. 2006. *Global Shadows: Africa in the Neoliberal World Order.* Durham: Duke University Press.

Ferguson, James, and Akhil Gupta. 2002. Spatializing States: Toward an Ethnography of Neoliberal Governmentality. *American Ethnologist* 29 (4): 981–1002.

Foucault, Michel. 1970. *The Order of Things: An Archaeology of the Human Sciences.* London: Tavistock Publications.

———. 1973. *Madness and Civilization: A History of Insanity in the Age of Reason.* New York: Vintage Books.

———. 1977. *Discipline and Punish: The Birth of the Prison.* New York: Pantheon Books.

———. 1978. *The History of Sexuality.* New York: Pantheon Books.

———. 1983. The Subject and Power. In *Michel Foucault: Beyond Structuralism and Hermeneutics,* ed. Hubert L. Dreyfus and Paul Rabinow, 208–226. Chicago: University of Chicago Press.

———. 1988. Technologies of the Self. In *Technologies of the Self: A Seminar with Michel Foucault,* ed. Luther H. Martin, Huck Gutman, and Patrick H. Hutton, 16–49. Amherst: University of Massachusetts Press.

———. 1991. Governmentality. In *The Foucault Effect,* ed. Graham Burchell, Colin Gordon, and Peter Miller, 87–104. Chicago: University of Chicago Press.

———. 1997. On the Genealogy of Ethics: An Overview of Work in Progress. In *Ethics: Subjectivity and Truth,* ed. Paul Rabinow, 253–280. New York: New Press.

———. 2001. *Fearless Speech.* Los Angeles: Semiotext(e).

———. 2007. *Security, Territory, Population: Lectures at the College de France, 1977–1978.* Houndmills: Palgrave Macmillan.

———. 2008. *The Birth of Biopolitics: Lectures at the College de France, 1978–1979.* Houndmills: Palgrave Macmillan.

Fox, James. 2004. Currents in Contemporary Islam in Indonesia. Paper presented at the Harvard Asia Vision 21 Conference. Cambridge, Massachusetts.

Friend, Theodore. 2003. *Indonesian Destinies.* Cambridge: Belknap Press.

Furnivall, John S. 1948. *Colonial Policy and Practice: A Comparative Study of Burma and Netherlands India.* Cambridge: University Press.

Gade, Anna M. 2004. *Perfection Makes Practice: Learning, Emotion, and the Recited Qur'an in Indonesia.* Honolulu: University of Hawai'i Press.

Geertz, Clifford. 1960. *The Religion of Java.* Glencoe, IL: Free Press.

———. 1963a. *Agricultural Involution: The Process of Ecological Change in Indonesia.* Berkeley: University of California Press.

———. 1963b. *Peddlers and Princes: Social Change and Economic Modernization in Two Indonesian Towns.* Chicago: University of Chicago Press.

———. 1973a. Deep Play: Notes on the Balinese Cockfight. In *The Interpretation of Cultures,* 412–453. New York: Basic Books.

———. 1973b. Thick Description: Toward an Interpretive Theory of Culture. In *The Interpretation of Cultures,* 3–30. New York: Basic Books.

———. 1980. *Negara: The Theatre State in Nineteenth-Century Bali.* Princeton: Princeton University Press.

———. 1983. From the Native's Point of View: On the Nature of Anthropological Understanding. In *Local Knowledge: Further Essays in Interpretive Anthropology,* 55–70. New York: Basic Books.

Geertz, Hildred. 1961. *The Javanese Family: A Study of Kinship and Socialization.* New York: Free Press.

Ginanjar, Ary. 2001. *Rahasia Sukses Membangun Kecerdasan Emosi Dan Spiritual ESQ* [Secrets of success in developing emotional and spiritual intelligence ESQ]. Jakarta: Penerbit Arga.

Goleman, Daniel. 1995. *Emotional Intelligence.* New York: Bantam Books.

Government of Indonesia. 2000. Memorandum of Economic and Financial Policies. Accessed December 15, 2006, from World Bank Indonesia website, http://www.worldbank.or.id/eap/eap.nsf/2500ec5f1a2d9bad852568a3006f557d/66af15a48da09728472569af001857b6?OpenDocument.

Gunawan, Hendra. 2000. *M. Natsir Dan Darul Islam: Studi Kasus Aceh Dan Sulawesi Selatan Tahun 1953–1958* [M. Natsir and Darul Islam: A case study of Aceh and South Sulawesi]. Jakarta: Media Da'wah.

Gupta, Akhil. 1997. Agrarian Populism in the Development of a Modern Nation (India). In *International Development and the Social Sciences,* ed. Frederick Cooper and Randall Packard, 320–344. Berkeley: University of California Press.

———. 1998. *Postcolonial Developments: Agriculture in the Making of Modern India.* Durham: Duke University Press.

Gupta, Akhil, and James Ferguson. 1997a. *Anthropological Locations: Boundaries and Grounds of a Field Science.* Berkeley: University of California Press.

——. 1997b. *Culture, Power, Place: Explorations in Critical Anthropology.* Durham: Duke University Press.

Hadiz, Vedi R. 1997. *Workers and the State in New Order Indonesia.* London: Routledge.

Hadler, Jeffrey. 2004. Translations of Antisemitism: Jews, the Chinese, and Violence in Colonial and Post-Colonial Indonesia. *Indonesia and the Malay World* 32 (94): 291–313.

Hale, Sondra. 1998. Islam in Africa: Particularisms and Hegemonies. *Reviews in Anthropology* 3:57–69.

Hannerz, Ulf. 1989. Notes on the Global Ecumene. *Public Culture* 1 (2): 66–75.

——. 2004. *Foreign News: Exploring the World of Foreign Correspondents.* Chicago: University of Chicago Press.

Hansen, Thomas Blom. 1999. *The Saffron Wave: Democracy and Hindu Nationalism in India.* Princeton: Princeton University Press.

Haraway, Donna. 1991. *Simians, Cyborgs, and Women: The Re-Invention of Nature.* New York: Routledge.

Harding, Susan F. 2001. *The Book of Jerry Falwell: Fundamentalist Language and Politics.* Princeton: Princeton University Press.

Hart, Gillian. 1986. *Power, Labor, and Livelihood: Processes of Change in Rural Java.* Berkeley: University of California Press.

Harvey, David. 1989. *The Condition of Postmodernity: An Enquiry into the Origins of Cultural Change.* Oxford: Blackwell.

——. 2005. *A Brief History of Neoliberalism.* Oxford: Oxford University Press.

——. 2006. *Spaces of Global Capitalism: A Theory of Uneven Geographical Development.* London: Verso.

Hefner, Robert W. 1996. Islamizing Capitalism: On the Founding of Indonesia's First Islamic Bank. In *Toward a New Paradigm: Recent Developments in Indonesian Islamic Thought,* ed. Mark Woodward, 291–322. Tempe: Center for Southeast Asian Studies, Arizona State University.

——. 1997. Print Islam: Mass Media and Ideological Rivalries among Indonesian Muslims. *Indonesia* 64:77–103.

——. 2000. *Civil Islam: Muslims and Democratization in Indonesia.* Princeton: Princeton University Press.

Heryanto, Ariel. 1988. The "Development" Of Development. *Indonesia* 46:1–24.

Hikam, Muhammad. 1995. The State, Grass-Roots Politics and Civil Society: A Study of Social Movements under Indonesia's New Order (1989–1994). PhD diss., University of Hawai'i.

Hill, Hal. 2000. *The Indonesian Economy.* Cambridge: Cambridge University Press.

Hirschkind, Charles. 2006. *The Ethical Soundscape: Cassette Sermons and Islamic Counterpublics.* New York: Columbia University Press.

Hirschman, Albert O. 1977. *The Passions and the Interests: Political Arguments for Capitalism before Its Triumph.* Princeton: Princeton University Press.

Hoesterey, James. 2008. Marketing Morality: The Rise, Fall, and Rebranding of Aa Gym. In *Expressing Islam: Religious Life and Politics in Indonesia,* ed. Greg Fealy and Sally White, 95–112. Singapore: Institute of Southeast Asian Studies.

———. 2009. Tele-Dai, The Muslim Television Preacher. *Indonesia* 87:41–43.

Hollan, Douglas, and C. Jason Throop. 2008. Whatever Happened to Empathy? *Ethos* 36 (4): 385–401.

Holmes, Douglas. 2000. *Integral Europe: Fast-Capitalism, Multiculturalism, Neofascism.* Princeton: Princeton University Press.

———. 2009. Economy of Words. *Cultural Anthropology* 24 (3): 381–419.

Holmes, Douglas, and George Marcus. 2005. Cultures of Expertise and the Management of Globalization: Toward the Re-Functioning of Ethnography. In *Global Assemblages: Technology, Politics, and Ethics as Anthropological Problems,* ed. Aihwa Ong and Stephen Collier, 235–252. Malden, MA: Blackwell.

———. 2006. Fast Capitalism: Para-Ethnography and the Rise of the Symbolic Analyst. In *Frontiers of Capital: Ethnographic Reflections on the New Economy,* ed. Melissa S. Fisher and Greg Downey, 33–57. Durham: Duke University Press.

Holston, James. 1989. *The Modernist City: An Anthropological Critique of Brasilia.* Chicago: University of Chicago Press.

Hotz, Robert Lee. 1997. Brain Region May Be Linked to Religion. *Seattle Times.* October 29.

Huczynski, Andrzej. 2006. *Management Gurus.* London: Routledge.

Huntington, Samuel P. 1993. The Clash of Civilizations? *Foreign Affairs* 72 (3): 22–50.

Imaduddin, Abdulrahim. 1985. Organizational Effectiveness of Universities in Malaysia. PhD diss., Iowa State University.

———. 1992. *Semangat Tawhid Dan Motivasi Kerja* [The spirit of tawhid and work motivation]. Kuala Lumpur: Institut Kajian Dasar Malaysia.

Inda, Jonathan Xavier, and Renato Rosaldo. 2002. *The Anthropology of Globalization: A Reader.* Malden, MA: Blackwell.

Jackson, Bradley. 2001. *Management Gurus and Management Fashions: A Dramatistic Inquiry.* London: Routledge.

Jackson, Karl, and Lucian Pye. 1978. *Political Power and Communications in Indonesia.* Berkeley: University of California Press.

Kartodirdjo, Sartono. 1966. *The Peasants' Revolt of Banten in 1888: Its Conditions, Course and Sequel.* 's-Gravenhage: Martinus Nijhoff.

Keane, Webb. 2003. Public Speaking: On Indonesian as the Language of the Nation. *Public Culture* 15 (3): 503–530.

Kimura, Ehito. 2007. Marginality and Opportunity in the Periphery: The Emergence of Gorontalo Province in North Sulawesi. *Indonesia* 84:71–95.

Kitley, Philip. 1999. *Pancasila* in the Minor Key: TVRI's *Si Unyil* Models the Child. *Indonesia* 68:129–152.

Klima, Alan. 2002. *The Funeral Casino: Meditation, Massacre, and Exchange with the Dead in Thailand.* Princeton: Princeton University Press.

Kohrman, Matthew. 2005. *Bodies of Difference: Experiences of Disability and Institutional Advocacy in the Making of Modern China.* Berkeley: University of California Press.

Kondo, Dorinne. 1990. *Crafting Selves: Power, Gender, and Discourses of Identity in a Japanese Workplace.* Chicago: University of Chicago Press.

Koning, Juliette. 2000. *Women and Households in Indonesia: Cultural Notions and Social Practices.* Richmond: Curzon.

Krismantari, Ika. 2008. Krakatau Steel Revives Talks with Strategic Partners. *Jakarta Post.* November 27.

Kresman, R. A., Y. M. Hadin, and D. W. Sumarni. 1989. Amok: Sebuah Ilustrasi Kasus [Amok: Illustrated cases]. *Jiwa* 22 (3): 49–52.

Kuhn, Thomas. 1962. *The Structure of Scientific Revolutions.* Chicago: University of Chicago Press.

Kusno, Abidin. 2003. Remembering/Forgetting the May Riots: Architecture, Violence, and the Making Of "Chinese Cultures" in Post-1998 Jakarta. *Public Culture* 15 (1): 149–177.

Laffan, Michael. 2003. *Islamic Nationhood and Colonial Indonesia: The Umma below the Winds.* London: RoutledgeCurzon.

Lansing, Stephen. 1991. *Priests and Programmers: Technologies of Power in the Engineered Landscape of Bali.* Princeton: Princeton University Press.

———. 2006. *Perfect Order: Recognizing Complexity in Bali.* Princeton: Princeton University Press.

Latour, Bruno. 1999. Circulating Reference: Sampling the Soil in the Amazon Forest. In *Pandora's Hope,* 24–79. Cambridge: Harvard University Press.

Lee, Doreen. 2003. Boxed Memories. *Indonesia* 75:1–8.

Lehigh, Scot. 2008. Struggling to Restore Faith in the System. *Boston Globe.* Accessed August 7, 2009, from http://www.boston.com/bostonglobe/editorial_opinion/oped/articles/2008/09/17/struggling_to_restore_faith_in_the_system/.

Leve, Lauren, and Lamia Karim. 2001. Privatizing the State: Ethnography of Development, Transnational Capital, and NGOs. *PoLAR: Political and Legal Anthropology Review* 24 (1): 53–58.

Li, Tania. 2007. *The Will to Improve: Governmentality, Development, and the Practice of Politics.* Durham: Duke University Press.

Lindquist, Johan. 2004. Veils and Ecstasy: Negotiating Shame in the Indonesian Borderlands. *Ethnos* 69 (4): 487–508.

———. 2008. *The Anxieties of Mobility: Migration and Tourism in the Indonesian Borderlands.* Honolulu: University of Hawai'i Press.

Livingston, J. Sterling. 1988. Pygmalion in Management. *Harvard Business Review* 65 (5): 121–130.

Lomnitz-Adler, Claudio. 1992. *Exits from the Labyrinth Culture and Ideology in the Mexican National Space.* Berkeley: University of California Press.

Luhmann, Niklas. 1998. *Observations on Modernity.* Stanford: Stanford University Press.

Luhrmann, Tanya. 2004. Metakinesis: How God Becomes Intimate in Contemporary U.S. Christianity. *American Anthropologist.* 106 (3): 518–528.

Lukács, Georg. 1972. *History and Class Consciousness: Studies in Marxist Dialectics.* Cambridge, MA: MIT Press.

Lutz, Catherine, and Lila Abu-Lughod. 1990. *Language and the Politics of Emotion.* Cambridge: Cambridge University Press.

Lutz, Catherine, and Geoffrey M. White. 1986. The Anthropology of Emotions. *Annual Review of Anthropology* 15:405–436.

Mackie, J. A. C. 1976. *The Chinese in Indonesia: Five Essays.* Honolulu: University of Hawai'i Press.

Mahmood, Saba. 2001. Feminist Theory, Embodiment, and the Docile Agent: Some Reflections on the Egyptian Islamic Revival. *Cultural Anthropology* 16 (2): 202–236.

———. 2005. *Politics of Piety: The Islamic Revival and the Feminist Subject.* Princeton: Princeton University Press.

Malinowski, Bronislaw. 1922. *Argonauts of the Western Pacific: An Account of Native Enterprise and Adventure in the Archipelagoes of Melanesian New Guinea.* New York: Dutton.

Malkki, Liisa. 1997. National Geographic: The Rooting of Peoples and the Territorialization of National Identity among Scholars and Refugees. In *Culture, Power, Place: Explorations in Critical Anthropology,* ed. Akhil Gupta and James Ferguson, 52–74. Durham: Duke University Press.

Marcus, George E. 1998. *Ethnography through Thick and Thin.* Princeton: Princeton University Press.

———. 2007. Ethnography Two Decades after Writing Culture: From the Experimental to the Baroque *Anthropological Quarterly* 80 (4): 1127–1145.

Martensson, Ulrika. 2007. The Power of Subject: Weber, Foucault and Islam. *Critique: Critical Middle Eastern Studies* 16 (2): 97–136.

Masaaki, Okamoto. 2004. Local Politics in Decentralized Indonesia: The Governor General of Banten Province. *International Institute for Asian Studies Newsletter* 34:23.

———. 2008a. Jawara in Power, 1998–2007. *Indonesia* 86:109–138.

———. 2008b. An Unholy Alliance: Political Thugs and Political Islam Work Together. *Inside Indonesia.* Accessed May 5, 2009, from http://www.insideindonesia.org/content/view/1101/47/.

Maurer, Bill. 2002. Anthropological and Accounting Knowledge in Islamic Banking and Finance: Rethinking Critical Accounts. *Journal of the Royal Anthropological Institute* (n.s.) 8 (4): 645–667.

———. 2005. *Mutual Life, Limited: Islamic Banking, Alternative Currencies, Lateral Reason.* Princeton: Princeton University Press.

Mauss, Marcel. 1990. *The Gift: The Form and Reason for Exchange in Archaic Societies.* London: Routledge.

Mazzarella, William. 2003. *Shoveling Smoke: Advertising and Globalization in Contemporary India.* Durham: Duke University Press.

McGregor, Katharine. 2002. Commemoration of 1 October, *"Hari Kesaktian Pancasila,"* A Post Mortem Analysis? *Asian Studies Review* 26 (1): 39–72.

Mehta, Uday Singh. 1999. *Liberalism and Empire: A Study in Nineteenth-Century British Liberal Thought.* Chicago: University of Chicago Press.

Meilink-Roelofsz, M. A. P. 1962. *Asian Trade and European Influence in the Indonesian Archipelago between 1500 and About 1630.* The Hague: Martinus Nijhoff.

Metal Bulletin Monthly. 1996. Krakatau Steel Expands in a Big Way. 5:77.

Mietzner, Marcus. 2007. Local Elections and Autonomy in Papua and Aceh: Mitigating or Fueling Secessionism? *Indonesia* 84:1–39.

Miller, Peter, and Nikolas Rose. 1992. Political Power beyond the State: Problematics of Government. *British Journal of Sociology* 43 (2): 173–205.

Mitchell, Timothy. 2002. *Rule of Experts: Egypt, Techno-Politics, Modernity.* Berkeley: University of California Press.

———. 2005. The Work of Economics: How a Discipline Makes Its World. *European Journal of Sociology* 46 (2): 297–320.

Miyazaki, Hirokazu. 2004. *The Method of Hope: Anthropology, Philosophy, and Fijian Knowledge.* Stanford: Stanford University Press.

———. 2007. Between Arbitrage and Speculation: An Economy of Belief and Doubt. *Economy and Society* 36 (3): 397–416.

Moody, Raymond A. 1976. *Life after Life: The Investigation of a Phenomenon—Survival of Bodily Death.* Toronto: Bantam Books.

Moody, Raymond A., and Paul Perry. 1993. *Reunions: Visionary Encounters with Departed Loved Ones.* New York: Villard Books.

Moon, Suzanne. 2009. Justice, Geography, and Steel: Technology and National Identity in Indonesian Industrialization. *Osiris* 24 (1): 253–277.

Moore, Donald S., Jake Kosek, and Anand Pandian. 2003. *Race, Nature, and the Politics of Difference.* Durham: Duke University Press.

Morfit, Michael. 1981. Pancasila: The Indonesian State Ideology According to the New Order Government. *Asian Survey* 21 (8): 838–851.

Mrázek, Rudolf. 2002. *Engineers of Happy Land: Technology and Nationalism in a Colony.* Princeton: Princeton University Press.

Muehlebach, Andrea. 2007. The Moral Neoliberal: Welfare State and Ethical Citizenship in Contemporary Italy. PhD diss., University of Chicago.

Multatuli. 1868. *Max Havelaar; or, the Coffee Auctions of the Dutch Trading Company.* Edinburgh: Edmonston & Douglas.

Noer, Deliar. 1973. *The Modernist Muslim Movement in Indonesia, 1900–1942.* Singapore: Oxford University Press.

Nurdin, Ahmad Ali. 2005. Islam and State: A Study of the Liberal Islamic Network in Indonesia, 1999–2004. *New Zealand Journal of Asian Studies* 7 (2): 20–39.

Obama, Barack. 2009a. News conference, April 2. White House website. Accessed August 7, 2009, from http://www.whitehouse.gov/the_press_office/news-conference-by-president-obama-4-02-09/.

———. 2009b. Weekly address, June 20. White House website. Accessed August 7, 2009, from http://www.whitehouse.gov/the_press_office/WEEKLY-ADDRESS-President-Obama-Highlights-Tough-New-Consumer-Protections/.

Olds, Kris, and Nigel Thrift. 2005. Cultures on the Brink: Reengineering the Soul of Capitalism—on a Global Scale. In *Global Assemblages: Technology, Politics, and Ethics as Anthropological Problems,* ed. Aihwa Ong and Stephen Collier, 270–290. Malden, MA: Blackwell.

O'Meara, Patrick, Howard D. Mehlinger, and Matthew Krain. 2000. *Globalization and the Challenges of a New Century.* Bloomington: Indiana University Press.

Ong, Aihwa. 1987. *Spirits of Resistance and Capitalist Discipline: Factory Women in Malaysia.* Albany: State University of New York Press.

———. 1990. State versus Islam: Malay Families, Women's Bodies, and the Body Politic in Malaysia. *American Ethnologist* 17 (2): 258–276.

———. 1999. *Flexible Citizenship: The Cultural Logics of Transnationality.* Durham: Duke University Press.

———. 2000. Graduated Sovereignty in South-East Asia. *Theory, Culture and Society* 17 (4): 55–75.

———. 2006. *Neoliberalism as Exception: Mutations in Citizenship and Sovereignty.* Durham: Duke University Press.

Ong, Aihwa, and Stephen J. Collier. 2005. *Global Assemblages: Technology, Politics, and Ethics as Anthropological Problems.* Malden, MA: Blackwell.

Ortner, Sherry. 1984. Theory in Anthropology since the 1960s. *Comparative Studies in Society and History* 26 (1): 126–166.

Park, Kyeyoung. 1999. "I'm Floating in the Air": Creation of a Korean Transnational Space among Korean-Latino-American Re-Migrants. *Positions: East Asia Cultures Critique* 7 (3): 667–695.

Peacock, James L. 1978. *Muslim Puritans: Reformist Psychology in Southeast Asian Islam.* Berkeley: University of California Press.

Peluso, Nancy. 2006. Passing the Red Bowl: Creating Community through Violence in West Kalimantan, Indonesia. In *Violent Conflict in Indonesia: Analysis, Representation, Resolution,* ed. Charles Coppel, 106–128. New York: Routledge.

Peluso, Nancy, and Emily Harwell. 2001. Territory, Custom, and the Cultural Politics of Ethnic War in West Kalimantan Indonesia. In *Violent Environments,* ed. Nancy Peluso and Michael Watts, 83–116. Ithaca: Cornell University Press.

Pemberton, John. 1994a. *On the Subject Of "Java."* Ithaca: Cornell University Press.

———. 1994b. Recollections From "Beautiful Indonesia" (Somewhere beyond the Postmodern). *Public Culture* 6 (2): 241–262.

———. 1999. Open Secrets: Excerpts from Conversations with a Javanese Lawyer, and a Comment. In *Figures of Criminality in Indonesia, the Philippines, and Colonial Vietnam,* ed. Vicente L. Rafael and Rudolf Mrazek, 198–209. Ithaca: Southeast Asia Program, Cornell University.

Pickthall, Marmaduke. 2000. *The Glorious Qur'an.* Elmhurst, NY: Tahrike Tarsile Qur'an.

Popkin, Samuel. 1979. *The Rational Peasant: The Political Economy of Rural Society in Vietnam.* Berkeley: University of California Press.

Postero, Nancy. 2007. *Now We Are Citizens: Indigenous Politics in Postmulticultural Bolivia.* Stanford: Stanford University Press.

Povinelli, Elizabeth A. 2002. *The Cunning of Recognition: Indigenous Alterities and the Making of Australian Multiculturalism.* Durham: Duke University Press.

Prasetyawan, Wahyu. 2006. The Unfinished Privatization of Semen Padang: The Structure of the Political Economy in Post-Suharto Indonesia. *Indonesia* 81:51–70.

Purdey, Jemma. 2006. *Anti-Chinese Violence in Indonesia, 1996–1999.* Honolulu: University of Hawai'i Press.

Purwadi, Dibyo Soemantri, Alfuzi Salam, Purwo Djatmiko, Sulaeman Ma'ruf and Zainal Muttaqien. 2003. *Sejarah P.T. Krakatau Steel: Memelihara Momentum Pertumbuhan* [The history of P.T. Krakatau Steel: Maintaining momentum for growth]. Yogyakarta: Pustaka Raja.

Rabinow, Paul. 1986. Representations Are Social Facts: Modernity and Post-Modernity in Anthropology. In *Writing Culture: The Poetics and Politics of Ethnography,* ed. James Clifford and George Marcus, 234–261. Berkeley: University of California Press.

——. 1989. *French Modern: Norms and Forms of the Social Environment.* Cambridge: MIT Press.

——. 1996. *Making PCR: A Story of Biotechnology.* Chicago: University of Chicago Press.

——. 1999. *French DNA: Trouble in Purgatory.* Chicago: University of Chicago Press.

——. 2003. *Anthropos Today: Reflections on Modern Equipment.* Princeton: Princeton University Press.

——. 2008. On the Anthropology of the Contemporary. Sir James Frazer Lecture. Cambridge University. Accessed June 30, 2009, from http://www.dspace.cam.ac.uk/handle/1810/205355.

Rabinow, Paul, and Talia Dan-Cohen. 2005. *A Machine to Make a Future: Biotech Chronicles.* Princeton: Princeton University Press.

Rahnema, Majid, and Victoria Bawtree. 1997. *The Post-Development Reader.* London: Zed Books.

Reid, Anthony. 1988. *Southeast Asia in the Age of Commerce, 1450–1680.* New Haven: Yale University Press.

Republika. 2006a. Ary Ginanjar Terpilih Sebagai Salah Satu Dewan Pakar ICMI [Ary Ginanjar selected to the ICMI Board of Experts]. Accessed February 18, 2006, from http://www.republika.co.id/koran_detail.asp?id=235146&kat_id=410.

——. 2006b. Rozy Munir: "ESQ Alat Pengasah Keimanan" [Rozy Munir: "ESQ is an instrument for sharpening faith"]. Accessed May 16, 2006, from http://www.republika.co.id/koran_detail.asp?id=248186&kat_id=410.

——. 2008. ESQ Peduli Pendidikan: 50.146 Guru Telah Ikut Training ESQ [ESQ Cares for Education: 50,146 teachers have already gone through ESQ training]. In *Jejak Langkah Menuju Indonesia Emas 2020: Kompilasi Artikel Dan Berita ESQ 165 Di Media Massa* [Steps toward a golden Indonesia 2020: A compilation of articles and news about ESQ 165 in the mass media], ed. Erwyn Kurniawan, Dadang Kusmayadi, and Ida S. Widayanti, 305–309. Jakarta: Arga Printing.

Richard, Analiese. 2009. Mediating Dilemmas: Local NGOs and Rural Development in Neoliberal Mexico. PoLAR: *Political and Legal Anthropology Review* 32 (2): 166–194.

Richard, Analiese, and Daromir Rudnyckyj. 2009. Economies of Affect. *Journal of the Royal Anthropological Institute* (n.s.) 15 (1): 57–77.

Ricklefs, M. C. 1981. *A History of Modern Indonesia.* Bloomington: Indiana University Press.

Ricœur, Paul. 1970. *Freud and Philosophy: An Essay on Interpretation.* New Haven: Yale University Press.

Riles, Annelise. 2000. *The Network Inside Out.* Ann Arbor: University of Michigan Press.

——. 2004. Real Time: Governing the Market after the Failure of Knowledge. *American Ethnologist* 31 (3): 1–14.

Rinaldo, Rachel. 2008. Envisioning the Nation: Women Activists, Religion, and the Public Sphere in Indonesia. *Social Forces* 86 (4): 1781–1804.

Robinson, Geoffrey. 1995. *The Dark Side of Paradise: Political Violence in Bali.* Ithaca: Cornell University Press.

Robison, Richard. 1986. *Indonesia: The Rise of Capital.* North Sydney, Australia: Allen & Unwin.

Robison, Richard, and Vedi R. Hadiz. 2004. *Reorganising Power in Indonesia: The Politics of Oligarchy in an Age of Markets.* London: RoutledgeCurzon.

Rock, Michael. 2003. The Politics of Development Policy and Development Policy Reform in New Order Indonesia. William Davidson Institute Working Paper No. 632. Ann Arbor: University of Michigan Business School.

Rofel, Lisa. 1997. Rethinking Modernity: Space and Factory Discipline in China. In *Culture, Power, Place: Explorations in Critical Anthropology,* ed. Akhil Gupta and James Ferguson, 155–178. Durham: Duke University Press.

———. 1999. *Other Modernities: Gendered Yearnings in China after Socialism.* Berkeley: University of California Press.

———. 2007. *Desiring China: Experiments in Neoliberalism, Sexuality, and Public Culture.* Durham: Duke University Press.

Roff, William. 1985. Islam Obscured? Some Reflections on Studies of Islam and Society in Southeast Asia. *Archipel* 29 (1): 7–34.

Roosa, John. 2006. *Pretext for Mass Murder: The September 30th Movement and Suharto's Coup d'Etat in Indonesia.* Madison: University of Wisconsin Press.

Rosaldo, Michelle Z. 1980. *Knowledge and Passion: Ilongot Notions of Self and Social Life.* Cambridge: Cambridge University Press.

Rose, Nikolas S. 1999. *Powers of Freedom: Reframing Political Thought.* Cambridge: Cambridge University Press.

Rostow, Walt W. 1960. *The Stages of Economic Growth: A Non-Communist Manifesto.* Cambridge: Cambridge University Press.

Rosyad, Rifki. 2006. *A Quest for True Islam: A Study of the Islamic Resurgence Movement among the Youth in Bandung.* Canberra: ANU E Press. Accessed April 9, 2010, from http://epress.anu.edu.au/islamic/quest/pdf/whole_book.pdf.

Rudnyckyj, Daromir. 2004. Technologies of Servitude: Governmentality and Indonesian Transnational Labor Migration. *Anthropological Quarterly* 77 (3): 407–434.

———. 2009. PowerPointing Islam: Form and Spiritual Reform in Reformasi Indonesia. In *Mediating Piety: Religion and Technology in Asia,* ed. Francis Lim, 91–112. Leiden: Brill.

Rush, James R. 1990. *Opium to Java: Revenue Farming and Chinese Enterprise in Colonial Indonesia, 1860–1910.* Ithaca: Cornell University Press.

Rutherford, Danilyn. 2003. *Raiding the Land of the Foreigners: The Limits of the Nation on an Indonesian Frontier.* Princeton: Princeton University Press.

Sachs, Wolfgang. 1992. *The Development Dictionary: A Guide to Knowledge as Power.* London: Zed Books.

Sahlins, Marshall. 1972. *Stone Age Economics.* Chicago: Aldine-Atherton.

Samudra, Jaida. 2008. Memory in Our Body: Thick Participation and the Translation of Kinesthetic Experience. *American Ethnologist* 35 (4): 665–681.

Sassen, Saskia. 1998. *Globalization and Its Discontents: Essays on the New Mobility of People and Money.* New York: New Press.

Sawyer, Suzana. 2004. *Crude Chronicles: Indigenous Politics, Multinational Oil, and Neoliberalism in Ecuador.* Durham: Duke University Press.

Schrauwers, Albert. 2003. Through a Glass Darkly: Charity, Conspiracy, and Power in New Order Indonesia. In *Transparency and Conspiracy: Ethnographies of Suspicion in the New World Order,* ed. Harry G. West and Todd Sanders, 125–147. Durham: Duke University Press.

Schulte Nordholt, Henk. 1997. *Outward Appearances: Dressing State and Society in Indonesia.* Leiden: KITLV Press.

Schulz, Dorothea E. 2006. Promises of (Im)Mediate Salvation: Islam, Broadcast Media, and the Remaking of Religious Experience in Mali. *American Ethnologist* 33 (2): 210–229.

Schwarz, Adam. 1994. *A Nation in Waiting: Indonesia in the 1990s.* Boulder: Westview Press.

Scott, James C. 1976. *The Moral Economy of the Peasant: Rebellion and Subsistence in Southeast Asia.* New Haven: Yale University Press.

——. 1998. *Seeing Like a State: How Certain Schemes to Improve the Human Condition Have Failed.* New Haven: Yale University Press.

Scott, James C., and Ben Kerkvliet. 1977. How Traditional Patrons Lose Legitimacy: A Theory with Special Reference to Southeast Asia. In *Friends, Followers, and Factions: A Reader in Political Clientelism,* ed. Steffen W. Schmidt, 439–457. Berkeley: University of California Press.

Sedgwick, Eve Kosofsky. 2003. *Touching Feeling: Affect, Pedagogy, Performativity.* Durham: Duke University Press.

Shever, Elana. 2008. Neoliberal Associations: Property, Company, and Family in the Argentine Oil Fields. *American Ethnologist* 35 (4): 701–716.

Shore, Cris, and Susan Wright. 2000. Coercive Accountability: The Rise of Audit Culture in Higher Education. In *Audit Cultures: Anthropological Studies in Accountability, Ethics, and the Academy,* ed. Marilyn Strathern, 57–89. London: Routledge.

Sidel, John. 2006. *Riots, Pogroms, Jihad: Religious Violence in Indonesia.* Ithaca: Cornell University Press.

Siegel, James. 1986. *Solo in the New Order: Language and Hierarchy in an Indonesian City.* Princeton: Princeton University Press.

——. 1998. *A New Criminal Type in Jakarta: Counter-Revolution Today.* Durham: Duke University Press.

——. 2001. Suharto, Witches. *Indonesia* 71:27–78.

——. 2006. *Naming the Witch.* Stanford: Stanford University Press.

Silverstein, Brian. 2008. Disciplines of Presence in Modern Turkey: Discourse, Companionship and the Mass Mediation of Islamic Practice. *Cultural Anthropology* 23 (1): 118–153.

Smith, Adam. 1976. *An Inquiry into the Nature and Causes of the Wealth of Nations.* Chicago: University of Chicago Press.

——. 2002. *The Theory of Moral Sentiments.* Cambridge: Cambridge University Press.

Soesastro, Hadi, and Chatib Basri. 1998. Survey of Recent Developments. *Bulletin of Indonesian Economic Studies* 34 (1): 3–54.

Stein, Steven J., and Howard E. Book. 2000. *The EQ Edge: Emotional Intelligence and Your Success.* Toronto: Stoddart.

Stewart, Kathleen. 2008. *Ordinary Affects*. Durham: Duke University Press.

Stoler, Ann. 2002. *Carnal Knowledge and Imperial Power: Race and the Intimate in Colonial Rule*. Berkeley: University of California Press.

Strathern, Marilyn. 1988. *The Gender of the Gift: Problems with Women and Problems with Society in Melanesia*. Berkeley: University of California Press.

——. 2000. *Audit Cultures: Anthropological Studies in Accountability, Ethics, and the Academy*. London: Routledge.

Suharmoko, Aditya. 2008. Krakatau, Garuda, BTN Cleared to Go Public. *Jakarta Post*. Accessed October 3, 2008, from http://www.thejakartapost.com/news/2008/09/19/krakatau-garuda-btn-cleared-go-public.html.

Sumanto, Al Qurtuby. 2003. *Arus Cina-Islam-Jawa: Bongkar Sejarah Atas Peranan Tionghoa Dalam Penyebaran Agama Islam Di Nusantara* [The China-Islam-Java flow: Deconstructing the history of the role of China in the spread of Islam in the Indonesian archipelago]. Jakarta: Inspeal Ahimsakarya Press.

Suryadinata, Leo. 2007. *Understanding the Ethnic Chinese in Southeast Asia*. Singapore: Institute of Southeast Asian Studies.

Sutan, Eries Adlin. 2008. ESQ Juga Melanda Malaysia [ESQ sweeps Malaysia too]. *Bisnis Indonesia*. Accessed May 26, 2009, from http://web.bisnis.com/edisi-cetak/edisiharian/oasis/1id87882.html.

Sutherland, Heather. 1979. *The Making of a Bureaucratic Elite: The Colonial Transformation of the Javanese Priyayi*. Singapore: Heinemann Educational Books.

Szakolczai, Arpád 1998. *Max Weber and Michel Foucault: Parallel Life-Works*. London: Routledge.

Thee, Kian Wie. 2003. *Recollections: The Indonesian Economy, 1950s–1990s*. Singapore: Institute of Southeast Asian Studies.

Thompson, Edward. 1971. The Moral Economy of the English Crowd in the Eighteenth Century. *Past and Present* 50:76–136.

Thongchai, Winichakul. 1994. *Siam Mapped: A History of the Geo-Body of a Nation*. Honolulu: University of Hawai'i Press.

Thrift, Nigel. 1998. The Rise of Soft Capitalism. In *An Unruly World? Globalisation, Goverance and Geography,* ed. Andrew Herod, Gearóid O'Tuathail, and Susan Roberts, 25–71. London: Routledge.

——. 1999. The Globalisation of the System of Business Knowledge. In *Globalisation and the Asia Pacific: Contested Territories,* ed. Kris Olds, Peter Dicken, Philip F. Kelly, Lily Kong, and Henry Wai-Chung Yeung, 57–71. London: Routledge.

——2005. *Knowing Capitalism*. London: Sage.

Tihami, M. A. 1992. Kiyai Dan Jawara Di Banten: Studi Tentang Agama, Magi, Dan Kepemimpinan Di Desa Pasanggahan, Serang, Banten [*Kiyai* and *Jawara* in Banten: A study of religion, magic, and leadership in Pasanggrahan village, Serang, Banten]. MA thesis, University of Indonesia.

Tirtosudiro, Achmad. 2002. *Bang Imad: Pemikiran Dan Gerakan Dakwahnya* [Bang Imad: The thought and practice of proselytization]. Jakarta: Gema Insani Press.

Tsing, Anna Lowenhaupt. 2005. *Friction: An Ethnography of Global Connection*. Princeton: Princeton University Press.

van Dijk, Cornelis. 1981. *Rebellion under the Banner of Islam: The Darul Islam in Indonesia*. The Hague: Martinus Nijhoff.

van Dijk, Kees. 2001. *A Country in Despair: Indonesia between 1997 and 2000.* Leiden: KITLV Press.

van Klinken, Gerry. 2007. *Communal Violence and Democratization in Indonesia: Small Town Wars.* London: Routledge.

van Leur, Jacob C. 1955. *Indonesian Trade and Society: Essays in Asian Social and Economic History.* The Hague: W. Van Hoeve.

Vann, Elizabeth F. 2006. The Limits of Authenticity in Vietnamese Consumer Markets. *American Anthropologist* 108 (2): 286–296.

Warouw, Nicolaas. 2005. Pekerja Industri Indonesia, Gerakan Buruh, dan New Social Movement: Merajut Sebuah Kemungkinan [Indonesian industrial workers, labor movements, and new social movements: Weaving a possibility]. *Jurnal Analisis Sosial* 10 (2): 1–18.

Watson, C. W. 2005. A Popular Indonesian Preacher: The Significance of Aa Gymnastiar. *Journal of the Royal Anthropological Institute* (n.s.) 11 (4): 773–792.

Weatherbee, Donald E. 1985. Indonesia in 1984: Pancasila, Politics and Power. *Asian Survey* 25 (2): 187–197.

Weber, Max. 1920. *Gesammelte Aufsatze Zur Religionssoziologie* [Collected works in the sociology of religion]. Tubingen: Mohr.

——. 1949. "Objectivity" in Social Science and Social Policy. In *The Methodology of the Social Sciences,* 49–112. New York: Free Press.

——. 1951. *The Religion of China: Confucianism and Taoism.* Glencoe, IL: Free Press.

——. 1958a. Bureaucracy. In *For Max Weber: Essays in Sociology,* ed. Hans Gerth and C. Wright Mills, 196–244. New York: Oxford University Press.

——. 1958b. *The Religion of India: The Sociology of Hinduism and Buddhism.* Glencoe, IL: Free Press.

——. 1990. *The Protestant Ethic and the Spirit of Capitalism.* London: Unwin Hyman.

Weix, G. G. 1998. Islamic Prayer Groups in Indonesia: Local Forums and Gendered Responses. *Critique of Anthropology* 18 (4): 405–420.

Wertheim, W. F. 1977. From Aliran towards Class Struggle in the Countryside of Java. In *Friends, Followers, and Factions: A Reader in Political Clientelism,* ed. Steffen W. Schmidt. Berkeley: University of California Press.

White, Benjamin. 1983. *Agricultural Involution and Its Critics: Twenty Years after Clifford Geertz.* The Hague: Institute of Social Studies.

Wiegele, Katharine L. 2005. *Investing in Miracles: El Shaddai and the Transformation of Popular Catholicism in the Philippines.* Honolulu: University of Hawai'i Press.

Wikan, Unni. 1990. *Managing Turbulent Hearts: A Balinese Formula for Living.* Chicago: University of Chicago Press.

Williams, Michael C. 1990. *Communism, Religion, and Revolt in Banten.* Athens: Ohio University Press.

Winchester, Simon. 2003. *Krakatoa: The Day the World Exploded, August 27, 1883.* New York: Harper Collins.

Winters, Jeffrey. 2000. A Review Essay: The Political Economy of Labor in Indonesia. *Indonesia* 70:139–150.

Winzeler, Robert. 1990. Amok: Cultural, Psychological, and Historical Perspectives. In *Emotions of Culture: A Malay Perspective,* ed. Karim Wazir-Jahan Begum, 96–122. Singapore: Oxford University Press.

Wolters, Oliver W. 1999. *History, Culture, and Region in Southeast Asian Perspectives.* Ithaca: Southeast Asia Program, Cornell University.

Woodward, Mark R. 1989. *Islam in Java: Normative Piety and Mysticism in the Sultanate of Yogyakarta.* Tucson: University of Arizona Press.

World Bank. 2003. Combating Corruption in Indonesia: Enhancing Accountability for Development. Washington, DC: East Asia Poverty Reduction and Economic Management Unit.

Yan, Yunxiang. 2009. *The Individualization of Chinese Society.* Oxford: Berg.

Yanagisako, Sylvia. 2002. *Producing Culture and Capital: Family Firms in Italy.* Princeton: Princeton University Press.

Yudhoyono, Susilo Bambang. 2006. *Indonesia on the Move: Selected Speeches and Articles by the President of the Republic of Indonesia.* Jakarta: Bhuana Ilmu Populer.

Yusanto, Ismail, and Karebet Widjajakusuma. 2002. *Pengantar Manajemen Syariat* [Introduction to Syariah managment]. Jakarta: Khairul Bayan.

———. 2003. *Manajemen Strategis: Perspektif Syariah* [Strategic management: A Syariah perspective]. Jakarta: Khairul Bayaan.

Zaloom, Caitlin. 2006. *Out of the Pits: Trading and Technology from Chicago to London.* Chicago: University of Chicago Press.

Zohar, Danah, and I. N. Marshall. 2000. *SQ: Spiritual Intelligence—the Ultimate Intelligence.* London: Bloomsbury.

INDEX

Page numbers in italics refer to figures and tables.